Special Use Vehicles

Special Use Vehicles

An Illustrated History of Unconventional Cars and Trucks Worldwide

GEORGE W. GREEN

McFarland & Company, Inc., Publishers
Jefferson, North Carolina, and London

The scripture quotation in Chapter V marked (NIV)
is taken from the Holy Bible, New International
Version (R). NIV (R). Copyright © 1973, 1978, 1984
by International Bible Society. Used by permission of Zondervan
Publishing House. All rights reserved.

Library of Congress Cataloguing-in-Publication Data

Green, George W., 1921–
Special use vehicles : an illustrated history of unconventional
cars and trucks worldwide / George W. Green.
p.   cm.
Includes index.

ISBN 0-7864-1245-3 (illustrated case binding : 50# alkaline paper)

1. Commercial vehicles.   2. Government vehicles.
3. Motor vehicles, Amphibious.   I. Title.
TL235.8.G74   2003   629.2—dc21   2002014697

British Library cataloguing data are available

Cover photographs: The Rev. Branford Clarke with the Model T Mobile
Chapel *(Collections of Henry Ford Museum and Greenfield Village)*,
Moulton B. Taylor and his Aerocar *(EAA Foundation Library Archives)*
and Emerson Drug's Bromo-Seltzer replica bottle on wheels
(American Truck Historical Society)

Manufactured in the United States of America

McFarland & Company, Inc., Publishers
Box 611, Jefferson, North Carolina 28640
www.mcfarlandpub.com

Contents

To Pauline, Norma and Mary
My "Treasure Trinity"

Introduction

It has been well stated that a civilization can best be judged by its transportation, since that has proved to be one of the prime catalysts in society.

Beyond the mundane, traditional purposes of motor vehicles moving passengers, goods, raw materials and mail from place to place lies a fascinating world of unconventional uses. These, surprisingly, embrace virtually all activities normally conducted from fixed-base, brick-and-mortar locations.

This study explores a remarkable array of disparate functions for vehicles, including use in sales, advertising, training, charity and public service, religion, and functional activities. Multimodal and government vehicles are also considered.

The object of this book is to present a factual, comprehensive, practical, and clear treatment of the subject that will be useful to a wide audience. Hundreds of representative examples and detailed case histories of unusual units are presented.

This book is not intended as an exhaustive collection of data on all special uses—there are simply too many of them, and identifying them would require too much subjectivity.

No attempt has been made to compare one effort directly with another or to conduct a critique, per se, of a particular vehicle's effectiveness for its unique purpose.

Data and photographs for the study have been steadily built up over the past 50 years of research. I was extremely fortunate in my business career to occupy executive positions in the transportation industry which yielded me access to a continuing flow of relevant information.

Although it is not possible to acknowledge individually all those who cooperated I should at least like to express my deep indebtedness and gratitude for their contributions on a collective basis. Especially I wish to thank my wife, daughter and sister for their unending support and contributions.

I welcome inquiries from readers, sent to me in care of the publisher.

George W. Green
Fall 2002

CHAPTER I

Sales Vehicles

Mobile sales of durable and non-durable consumer and industrial goods and services may be defined as a channel of direct distribution involving a self-propelled vehicle operated over a fixed territory or route or at random locations. This technique can be the sole means of sales or may supplement other channels like traditional fixed location retail or wholesale outlets, catalogs, telemarketing, multi-level marketing (MLM), party plan, on-line Net shopping, etc.

Virtually every phase of the marketing structure has been affected by mobility at one time or another.

Early special use vehicles of perambulatory sellers consisted largely of passenger cars, pickup trucks or small vans crammed with deliveries, samples and brochures. In the 1920s and 1930s and for a short period in the late 1940s and 1950s agents were knocking on doors for encyclopedias, cosmetics, vacuum cleaners, brushes, cookware, vitamins and a host of other products. These efforts gave way in evolutionary periods to today's wide variety of elaborate, custom-made or converted selling vehicles outfitted as verita-ble traveling stores in every sense of the word to sell or dispense offerings to customers. In addition to unique body features involving functional doors, windows and raised roofs, these vocational vehicles were typically ordered with all heavy-duty equipment and extra-large gas tanks.

Vagabond sellers may operate year round, only seasonally, or may be set up when a business is being built or is closed temporarily.

Sending out these sales vehicles are manufacturers, wholesalers, and independent, cooperative and franchised retailers. The latter trend proliferated beginning in the 1960s and extending into the 1970s and 1980s.

Mobile sales service is particularly attractive to several segments of the consumer market. Significant global social, economic and topographical patterns reflect lifestyle changes which have resulted in a revolution in the mercantile world. These changes include two-income families often too busy to get to stores; buyers lacking ready transportation (senior citizens, parents with young children, handicapped, college students, teenagers), affluent singles, and customers in relatively remote, isolated locations.

In 1980 Selame Design Associates, specialists in corporate and retail identity, actually envisioned an innovative concept embracing a computer-age shopping mall featuring mobile retail stores that could travel from site to site. Truck trailers would unfold to plug into the mall's central core. Through the developer's programming, retail and site locations could be switched and positioned for maximum selling power.

This whole idea of "mobile marketing" is far from new. Historical caravan trade through the ages in many countries is well documented. In America today's sleek units have come a long way from the humble Yankee Peddler whose rich pioneer heritage set the precedent. He roamed the hinterlands in the 18th and early 19th centuries as a fixture in the colonial period, on foot with a pack on his back, on muleback, on horseback, or with a carriage or two-horse wagon. Some even doubled as spies during the American Revolution.

We must not overlook the old traveling medicine show that offered fabulous cure-all elixirs from town to town, to say nothing of the itinerant journeymen printers, surveyors, gunsmiths, photographers, barbers and scissors grinders.

Sales have been accomplished worldwide not only from motor vehicles but also from such unlikely conveyances as baby carriages, bicycles, tricycles, carriages, pushcarts, express wagons, motorbikes, mopeds, motor scooters, sleds, sleighs and even wheelbarrows.

Portable sales don't even need wheels when implemented by booths, portable

This mobile mall concept was developed by Selame Design in 1980. *(Courtesy Selame Design Associates)*

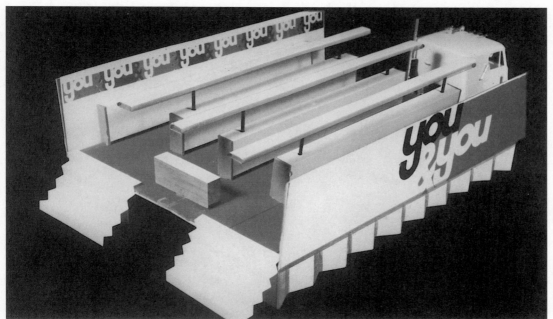

Top: **Mobile retail units travel to and from a mall site. The cutaway roof shows the compacted store interior.** *Bottom:* **The unfolded store is ready to shed cab and plug in to the mall's center core.** *(Courtesy Selame Design Associates)*

buildings, kiosks, shacks, stalls, tables, geodesic domes, tents and canopies, and vending machines.

The following significant, representative examples of motorized sales vehicles show them in detail in a wide variety of settings.

Sales of food, household goods, transportation, apparel and general merchandise are covered. Services described are automotive, personal, financial, insurance, real estate, legal, amusements, health care, pet care, lodging, education, communications, social, advertising and repair.

Sales to the General Public from Vehicles

GROCERIES

Probably the largest ongoing sales volume to consumers from sales vehicles involves food, both groceries and prepared foods.

Food items sold on the road predate motor vehicles with horse and wagon operations. A peak of 5,000 routes was served in the late 1800s when A & P operated a fleet of distinctive, high-wheeled vermilion, gold and black wagons in the heartlands selling staples to farm wives.

Sales proliferated after World War I for mobile grocery stores when War Department surplus trucks were put into civilian service in the 1920s.

In the Depression years of the 1930s fleets of huge vans sold groceries in such cities as Detroit, while in the rural South and other remote sections old sedans or even school buses, crude but functional, were converted to traveling stores. Some of these still operated for several years after the end of World War II.

In the 1960s several large chain grocery stores experimented with traveling food stores on trucks.

A kosher delicatessen on wheels, the Brooklyn Bagel Box, a specially-built Dodge motor home with a large side dis-

In the late 1920s and 1930s it was common to see neighborhood mobile grocery stores in major U.S. cities. This motor store in Detroit, Michigan, in December 1926 was a great convenience for shoppers who needed to replenish staples, especially in inclement weather. *(Manning Brothers Historic Photographic Collection)*

Motor home designs lend themselves to many different commercial uses, as evidenced by this custom Dodge model made into a traveling delicatessen, the Brooklyn Bagel Box. It served kosher customers in Fullerton, California, in the 1960s. The display case allowed shoppers an excellent view of the many different varieties offered. *(Courtesy Brooklyn Bagel Box)*

play case, began to serve customers in California in 1965.

Jewel Tea reached its peak in about 1966, boasting 2,111 routes in 44 states with 1,000,000 customers. Seven-foot-high Chevrolet step vans operated in the suburbs and subdivisions. Many non-food items were also sold.

As late as 1986 a custom-built Winnebago motor home Mobile Mart was introduced, designed specifically for higher-income residential areas.

Nonprofit mobile markets continue to serve retirees in high-rise apartments and housing complexes in Cleveland, Toledo, Boston, Chicago and Denver. Starting out in converted 23-foot bookmobiles and buses they have graduated into such vehicles as customized 32-foot Fruehauf double-wide vans.

On foreign shores mobile groceries were in Germany as early as the 1920s, and after World War II in West Germany. They have been popular in rural Scotland at outlying farms.

The Federation of Migros Cooperatives in Zurich, Switzerland, a series of regional cooperatives, operates 133 truck stores carrying both food and non-food items for customers in out-of-the-way places. Both walk-through service and self-service stores stock up to 900 different items. They started out with five Model T Ford trucks in 1925 on a predetermined route. Today sales area in the truck is 70 square feet. Most are Magirus-Deutz, Mercedes or Berna. Other Swiss organizations involved in mobile marketing are Coop Schweiz in Basil and Konsumver in Zurich.

When it comes to specific food items like milk; bakery products; fruits and vegetables; meat and fish; natural organic foods; and potato chips, the pattern ap-

Mobile marketing developed into a worldwide enterprise. There have been several traveling store chains in Switzerland. Shown is one operated by the Federation of Migros Cooperatives in Zurich. Since 1925 it has offered both food and non-food items. *(Courtesy Federation of Migros Cooperatives)*

proximates that of the general mobile grocery vehicles. Home delivery routes carried on in the 1920s and 1930s but virtually stopped in significant numbers at the end of World War II, although a few continued into the 1970s and 1980s. For example, the incidence of home delivered milk fell from an estimated 75 percent in the 1930s to less than one percent today.

Vehicles of choice used on home routes were modified step vans and panel trucks. Two-speed electric food trucks came into use in England in the 1970s with a range of 52 miles and top speed of 21 mph.

Also in the 1970s two Canadian dairies came up with 55 × 20 foot prefabricated shops on wheels which could be removed and set on permanent concrete foundations or jacks. They were split down

the center to form two sections for transport and used mostly in subdivisions, high-rises and summer resorts.

PREPARED FOODS

Turning now to the sales of prepared foods and drinks from vehicles, we discover an insatiable demand for both on and off-premises immediate consumption, sustaining a large, continuing industry segment in not only the United States and Canada but in such countries as England, Germany, Russia and Poland.

Prepared foods find their way to consumers through five principal avenues: 1) mobile restaurants; 2) neighborhood street sales; 3) concessions at crowd venues; 4) caterers; and 5) portable vending machines.

Mobile restaurants or canteens, whether independent or franchised, are housed in specially-built vans, trailers and converted buses with fold-down counters on the sides. One of the first motor-driven lunch stands in the United States was operated by Zack Benn of Anacortes, Washington. He also sold souvenirs at fairs, picnics and carnivals in the Pacific Northwest in 1912.

The popular Manhattan restaurant Tavern on the Green sends a restaurant truck every day to Sixth Avenue near the Rockefeller Center complex. Steve's World of Food, Detroit, built a comestibles vehicle with seven ovens, a ten-foot-long grill, refrigerator, freezer and its own power plant and set up at the Olympic Games in Atlanta in 1996. In Europe a double-decker bus, the Walnut Tree Branch Line, has been successfully converted into a restaurant seating 22 on the upper deck with the bar and kitchen below.

Movie and television actor Patrick O'Neal, of Beverly Hills, California, has his Str*eat*car, an aluminum van restaurant featuring an all-vegetarian menu, his sixth foray into the business.

Gino's Restaurants, King of Prussia, Pennsylvania, uses a 30-foot self-contained, aluminum motor home to serve Kentucky Fried Chicken to up to 300 customers per hour. All the equipment was customized to fit into a small space.

Ice cream is the principal product still sold in neighborhoods from a vehicle. These sales began in the 1920s using a Model T Ford, then moving into reconstituted, boxy former mail trucks, step vans and specially-built trucks. Virtually all have been franchised.

Concessionaries roam around to park their vehicles known as "grab joints" wherever there are crowds. Fairs, sporting events, carnivals, charity and fund-raisers, college campuses, flea markets, beaches and parks are popular venues. They sell such food as sandwiches, particularly hot dogs and hamburgers; candy apples; popcorn; peanuts; cotton candy; donuts; pizza; frozen yogurt; waffles; cookies; cinnamon rolls; chili; hot tamales; baked potatoes; fish and chips; coffee and carbonated beverages. Both McDonald's and Burger King have tested mobile sales. Frozen pizza maker DiGiorno operates a large mobile kitchen and vending trailer that follows golf's PGA tour.

Colorful sales vehicles include restored 1909 vintage Cretors popcorn trucks; Cookie Coach replica 1901 red pie wagons; and donuts in a trailer designed to resemble a railroad car.

Most of the street vehicles and concession units are manufactured by specialized body companies. These firms consistently offer to the trade a variety of customized light, medium and heavy-duty models expressly designed in every single feature so far as the chassis, body and all equipment are concerned to accommodate food sales.

Another segment of this market, mobile catering, uses vehicles ranging from industrial route vans visiting factories, construction sites and office buildings to huge vehicle fleets serving society weddings for hundreds of guests, commercial events, movie crews on location and snowmobile rallies.

Vince Gile's rolling, up-scale restaurant fleet of five serves entertainment stars on tour with his Ritz Mobile Gourmet. This custom-made bus contains a fully equipped commercial kitchen with a dining room for ten and a back bedroom and bathroom. Accompanying it is a 20-foot refrigerated trailer with an outside grill.

Pubs on wheels are relatively rare, although beer has been sold from trucks at car races.

Top: Anyone who visited a fair, carnival, beach, park or other such recreational or amusement site beginning about 1909 would no doubt run into a Cretors fresh buttered popcorn truck, shown above in 1913. Available in addition were Coney Islands, red hots, ice cream cones, Cracker Jack, fresh roasted peanuts, and cold drinks. Vintage trucks have been restored for the benefit of younger generations. *(Courtesy Cretors & Co.)*. *Bottom:* The Jolly Trolley street vending franchise sells Sno-Cones both on daily routes and at special celebrations. Built by hand, they have an aluminum top, solid walnut or cypress wood trim, and a top speed of 30 mph. The top and signs are well lighted for nighttime. Children constitute about 70 percent of the trade. *(Courtesy Tooterville Trolley Co.)*

HOUSEHOLD GOODS

Since at least the mid–1970s local firms engaged in home remodeling, heating and air conditioning have sent out showmobile vans to prospects' houses with hands-on displays to augment their fixed-base showrooms.

In addition to vans used by independent retailers there are over 30 franchises in the United States and Canada which provide custom-made vans with samples for interior decoration products like wallpaper, floor coverings, upholstery and window treatments. At least one specializes in children's room designs.

In the Detroit area a furniture dealer started in 2000 taking trucks with portable showrooms in them to three university campus student dormitories.

Mobile sales units are also active carrying kitchenware, bedding, housewares, wall hangings and picture frames.

Television sets, radios, pianos, organs and musical instruments have been taken to prospects, as well as video hardware and software. Depending upon the product offered, vehicles used include special vans, trailers and buses.

Service organizations on wheels offer cleaning and repair facilities for virtually any household item. Many of these also solicit business in the commercial, industrial and institutional markets.

TRANSPORTATION

In the late 1940s automobile dealers began using roving showrooms, offices, closing rooms and demonstrators for several different major makes. These were mostly special converted vans with folding steps and high ceilings and in some cases Continental Trailways buses, motor homes or trailers filled the bill. Effective use of these vehicles has been reported in shopping centers, drag strips and at farms.

Other automotive related products sold out of vehicles have included tires, car wax and hubcaps.

Mobile refueling services have been a business practice for many years in all phases of the transportation industry (cars, trucks, trains and airplanes). Beginning with portable hand pumps mobile gas stations operated later in the early 1900s through the 1920s with fuel vended from truck-mounted pumps. Farrell Manufacturing Company built one on a Reo chassis, and the Sinclair Refining Company Gas-O-Car was a White Model 51–190 W.B. In 1925 Ford Motor sold Benzol (motor fuel blended with gasoline) from 25-horsepower trucks, a by-product of the Rouge complex in Dearborn, Michigan.

Mother Earth News, a Hendersonville, North Carolina, counterculture magazine, provided in 1979 alcohol (ethanol gasohol) from its mobile still for Manhattan taxis.

In 1972 a service was provided in Greensboro, North Carolina, for employees of industrial or business firms who parked in company lots. Their cars were serviced on a fixed, periodic schedule by gasoline distribution trucks with 850-gallon tanks and computerized metering systems under exclusive site license agreements. Coded stickers on customer windshields guided the operators.

Since 1965 in England "pirate tankers," large trucks with two full-sized pumps attached to the rear, have toured main roads in such areas as Kent to sell cut-rate gas to motorists on their way to work or sports events under such provocative names as Zoom and Whoosh. In Sweden the Swedish Oil Consumers Cooperative has opened 30 self-service, fully automatic mobile stations in shopping centers and small communities. Self-contained, each station consists of three aboveground tanks, two pumps and a money machine.

Both bicycle repair and motorcycle

Too busy to get to a gas station? Back in the early 1900s through the 1920s truck-mounted portable pumps would be brought to the motorist. Prominent was the Sinclair Refining Company's Gas-O-Car, a White Model 51-190 WB, shown above about 1926. Note the handy bicycle air supply available. Whites were manufactured from 1900 to the late 1950s. *(American Truck Historical Society)*

rentals have been taken directly to consumers.

When on trips travelers encounter mobile ticket offices, waiting rooms, travel agencies and baggage inspection. At O'Hare International Airport in Chicago a Calumet Coach combines conveyor-belt speed with X-ray vision.

APPAREL

All lines of apparel have been sold out of vehicles: men's, boy's, women's and girl's, by traveling merchants in the United States and Canada. Custom-fitted vans with dressing space are provided. A typical operation was The Pants Man in Detroit in 1973, who used two large, radio-equipped vans, each with a 300-pants

inventory complete with alteration and pressing services. In 1967 Bird's Paradise boutique on wheels—a converted horsebox—made an appearance in North London. In 1989 Amen Wardy sent out his custom-fitted Clothesmobile mobile home in Beverly Hills featuring top design clothes for women. Expanded women's wear lines embraced jewelry and other products. Some firms including franchises have specialized in serving nursing homes and state hospitals while others focus on moving uniforms and career apparel from their showrooms.

Specific segments of the market are served by such organizations as Mandel Brothers Department Store in Chicago, which in 1970 used a 28-foot trailer to merchandise sports apparel and equipment

This Timberland shoe store shows how quickly and easily a highway four-wheel trailer can be set up as a full-fledged "retail outlet" complete with such amenities as benches, mirrors and a floor. With swing-out displays on both sides and hinged signs that stand above, it is ready for business. *(Courtesy Mobilexhibit)*

at nearby sporting events. Combining country music and racing in 1997, the Brooks and Dunn Legends traveling display in a 73-foot custom trailer rig featured a complete line of apparel and related souvenir merchandise. Distributors for Miller Beer in the mid–1980s sold clothing with Miller logos from mobile units. Gucci discount outlets have chosen state fairs for their rolling displays.

Large trailer shoemobiles became a familiar sight after World War II at industrial plants, building sites and warehouses, selling protective footwear to employees. By the 1970s there were at least a dozen show companies in this business, ei-

ther selling directly or through local distributors in the United States, Canada and Great Britain. A few independent mobile shoe operations began as early as the 1950s, some concentrating on athletic shoes for joggers. At least one firm negotiated a combination deal to have its work shoes sold in tool vans selling to automobile mechanics.

Custom tailors now make home and office calls in some cases.

GENERAL MERCHANDISE

Examples of general merchandise stores in the United States with mobile units include Belk in Greensboro, North Carolina.

A variety store on wheels was sent into Florida in 1962 by McCrory-McLellan-Green Stores. This custom-built, 35-foot Suburban Shopmobile had skylight openings, regular counters, checkout and display windows as well as outside vending machines.

The Ammex Duty-Free store has operated out of a trailer since 1970 in Detroit near the Detroit-Windsor Tunnel, selling liquor, tobacco, perfume and other goods.

Country general stores began operation in the rural United States in the 1930s in states including Alabama, Georgia, Mississippi, West Virginia, New Mexico and New York. These ranged from campers or old school buses to specially outfitted, two-ton trucks. Weekly visits put about 60 miles a day on the vehicles. Small mobile stores are also found in such locations as lumber camps selling clothes and tobacco.

A very large number of disparate miscellaneous merchandise has also been sold out of vehicles in the United States and abroad. This includes such items as patent medicine, antiques, phonograph records, firearms, golf balls, books, jewelry, toys, cameras, gifts, souvenirs, fresh flowers, cigars, magazines, ceramic tile, hardware, fertilizer, paint spray guns, fireworks, pet food and kites. Customized vans are used mostly for these sales, as well as special trucks, buses, trailers and recreational vehicles.

Consumer Services

The service industries also use mobile selling extensively.

AUTOMOTIVE SERVICES

Consumers in the United States, Canada, Great Britain and Australia have been most fortunate to be recipients of a long list of handy mobile automotive services: windshield repair; mechanical repairs; tune-ups; detailing; lube and oil change; diagnostic; tires; and dent repair. Other less frequently offered are window tinting; theft prevention; radio service; undercoating; gold plating and odor elimination. Some operations extend services to recreational vehicles, snowmobiles, boats and even airplanes. It is common to find a trade segment of many of these businesses serving fleet accounts. Mechanical specialists focus on brakes, mufflers, radiators or air conditioners.

While independents maintain a foothold in this market the franchisers clearly dominate, coming in the 1970s and maintaining momentum in the 1980s and 1990s. Automobile dealers, manufacturers, parts makers, chain department stores and membership automobile clubs have taken brief forays into this field from time to time. Dealer service has been devoted mostly to installing accessories, warranty work, recalls and repairing and retrofitting from mobile units.

Depending upon the specific automotive service provided, vehicles have ranged from cargo vans and panel trucks to huge, maximum-length truck-trailer

Opposite, top: **Auto Critic mobile used vehicle inspection franchise responds to calls within 24 hours, offering a bumper-to-bumper, 92-item checklist for prospective buyers of cars and light trucks. The work is performed by a certified mechanic in about an hour. A test drive is included in the compelte service. The fully equipped van contains an array of diagnostic equipment. It meets customers at home, work, bank and elsewhere.** *(Courtesy Auto Critic). Bottom:* **On-the-spot windshield repair and quick lube and oil change are offered by the Mobile Oil Butler franchise. The custom-designed vehicle serves both residential markets and fleets through one-time service and contracts.** *(Courtesy Oil Butler International Corp.)*

combinations. Undercoating is performed in custom-built ramp trailers and mufflers are installed in special trucks with hydraulically-powered lifts and nonskid ramps.

A mobile car washer that is driven to a shopping center or company lot has a closed, over-the-road position, but is extendable to scour pass-through cars and trucks of different sizes, draining, filtering and reusing water stored in tanks.

The earliest attempts at mobile service were rather crude. Said to be the first glass replacement vehicle was a jerry-built 1926 Willys Whippet which had the rumble seat replaced with glass-grinding and polishing apparatus.

PERSONAL SERVICES

Personal services run the gamut. Mobile barbers come to the customer, such as the quarter-million-dollar, 40-foot Ruffles salon van serving exclusive Beverly Hills, California, patrons. It boasts a kitchen and showers. Barbers also hit office buildings and fire stations. Traveling beauty parlors are a boon to the elderly, handicapped and shut-ins, as is home massage.

Shoe repairing has been implemented with vehicles shaped like shoes and boots and fleets of scooters visiting homes, high rises and offices.

Franchised diaper services also usually sell baby products and distribute samples and coupons.

Dry cleaning goes way back. A 1909 advertisement in Los Angeles read "Suits sprayed and pressed weekly @ $1.50/mo.; cleaned and pressed $3 from the Valet Services Department of City Dye Works." Modern vans now operate on routes and also at commuter railroad stations in New York and Connecticut. Some have expanded to handle also laundry, film processing and UPS shipping.

Surprisingly enough even funeral services have taken to the road. There is a freezing cryogenics van and a specially equipped mortuary van in Michigan which travels anywhere in the state to carry a body to the nearest crematory and arrange memorial services. In 1981 Airstream introduced its massive, 28-foot funeral coach accommodating a casket, 20 standing flower baskets and 20 people in plush comfort, replacing the traditional hearse and several limousines. A removable nameplate allowed other uses by the undertaker such as film presentations to schools and civic groups.

Portrait photographers with portable studio-darkrooms often show up at carnivals, fairs, resorts, grand openings, fundraisers and other special events.

An outstanding example of adaptive marketing occurred in 1970 when H & R Block hired a horse-and-buggy tax representative for the isolated Amish area of Millersburg, Ohio.

Mobile weddings in Las Vegas take place in 19-foot Winnebago motor homes, and in Japan you can get a tattoo in a trailer.

FINANCIAL SERVICES

Since the end of World War II well over 100 different financial institutions have found that mobile units are a valuable adjunct to their fixed-base headquarters and branches. These include banks, savings and loan associations, credit unions and check cashing companies.

They can be found in the United States, Canada, Dominican Republic, South Korea, Bosnia, Republic of Panama, China, Japan, Puerto Rico, Russia and South Africa. In the Congo three banking vehicles with Dodge Power Wagon chassis have been put in service which at night are transformed into living and sleeping quarters for the traveling personnel. Mobile banks are very evident all over Great

Britain, while in the Philippines they serve chiefly farmers, fishermen and vegetable growers. The U.S.S.R. provided mobile currency exchanges for the 1980 Olympic Games, handling 300 customers an hour with vans.

Several firms specialize in making bank vehicles, such as a 23,500-pound, 41-foot, self-contained van designed to accommodate heavy weight, as well as special communications and security equipment patterned after existing branch facilities. Precautions are taken to restrict unwanted movement. In this category are found GMC Model P6S042 Forward Control chassis and GMC 6H-5308A transit coaches. Less elaborate approaches cover custom conversions of vans, buses, campers, motor homes and mobile homes. Vehicles that maintain a regular route have sites prepared for them in the form of a wooden building shell, designed as a shake-proof shelter in California. Vehicles boast wheelchair lifts and some even have hydraulically-controlled folding roof signs.

Why mobile banks? There are several obvious advantages:

- Cost less than one-half of the price of building a branch and require much less to operate
- Fulfill temporary needs, such as branch under construction or repair, emergency or disaster
- Serve temporary college or university registrations
- Handle special community activities like sports events or parades
- Serve market segments where branches not feasible
- Fulfill need for additional peak hour windows
- Reach inner-city poor neighborhoods; scattered rural and suburban customers; senior citizens centers, nursing homes, hospitals and parking lots of factories,

small businesses, shops, offices and hotels

Moving bank staffs vary from two to six, averaging three.

One of the largest fleets of mobile banks—eight units—has been operated by Bank of America in California.

In addition to full-service banks (with the exception of safe deposit boxes and night depository), roving armored cars with tellers take deposits at places like shopping centers; mobile check cashing vehicles are active on paydays; and portable ATMs are carried around on trailers or customized cargo vans.

Boats and planes have also been called into service as banks.

To reach customers at shopping centers financial planners have converted a 7.5 meter motor home into an executive suite on wheels complete with office, reception area and washrooms.

A Southern California stockbroker uses a converted Dodge mobile home to transact rural business, traveling up to 5,000 miles a month.

Black-operated Universal National Bank has operated its Stockmobile van from Wall Street to Harlem in New York City seeking to interest small investors in capitalizing the recently-formed bank.

INSURANCE SERVICES

Since the late 1960s major U.S. and Canadian insurance companies like Travelers, Aetna and Nationwide have used custom-built vans and converted motor homes as disaster offices for expediting windstorm damage claims and similar catastrophes like earthquakes. Mobile units are also in use for processing motor vehicle accident damage claims and to contact local agents, who themselves in some cases sell out of rolling offices in vans and buses. These typically contain a raised roof, sky-

This branch office of the Bank of Lenawee, Adrian, Michigan, is said to be the first mobile bank in the state. The 41-foot converted motor home offers two automatic teller machines and full service to locations where no banks are available. It makes its trips on a regular schedule. *(Toledo Blade photograph by Diane Hires)*

lights, bay windows and baseboards throughout. Secondary uses of these insurance vehicles include small meetings, recruiting at college campuses and personnel training. Travelers modified a Dodge Commercial Traveler custom-built on an International Harvester chassis which ended up at the 1968 Republican National Convention in Miami because the firm carried several coverages on the event and many individual delegates were policyholders.

Blue Cross of Western Pennsylvania in 1963 carried on a month-long enrollment program for non-group subscribers in a trailer which contained a desk and six chairs.

REAL ESTATE SERVICES

Rolling real estate offices offer the advantage of speeding up all phases of residential and commercial transactions. Specially outfitted van conversions such as the Ford Windstar GL contour have such accouterments as rich paneled walls and ceilings, laminate tables, and cushioned seats and files for both independent agents and company salespeople. With their computers, printers and cell phones riders don't miss being "back at the office." A Costa Mesa, California, realtor uses a motor home at the Orange County swap meet which draws about 70,000 high-income people each weekend, while a New York saleswoman moving exclusive Park Avenue property tools around now in a 1994

If you wanted to visit the "office" to discuss some private legal matter with the late criminal lawyer Charles Campbell, this was it! *(*Detroit News, *Edwin C. Lombardo, photographer)*

Rolls Royce Silver Spur II with video screens affixed to each front seat headrest. A Dallas title and abstract company carries the process of closing a real estate deal directly to the principals concerned with its Cruising Completer van for home buyers, builders and agents. Typical mobile subdivision trailer sales offices are a logical choice, too, for project developers who can now show not only models but also virtual conceptions on the computer to prospects.

LEGAL SERVICES

For ten years from 1981 until his death the flamboyant defense attorney Charles Campbell operated his law "office" from his cocoa-brown Dodge minivan. He parked it daily near downtown police headquarters to transact business on the street in Detroit. In 1990 one of the largest law firms in Toledo, Ohio, set up a specially equipped van as an office to use on out-of-town trips and for confidential client conferences. When a chemical company accident in Bogalusa, Louisiana, sent up a toxic orange cloud in 1995, dozens of lawyers quickly descended upon the community seeking prospective plaintiffs. Many drove their campers onto vacant lots, designating the vehicles as temporary mobile law offices.

AMUSEMENTS

Portable amusements have historic origins in circuses, carnivals and parades.

Mobile museums in trailer tours have been sent out by Ripley's Believe It or Not and similar weird collections. A 1967 traveling exhibit of a 38-foot sperm whale was housed in a 20-ton show rig, a converted Kenworth Utility with a completely chrome frame. In Paris in 1971 there was a miniature art gallery atop a 10-ton truck with transparent walls.

Moviegoers in Germany and Japan view film screens mounted on trucks and buses at malls, campgrounds and beaches.

Stage shows and puppet shows can be easily moved around on vehicles. A Seattle mobile stage was a Ford 2½-ton Model AA flatbed truck outfitted with a collapsible stage that unfolded from a rear compartment and rested upon removable legs. A trap door on stage was provided for special pop-up effects. Volkswagen minibuses have been used widely for puppet shows.

Games on wheels include miniature basketball, slot car races, video arcades and fishing holes.

Musical mobiles list pianos, Dutch street organs, calliopes, carillons and an impromptu Rolling Stones concert on a flatbed truck in Greenwich Village in New York City.

For those who like to gamble, a Reno, Nevada, truck stop/casino complex provides a 1963 Kenworth cabover with a 36-foot trailer holding 31 slot machines.

A mobile ticket trailer in New York City provides ducats to Broadway shows.

The Livonia, Michigan, Jaycees hold at shopping centers an annual open house for children that consists of four connected Kroger semis designed as rooms with names like Dracula and Star Wars.

Gus the Party Bus is a 28-foot, customized motor home remodeled as a game room on wheels with video games, pinball

Reminiscent of the Chicago Fire of October 8, 1871, is the O'Leary Firetruck Tour for visitors to the Loop business section. The city burned to the ground in one of the most disastrous fires in history. A high spot on the trip is a visit to the Water Tower and Pumping Station (in background), one of the few landmarks which escaped. *(Courtesy O'Leary Firetruck Tours)*

Ever wish you were a kid again? The Tumblebus, a franchised mobile physical exercise program for children, provides a supervised plan for fitness combined with a play atmosphere. The converted bus has all the necessary equipment to keep the little tykes in top form without having to drive them anywhere, a boon to busy parents. *(Courtesy Tumblebus)*

machines, jukebox and party favors. Able to accommodate up to 20 people, it is often rented for birthday celebrations or fund-raisers.

HEALTH CARE

Consumers can now rely on convenient health care services which they pay for directly or through insurance plans in both urban and rural areas in two ways: reactivated home calls by doctors, a real boon to retirees and the housebound; and at mobile units at shopping centers, health fairs, conventions and supermarkets. These are operated by independent companies, hospitals, charitable and trade organizations, medical and dental schools and labor unions.

Specially equipped vans, trucks, buses,

RVs and trailers have been turned into virtual medical clinics offering screenings, diagnosis and treatment involving teeth, hearing, vision, kidneys, cholesterol, cancer, tuberculosis and cardiac catheterization. Some chiropractors, psychologists and chiropodists now meet their patients in a vehicle. There are even mobile anesthesia and autopsy vehicles. The typical clinic is 40 feet long with two examining rooms, reception and processing areas.

Several hospitals in an area typically share a unit with very expensive equipment like the lithotripter (kidney stone locator) or 22-wheeler MRI. These machines have hydraulic patient lift assemblies.

In China there is an abortion clinic on wheels providing sterilization and a birthing hospital plus family planning in

Autopsy/Post Services in La Crescenta, California, does just what the name implies: independent post-mortems. Vidal Herrera above serves private clients and hospitals with three fully equipped vans. He also offers organ recovery, tissue procurement/retrieval services and medical appliance recycling. *(Courtesy Autopsy/Post Services, Inc.)*

remote regions, and an old double-decker bus in Germany dispenses venereal disease counseling.

In the early part of the twentieth century several automobiles were so chosen by physicians that they became known as "doctors' cars": the 1904 Maxwell Model N, Duryea Phaeton, Model T Ford, 1926 Packard coupe and Buick.

Health clubs, too, have literally taken to the road. Specially designed and constructed vans and trailers have served individuals or groups for exercise since the 1980s, reaching homes, schools, churches, day-care centers and businesses. Some are franchised. Overall physical fitness is stressed and the specific focus may be weight reduction, stress management or injury rehabilitation. Medicinal herbs and health foods are available also. Two or

three weekly workouts to stereo music are common. Over half a dozen franchises concentrate on children. One takes an old fire engine to shopping centers to teach preschoolers to swim. A physical fitness trailer now follows the Senior PGA Tour; this 45-foot unit expands to a 24-foot-wide interior when parked.

PET CARE

Pet care takes in veterinary services and mobile grooming.

Mobile veterinarians cater to small animals and have been operating at least since the mid–1970s in every state, with higher numbers in California and New York states. Most of these units normally are not able to serve animals which require intensive care or surgical procedures, but some vans have been modified to provide for large animals as well as surgery. Vehicle length varies from 18 feet to 26 feet. There are some trailers, pickup trucks and recreational vehicles used for animals. One deluxe custom mobile hospital boasts an office, reception room, examination room, operating room, bathroom, kennels and waiting room. Custom-equipped veterinary vehicles include fold-out examining tables, counters, refrigerator, sink, X-ray, anesthesia unit, storage and hot and cold running water. Stainless steel cages have access from the inside while multi-drawer models use the rear doors. These units with drawers have two-way slides in the transverse compartment which permit them to be pushed to either the right or left sides.

Some services, including at least one franchise, stress preventive care with vaccinations and diagnosis while others offer veterinary dentistry and rescue squad services. A few combine small animal practice with traditional farm calls for livestock. One even conducts elementary school workshops on animal care with his van. They may either operate on an "on call" basis or park at specific locations certain hours and days on a schedule. It is not uncommon for a mobile veterinarian to serve 10 to 12 a day, with a thousand clients or more and 100,000 miles a year travel.

Mobile grooming for pets is carried out in fully-equipped, self-contained salon vans such as converted Dodge Sportsman models. Customized interiors typically contain stainless steel cages, adjustable tubs, hydraulic tables, counters, sinks and storage areas for supplies. They have hot and cold running water and are climate-controlled with fluorescent lights, and sometimes even piped-in music. Special

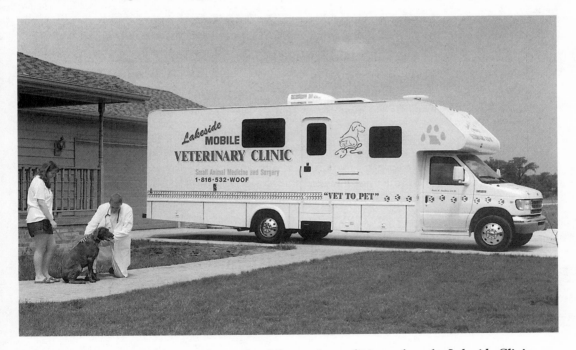

Pet owners appreciate the convenience of mobile veterinary clinics such as the Lakeside Clinic, above, in Kansas City, Missouri. Under the provocative slogan "Vet to Pet" it offers small animal medicine and surgery in a completely equipped custom vehicle. *(Courtesy Lakeside Mobile Veterinary Clinic)*

The Petential franchise offers free home delivery of pet food. As a pet store on wheels it also provides pet washing and free health checks. Note the display area in the van itself and on the doors. This is especially attractive to senior citizens and others who experience difficulty in traveling. *(Courtesy Petential)*

vehicles are designed for larger dogs with roof extensions. In major metropolitan areas fleets of nine or more vans may serve up to 6,000 customers. Franchising entered the picture in 1970 with the Ultrapet Groomibles which also sell dog food and pet supplies. There are several other similar organizations operating nationwide. Most serve the year around with day, evening and weekend appointments. These services are characterized by such clever, innovative names as Suds and Scissors, Petmobile, Galloping Groomer, Pet Pamperers, Wag 'n' Tails, Puppy Love, K 9 Care, Clip & Dip, Going to the Dogs and Bowzer Barber. Other pet services include transporting animals in limousines complete with fur-lined cages, air conditioning and TV, and on-site training.

LODGING

In 1951 a custom-built boarding house trailer became available for pipeline welders who followed construction jobs from Texas to California. The soundproofed, self-contained vehicle built with an extra heavy channel iron frame had 20 by 25 square feet of floor space and 80 inches of headroom. It contained eight double-decked bunks each with a window, lockers, washing facilities, shower and toilet. A smaller accompanying trailer housed an office, kitchen and dining room.

In 1958 a West German travel agency began offering 42 hybrid rolling hotel tours in 12 countries with a 39-foot passenger bus in front and a 40-foot red trailer dormitory hitched to the rear. These Rotels had a driver-mechanic-cook and tour guide. Later versions emerged in 1966: six triple-deckers for 27 passengers in oversized buses with a kitchen, bed-cabins, toilet and shower on the second floor. Meals were served on between-the-seat tables, with a refrigerator and bar downstairs. They were designed with theatrical troupes, sports teams and corporate management tours in mind. A 59-foot, articulated, double-decker Car-O-Tel su-

perbus for 14 passengers was a later approach by a tour group, as was a twin-decker omnibus converted into a portable motel that sleeps 11 with the top deck as bedrooms for a two-year world tour.

EDUCATION

Sheila Dawson is now on her third vehicle offering a mobile woodworking classroom to children in the San Diego, California, area. Starting out in a converted 1955 bakery truck, she moved up to a bigger 1958 school bus and finally now has ten adjustable workbenches set up in a 35-foot remodeled bus.

Trailside Country School since 1965 has taken students of high school age and

Starting in 1959 Howard Early offered his Norwood mobile music studio in the Cincinnati, Ohio, area. Parking in different shopping centers daily he provided instruction to children in guitar, accordion, etc., while their parents shopped. Two assistants went along in the two-room facility. *(Courtesy Norwood Music Center)*

older on annual ecology expeditions across the country in a special bus. They enjoy fully-accredited recognition.

Music schools in soundproof trailers now operate in Virginia, Michigan, Massachusetts, Ohio and Colorado, parking in shopping centers.

Probably the most novel training academic effort is that of magician Mark St. John, who has run his Hat 'n' Hare mobile magic school since 1990.

Several educational institutions in the 1970s and 1980s set up vans and minibuses as mobile offices to recruit and register off-campus. They visited shopping centers, churches, high schools and community colleges, and were staffed by faculty advisers. These included faculty from the University of Michigan College of Engineering, University of Toledo, State University of New York, Tampa Technical College, Monroe County Community College, Universidad de las Americas and Parsons Business School.

COMMUNICATIONS

Ameritech Michigan in 1996 sent out its 16,000-pound, 34-foot Winnebago van as a store on wheels. It was stocked with products and services including telephones, pagers, accessories, laptop computers, printers, TVs and VCRs. A refrigerator and coffee maker came in handy in visiting over 150 events. Since 1993 Air Touch Cellular has had a similar unit out.

SOCIAL SERVICES

Members with young children of the Ladies Professional Golf Association (LPGA) have access to a traveling day care center trailer during the nine-month tour season.

ADVERTISING SERVICES

Classified ads for consumers have been sold from a van in England by the *Lankshire Evening Telegram*.

REPAIR SERVICES

Both independent and franchised sharpening services often combined with locksmithing, have been on the road since the 1950s. Vehicles adapted to such service run the gamut from a converted laundry step van to a 72-foot custom trailer with built-in, track-mounted cabinets and shelving. Even three-wheeled Cushman trucks have been used. Many of these firms also serve commercial accounts. (Quite an improvement from the old "scissors grinder" with all his equipment on a bent back.)

Householders can also depend on having repair people come on wheels when they need services on TVs, VCRs, sound systems, clocks or firearms.

Sales to Businesses from Vehicles

DURABLE GOODS

There are two distinctly different segments of sellers and buyers involved with product sales from mobile units at the wholesale level: 1) sales of a variety of products by manufacturers' salespeople, industrial distributors and independent manufacturers' representatives to industrial, commercial, institutional, farm or professional business users, wholesalers and retailers (a few of these are franchise operations); 2) sales largely dominated by franchisers of automotive parts, accessories, supplies, equipment and tools by manufacturers, wholesalers, and car dealers to automotive service outlets and car and truck fleet operators.

In this first group a wide range of products is sold out of mobile units with some concentrations readily apparent in electrical and electronic machinery, equipment and supplies; chemicals; furniture; and fabricated metal products. Also present are instruments, paper, transportation equipment and textiles.

Vehicles of choice are display vans but also involved are trailers, goosenecks, buses and recreational vehicles. This category is very well represented in units on the road in Great Britain, mostly franchises.

In the automotive replacement or aftermarket most of the significant activity took place after the end of World War II in the United States, Canada and Great Britain. Independent wholesalers began to make their presence felt in the late 1940s; car and truck dealers in the 1960s; and manufacturers and franchises in the 1970s. In the early days such vehicles as converted school buses, motor homes and bakery trucks were drawn into service. As the business matured the vehicles became customized vans and panel trucks and in some cases even semi-trailers ranging in length from 10 feet to 42 feet and in weight from one ton to six tons. Fleets have gone up as high as 36 vehicles. The better units boast full-headroom, all-aluminum bodies and completely heavy-duty equipment. Interiors contain fiberglass skylights, dome lights, carpeting or tile floors, built-in tables, special walnut shelving, cabinets, steel bins, racks and drawers. Open stock displays may be on plywood or pegboard panels on walls and doors which swing out.

Drivers maintain a float stock of the most popular items, and have regular routes with schedules ranging from weekly to every six months. Performance parts are sold largely at Sunday drag strips. In addition to sales activities driver-salespeople maintain model stocks, pick up scrap, handle warranties and promotional aids.

Nondurable Goods

Wholesale nondurable goods sold from mobile units cover a disparate list of shoes, children's apparel, grocery items, books, gifts and novelties. Much of these sales are by manufacturer's representatives.

Business Services

Transportation

Serving trade elements in the United States and abroad with mobile automotive maintenance and repair services are vehicle manufacturers, jobbers, truck and trailer dealers and franchises. Served on a contract or "as needed" basis are new and used car, truck and motorcycle dealers; leasing firms; truck lines; public utilities; transit and tour operators; limousine companies and the like. Specialty services are provided for lift trucks, golf carts, marine items and aircraft.

Vehicles are designed to offer a complete range of specific services with special features like floodlights on top for night work on downtime trucks. Some tire repair trucks have a 125-ton hydraulic press for working on lift truck tires; a model for farm trucks is crane-mounted. A complete 40-foot mobile machine shop is a fixture at the Indianapolis 500 Races and between races it is taken to visit schools. Trailers serving refrigerated trucks drive the unit into the front of the reefer because the floor height of the trailer is designed to be the exact working height required. Laser-assisted trailer axle alignment is available and mobile auto crushers serve junkyards.

Mobile power water and chemical washing is active not only for vehicles but extends to virtually any exterior washable surface: buildings, signs, animal pens, poultry houses, bulk tanks, etc. With such power equipment operators extend their basic washing services to embrace paint and decal stripping, lawn fertilizing, degreasing, sewer and pipe flushing, duct cleaning and detailing. Typical washing vehicles are modified all-steel vans, some diesel-powered, with double reinforced frames, rear roll-up doors, side vent doors and heavy-duty equipment. Liquids are recycled. Franchises dominate this mobile segment of the market. Most washing organizations formed in the 1960s; the other automotive service franchises came in the 1970s with a tapering off after that.

To serve branch line shippers more adequately in smaller communities railroads have turned to customer service freight office vans, typically a custom ¾-ton Ford P400 compact Sportsvan. This trend began in 1967 and has involved the Burlington Northern, Grand Trunk Western, Illinois Central, Long Island, Northern Pacific, Great Northern and Union Pacific.

TESTING

Mobile testing involves both conditions directly affecting business or municipal activities and also employee health concerns.

Mobile commercial testing scientific research laboratories on wheels can be called by clients to monitor on site almost anything for which there are sensors. Typical assignments cover air, water, noise, soil, boilers, passenger vehicles, steam engines, electrical cable, meteorology, home heat loss and pavement conditions. The consulting engineers and planners use custom-built, state-of-the-art vans filled with the latest sophisticated monitoring equipment.

Mobile health services retained by businesses in the United States, Canada and Great Britain take two forms: testing and treatment. They are operated by independent firms and manufacturers. Custom-made vans began to go on the road in the 1960s and the number substantially expanded in the 1970s and 1980s. Screenings are offered on a wide range including vision, hearing, heart, pulmonary functions, drug-testing and complete multiphasic checks. On board is equipment for X-rays, audiometric booths and computers. They are used for pre-employment physicals and especially for periodic employee monitoring in hazardous occupations. They can either augment or entirely supplant in-house medical facilities.

Vehicles range all the way up from X-ray equipment transported in a panel truck to specially-built motor homes and vans, 35 feet to 48 feet long with private dressing and examining rooms featuring stainless steel and aluminum construction. Depending on the specific equipment they may have walls and ceilings of double fiberglass with corrugated aluminum fiber centers two inches thick; sliding doors on the side; solid ¾-inch, vertical grain oak floors with tempered Masonite overlay; leveling jacks and special shielding systems to prevent outside radio signals from penetrating. Some independent services also sell glasses, goggles, visors and other items onboard.

MARKETING RESEARCH

Mobile marketing research labs offer flexibility not available with traditional personal, mail, telephone or Internet survey methods. Firms with vehicles can more readily and cheaply contact such respondent groups as farmers, teenage girls and ethnic minorities at shopping centers, fairs, schools, campuses construction sites, beaches, supermarkets, industrial parks, flea markets, senior citizen housing or discount houses.

All sorts of vehicles have been successfully employed by research firms: vans, trailers and buses, up to 50 feet long. Nor-

A favorite technique of marketing research firms in the 1950s was intercepting housewives in shopping centers. Here Amro Research is interviewing a respondent who probably represents a good cross-section of the population. Exhibits in the Volkswagen van form a focus for questions. Note the handy podium for writing. Often coupons, small gifts or premiums were rewards. *(Courtesy Amro Research)*

mally they accommodate from four to eight people. Some are maintained as empty shells so that a variety of successive changing formats can be used, such as displays, TV screenings, model kitchens for product pre-testing or simulated stores. One alternative is to use two trailers side-by-side, one for signing-up and the second for actual interviews.

When research vehicles are located at a shopping mall, the most common site, a coupon check and ad test can be accomplished. Two groups are given coupons redeemable immediately in an adjacent store. One group is shown the ad and the other acts as a control to see any different level of redemptions.

Mobile research had its origin in the late 1950s in Volkswagen microbuses with projectors mounted inside to show TV commercials to respondents standing outside.

The ultimate in mobile testing, perhaps, was the Tanner Electronic Survey Tabulator, a TV rating system using a van with a high directional circular antenna mounted on a front bumper. The car moved through the residential neighborhood in the evening "prime time" hours recording and tabulating channels in operation. Experimentation was also carried out on a possible airborne unit utilizing a helicopter.

PRINTING AND PUBLISHING

Vehicles used in publishing newspapers and magazines have allowed editors and reporters to leave their desks behind to contact the public in person. When the Grand Coulee Dam was being built across the Columbia River in western Washington in 1938, a newspaper office on wheels turned on the *Grand Coulee Booster* in a frontier town near Spokane. Beginning in the 1960s the *Chicago Tribune* Action Express mobile city desk, a Travco Commercial Traveler, toured the city for interviews and provided on-the-spot coverage for major news events. It contacted an average of 5,000 people a week. In 1977 the *Cincinnati Post*, a metro daily, rented a van for a salesman and artist to solicit suburban advertising. In 1987 the daily newspaper *USA Today* inaugurated a six-month news junket in all 50 states with its "Bus Capade USA" in a specially built 40-foot Blue Bird Wanderlodge motorcoach. It had an office, kitchen and bath with a minicam mounted on the back. Regional and local staff people joined the news team en route. The follow-up newsgathering venture for Gannett saw it take to the air with its "Jetcapade." Also in 1988 the quarterly tabloid newspaper *Out West*, covering the back roads of 11 Western states, emanated from an 18-foot Carita minimotorhome newsroom and typesetting facility. In England Wolverhampton newspapers have used a mobile publishing office.

Magazinemobiles include *Commercial Car Journal* (1958), *Overdrive* (1972) and *S9 CB Radio Monthly* (1974).

Printing and allied manufacturing industries which perform services for the printing trades have spawned a variety of mobile operations. A self-contained mobile printing business became available in 1991 in the form of the Printmobile. This 16-foot step van featured a Grumman Olson Route Star body on a Chevrolet chassis capable of printing, platemaking, binding and desktop publishing with a two-person crew, designed for large institutions like hospitals and corporate training facilities.

Typesetting in recreational vehicles and vans is also offered for on-site work.

Traveling bookbinders have operated out of campers and 36-foot GMC Eleganza motor homes mostly in small towns repairing the bindings of 50 to 60 books a day. They specialize in plat books, deeds and other official records that can't be moved. They travel some 50,000 miles a year on average.

COMMUNICATIONS

The advent of television after World War II generated the need for mobile remote studio and control room facilities. One of the first units was that of WKBD in Chicago in 1948, with a broadcast unit with a body entirely hand-built of wood and sheet metal. The growth of color by the middle of the 1950s brought a need by the networks, their affiliates and local independent stations for studios at remote locations to produce live broadcasts. Advertising agencies entered the picture shooting commercials all over the globe. Independent production houses met the challenge with rental units for those without in-house vehicles. Hundreds of thousands of dollars worth of equipment is aboard these 18-wheelers close to 50 feet long, which may contain as many as 14 cameras. Besides the entertainment industry other customers use vans for training programs, sales presentations, seminars and meetings. Refinements have come in with cable television, pay television and satellite broadcasting. Remote radio broadcasting is done from vans, motor homes and trailers. A pioneer: WPIF in Raleigh, North Carolina, in 1930.

Cinemamobiles came in 1964 for remote motion picture production. These self-contained mobile studios house vast quantities of 3,600 different pieces of equipment. Eleven years in development, the fleet of 18 vehicles is leased individually. The largest unit, a 35-foot double-decker, has a lounge on top which seats 36 people and can transport a cast and crew of 60. Included are dressing rooms, lavatories, kitchens, wardrobes and mobile telephone systems. Custom-built in Europe, each unit has five complete departments.

Creativity has been displayed by the use of golf carts to cover matches, amphibians for water sports and motorcycles for Olympic foot races.

There are also traveling sound and recording studios.

SHREDDING

In the 1980s mobile shredding began to serve lawyers, engineers, accountants, detectives, hospitals, credit bureaus, insurance companies, restaurants and governmental agencies. Mobiles range from panel trucks to five-tonners. In some cases the shredding itself runs off the truck's transmission. Capacities may also handle wood, plastic and metal; schedules vary

One of the earliest users of mobile satellite dishes was WBTV Newstar 3 Live in Charlotte, North Carolina. This Piedmont facility also was a pioneer in the use of mobile color cruisers for remote telecasts. *(Courtesy WBTV3)*

The mobile shredding service Data-Grater leaves 600-pound security storage hampers with customers, to be picked up on a contract basis. The special vehicle can shred, compact, and empty automatically. *(Courtesy Data-Grater)*

from three times a week to yearly; and evening and weekend requests are honored. Compacting and recycling wrap up the sequence.

INVESTIGATIONS

Security considerations and other situations require businesses to retain private detective bureaus which employ mobile units in their repertoire. They serve as offices, patrol units, strikebreaker transport, polygraph testing and vehicles with surveillance equipment like video cameras. Typical assignments involve pay TV picture pirates and worker compensation fraud.

ADVERTISING AND PUBLIC RELATIONS

To service present clients and look for new accounts advertising agencies use mobile branch offices occasionally. They favor plush motor homes or buses adapted to their businesses with hospitality high on the menu: kitchens, lounge/bedrooms and bathrooms. These can seat from eight to 12 and often are taken to trade shows as well as clients. Some have photo studio darkrooms and/or roof deck photograph platforms. At the San Francisco Airport a public relations man maintains a 22-foot motor home with telescopic roof, used to photograph models and celebrities and for client rentals. The QVC mobile TV bus studio toured the nation in 1995 and 1996 looking for state and regional products to advertise live on its three-hour home shopping program.

COMMERCIAL PHOTOGRAPHY

Horse-drawn darkrooms have served Mathew Brady covering the Civil War; A.J. Russell photographing the Pacific Railway being built in 1869; Solomon D. Butcher concentrating on Nebraska sod houses in the 1880s and W.K.L. Dickson in the Boer War of 1899–1902. From 1930 to 1940 in New York City photojournalist Weegee (Arthur Fellig) developed photos in the trunk of his two-seater blessed with a special extra-large luggage compartment. For several years Zachary Bloom traveled with the Ringling Brothers Barnum and Bailey Circus, using a 36-foot trailer for his mobile darkroom. An engineering consulting firm has a 1963 Ford Econoline cargo van with the cargo area housing the camera body and the rear doors serving as its lens cover. A traveling 38-foot aerial photography cruiser has been built from a heavy-duty inter-city highway coach. It has a hydraulically-operated, 25-foot ladder and catwalk along each side to give a rigid shooting platform with four leveling jacks. It sleeps seven with a galley and shower.

ACCOUNTING

In the 1980s several franchised mobile accounting services were introduced for small and medium sized businesses. Working out of customized commercial van offices the franchises offer, in addition to computerized bookkeeping services, tax returns and financial management and counseling.

MAPPING

In 1992 Geospan, a geographical-information systems company, began to offer its custom vans to inventory the nation's infrastructure for utilities, real estate firms, governmental agencies and banks. Global-positioning systems satellite receivers and terrestrial-navigation gear create electronic street maps.

AGRICULTURAL SERVICES

Dairy farmers have had mobile herd management services since the 1980s. Operations in micro-computer equipped vans provide cost, production and breeding data. In 1979 a mobile slaughterhouse in New England began to serve pig farmers from a 1969 GMC school bus at the rate of 1,000 pigs a year. It was modified by taking out all of the seats and installing cutting tables, coolers, shelves, water bins, a band saw and a mobile winch.

REPAIR SERVICES

Repair services on a mobile basis offered at the commercial level include waste containers, computers, hydraulic hose, surgical instruments, pillows and stringed instruments, involving such operations as mobile welding.

OTHER MISCELLANEOUS SERVICES

Mobile services available also are listed for blueprints, auctions, balancing for auto racers, sign painting, computerized bartering, blacksmithing, disaster control, weather modification and water tanks.

Unacceptable Enterprises

Unfortunately but perhaps inevitably, vehicles have proven to be a boon to the unscrupulous, unethical and downright criminal; mobility aids and abets rampant antisocial activities worldwide. Ranging from misdemeanors to murder, the demi-monde needs its wheels as a vital adjunct for its warped lifestyles and evil vices. Vehicles figure in opportunistic business solicitations, pirate radio, fraud, counterfeiting, gambling, pornography, prostitution, escapes, theft, illegal purchases and sales, medical malpractice, rape and murder.

What would the underworld do without cars and trucks? The 1932 V-16 Cadillac Phaeton gained an unsavory reputation as the favored car of such mobile miscreants as bootleggers and robber barons. Infamous, nefarious nomads of the 1930s Clyde Barrow of Bonnie and Clyde fame and John Dillinger wrote Henry Ford to say how much they appreciated his powerful, speedy eight-cylinder cars, ideal for getaways from bank robberies. Totally successful getaways have been achieved by criminals using golf carts, snowmobiles, bicycles and motorcycles. More recently Mafia organizations in cities like Chicago have established plush mobile headquarters on top of a truck chassis complete with salon or drawing room appointments like bars, sofas and card tables.

OPPORTUNISTIC BUSINESS SOLICITATION

Lawyers in large metropolitan areas employ "runners" who drive around in a car equipped with a radio that can listen in on the public transportation radio system. When they hear of an accident they rush to it immediately to solicit business from those claiming to be injured so that they can sue the city transit line or others. The practice is characterized as "ambulance chasing."

Gypsy tow-truck operators employ unscrupulous tactics to haul away wrecked vehicles from accident scenes and then charge exorbitant storage prices. They too listen to accident reports on the short-wave radio and sometimes even beat the police to the collision.

PIRATE RADIO

Unlicensed, so-called pirate radio operators run their stations with a bootleg broadcast transmitter in trucks, as well as offshore.

FRAUD

A gypsy diagnostic medical laboratory company on wheels with RVs converted to "clinics" carrying testing equipment sent in false claims to insurance companies until the scam was uncovered in the 1980s. They offered free physicals not covered by Medicare on site to members of fitness and diet centers. Inept personnel and lack of basic hygiene were rampant.

Venal casting outfits in Hollywood send out bogus "talent scouts" in vans to Phoenix, Las Vegas, Kansas City, Minneapolis and New York City looking for the young, eager star-struck who pay for photographs and résumé counseling which never materialize.

COUNTERFEIT DOCUMENTS

Phony travelers' checks and a large assortment of false identification are printed on portable presses carried in campers, trucks or vans which travel through Southern states. The roving rings behind these scams prey especially on people in shopping centers, restaurants and hotels and motels. Bogus "winning" tickets on horse races also emanate from mobile print shops.

GAMBLING

Mobile bookies meet their customers at prearranged locations and times to place bets. Some have even driven ice cream trucks.

Cheating gamblers at casinos playing blackjack have a system whereby they are wired up to broadcast a picture of a card's underside to an accomplice with a receiver in a covered pickup in the parking lot.

PERAMBULATORY PORNOGRAPHY

In Los Angeles some pornographers run studios on wheels, picking up juveniles on the street in a van and photographing them on the spot.

PROSTITUTION

The Everleigh sisters with one of their stunning stable girls in Chicago in the early part of the twentieth century rode through the streets in a huge, open automobile painted a bright yellow with an enormous bunch of artificial flowers attached to the hood.

The *auto*erotic aspects of sin bins have been reported in New York City, where some pimps set up women in roving vans and limousines. Motorized massage parlors also are operated in the suburbs of large metropolitan centers. Nevada has had legal bawdy houses set up in trailers strung together. Camp followers in vehicles congregate around military bases. Seasonal opportunists find a spot for their bagnios in California and the Northwest at harvest time and in Northern Michigan during hunting season. Truckers are solicited over the CB airwaves by hookers in bordello vans; some work in shopping centers in the parking lots and at the Indianapolis 500 auto race in the infamous infield. In the military of some nations during wartime there have been mobile field and reserve houses of joy.

ESCAPES

Prison escapees in laundry trucks are legendary. In 1971 two convicts escaped from a Florida prison in a homemade bulletproof tank which rammed through the gates. The vehicle: a fork-lift truck hastily covered with 10-gauge sheet metal made in the furniture factory. In California a homemade armored car was used in an unsuccessful attempt to avoid arrest.

Thieves with customized trucks have stolen thousands of gallons of gasoline from service stations at night after closing hours after cutting the locks on the pumps. The trucks are equipped with a 500-gallon tank and a pump for siphoning. They cut a two-foot hole in the truck floor so that they can drop a hose into a tank and empty it without getting out.

In 1947 in New York City a man bought a second-hand vehicle and painted it to look like a U.S. mail truck. He pulled up daily at a branch post office which handled particularly valuable shipments from the New York ladies-wear garment center and loaded the truck with his accomplices and took off. Eventually they were nabbed.

To facilitate auto theft the "motor Mafia" maintain a number of mobile locksmith shops to manufacture duplicate keys for any model car on the spot.

In some countries humanitarian aid coming in is diverted to the black market and sold out of army trucks to unscrupulous merchants. Military corruption takes it away from hospitals, orphanages and food warehouses. Black market activities in Moscow center on auto parts on Saturday mornings on Ring Road.

Precious metal thieves melt their silver loot right in the van.

In Holland cable TV pirates operate from mobile studios fixed up in vans. They sell time to companies and agencies, use aerials for nothing and break in to disrupt reception with interruptions.

One of the tools of the trade of modern-day cattle rustlers is a rolling butcher shop in a truck.

Truck hijacking is fought by marking truck roofs for visual sightings by helicopters.

ILLEGAL PURCHASES AND SALES

Illegal purchases of food stamps are made at 50¢ on the dollar with criminals working out of vans where people congregate at the government offices.

During Prohibition bootleggers used trucks to haul their cargo. The rumrunners hid booze under furniture, hardware and groceries.

Distributors in New York City of fake clothing knockoffs use a fleet of vans to sell to street peddlers. Sellers of tools, bootleg tapes and stolen beef and pork also use vans.

A couple of hustlers operating out of a van have worked gas stations offering a kit that is supposed to enable a mechanic to remove the restrictor neck from gas tanks on cars requiring no-lead so owners can use regular without mutilating the filler tube in violation of federal law.

When it comes to narcotics, synthetic drugs are manufactured in vans. Home or office delivery of marijuana, rolling pipes and matches is available in New York City and Los Angeles. Some drug dealers have used ice cream or candy trucks as a front to sell to elementary school students. An international heroin ring successfully operated right *inside* a Mexican prison for four years in a plush house trailer command post, parked in the compound.

MEDICAL MALPRACTICE

An unlicensed dentist was caught treating patients in his vehicle "office" in Miami recently.

MURDER AND RAPE

During World War II in Germany the Nazis conducted fatal medical experiments in their genocide program in vans ("Sky Ride Wagons") with an observation window on the side.

They also employed "Black Raven" Gasenwagens, converted trucks with Red Cross markings or shingles to resemble house trailers. These asphyxiated at a time from 15 to 20 Eastern European Jews and other "undesirables." These windowless death vehicles resembled refrigerator vans and were painted a dark green with a hermetically sealed double door in the rear. The interior was lined with steel with an intake grating in the floor for gas to come in, released through a vent next to the cab or through pipes from the exhaust. An estimated 250,000 perished by this method.

A sadistic New Mexico villain abducted scores of women and held them captive inside his specially-equipped truck, the "toy torture box" where they were systematically raped and killed.

Although most marketing textbooks have never so far acknowledged "mobile marketing" adequately as a discrete channel of distribution, the sheer number of examples and persistence of the activity point toward a deserved recognition, beyond scattered and obscure references.

CHAPTER II

Advertising Vehicles

When passenger cars and trucks first began to appear on the roads in growing numbers it did not take long for perceptive advertisers to recognize their provocative potential for advertising, sales promotion, merchandising and public relations applications.

Vehicles have long since proved themselves to be effective both in the United States and abroad for moving both durable and nondurable consumer and industrial goods and services in the original equipment and replacement markets.

The list is impressive for a variety of techniques including displays and exhibits, demonstrations and sampling used by manufacturers, wholesalers, retailers, service providers, institutions, manufacturers' agents, public utilities, membership organizations, communications media, politicians and advocacy groups.

This chapter will describe in detail representative examples of unique vehicles initiated by individual advertisers, groups and outside commercial organizations.

Productmobiles

Beyond the obvious use of signs with names and logos on the outside of cars and trucks there eventually emerged a breed of new and exciting novelty visual vehicles with the body shaped like a huge replica of a product: productmobiles. They clearly correlate their design contours to focus on product identification at the buying level. It is easy to see how they quickly became in demand for retail store appearances, parades, fairs, sports events, schools and other civic activities. A comprehensive list of productmobiles appears in the Appendix.

Several of the earliest entries in the field deserve mention. In 1910 the American Thermos Bottle Company sent out its Thermos Bottle vehicle, custom designed as a light blue mammoth replica of Model 24 forming the body, cast in aluminum and finished inside in mahogany. The big flask toured the country with the slogan "Keeps Hot—Keeps Cold" inscribed in large letters on the wheels and "It's a Thermos or Just a Vacuum Bottle" (the Thermos name on the bottle will tell

In the past no picnic was complete without a Thermos bottle, and this custom vehicle did not let anyone forget it. This replica of a huge 1924 advertisement was seen all over the country in the 1920s. "Keeps Hot—Keeps Cold" was the message inscribed on the wheels. *(Courtesy King-Seeley Co.)*

you the difference) on both sides. The hood had a shiny aluminum screwcap and the rounding neck of the bottle held the driver and several passengers. It made an appearance at the 1924 Democratic Convention in New York City.

Pep-O-Mint Life Savers appeared on the streets as a motorized roll of candy on a Dodge truck chassis in 1918. The *Milwaukee Journal* in Wisconsin in the 1920s used a Model T Ford with a body shaped like a Graflex camera with an interior darkroom.

The famous productmobile advertising hot dogs and cold cuts enjoying the most ongoing media attention has been undoubtedly the Oscar Mayer Wienermobile, described as a true icon of Americana. The company is now a Kraft Foods division.

The original 1931 vehicle was designed by Carl G. Mayer to cruise around downtown Chicago. It was a 13-foot metal hog dog built by the General Body Company of Chicago and it had open cockpits in the center and rear.

All subsequent models evolving through the years (style changes in 1936, 1952, 1958, 1969, 1988, 1995 and 2000), have been specially designed and custom-built. The 1958 version saw for the first time the hog dog on the bun. Prior to that it was towed behind on a trailer.

Each of the units in today's fleet of eight is 27 feet long, eight feet wide, 11 feet high and weighs 14,050 pounds. The

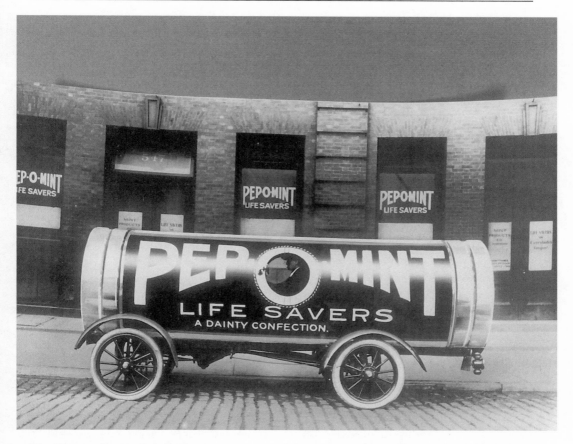

The Nabisco Foods Group of RJR Nabisco now includes Pep-O-Mint Life Savers among its 364 different branded products, but in 1918 the candy was promoted on this Dodge truck chassis as a "dainty confection" by the Mint Products Co. Note the driver behind the round window. *(Courtesy the Nabisco Foods Group, RJR Nabisco)*

bright red and yellow hot dog replicas with the familiar rhomboid emblem have been designed both by in-house draftsmen and professional industrial vehicle designers. A variety of truck chassis have been used: Willys Jeep, Dodge, Ford and now GMC W Series. Models have been produced in the firm's own body shop and at outside specialty vendors.

The bodies are carved from Styrofoam, sprayed with fiberglass and feature lightweight metals. The vehicles have a gull-wing door, a "bunroof" hatch on top, big side view mirrors, a 32-gallon gas tank, Pontiac Firebird taillights, and Pontiac Grand Prix headlights. Top speed: 100 miles

per hour. Both the dashboard and glove box are hot dog–shaped. Relish colored upholstery on the six captain chairs draws out the theme. A steamer on the lower side sends out a tantalizing aroma of freshly-grilled hot dogs while the loudspeaker blares out the familiar jingle "I Wish I Were an Oscar Mayer Wiener," thanks to its own radio station broadcasting at 88.3 FM. Such appropriate license plates as "WNR MBLE" and "I WSH IWR" round out the promotional package. For many years in the beginning Little Oscar mascots gave out toys to children. Outside the United States, tours have gone to Puerto Rico, Spain and Japan. It is not uncommon

More people have seen the custom Oscar Mayer Wienermobile than any other productmobile. In the early years the "world's smallest chef," above, gave out little trinkets to children. The vehicles are still going strong on the road afer 65 years pushing Yellow Band hot dogs and luncheon meats in the United States and abroad. *(Courtesy Oscar Mayer Division, Kraft Foods)*

for a Wienermobile to rack up 1,000 miles in one week. They are registered as trucks and every two weeks contract service is performed at a local outlet on the rolling wieners. To minimize wear they are only actually driven inside towns; between stops they ride on flatbed trailers.

Wienermobiles have been used in fund-raising efforts for Second Harvest National Food Bank Network to battle domestic hunger, and Toys for Tots. One of the 1950s vehicles is now on display at the Henry Ford Museum in Dearborn.

While many different products and services have appeared on advertising vehicles, certain concentrations or categories are apparent: beverages (liquor and carbonated drinks); foods and candy; sports

and amusements; footwear; auto parts and accessories; musical instruments; drugs; and tobacco.

All types of containers lend themselves readily to bodies because of their compatible configurations. Cartons, bottles and cans have become mechanized packaging.

For 30 years beginning in 1906 Bass and Worthington Brewery in England used a fleet of bottle lorries to deliver and promote original White Shield Pale India Ale. The first vehicles were round-radiatored Spykers made in Holland. After the end of World War I a switch was made to the six-cylinder, 1924 Daimler TL 30 chassis because its traditional fluting on the radiator echoed the shape of the crown

Productmobiles have always been very popular in the United Kingdom, and a pioneer in this category was the Bass and Worthington bottle vans for White Shield Original Pale India Ale. A Japanese beer used a similar vehicle. *(National Motor Museum)*

stopper on the bottle's neck. The bottle itself was made of sheet-iron. One is now on display at the National Motor Museum in England. A popular Japanese beer has used a similar vehicle.

The Heineken Brewery in Amsterdam, Holland, has a vehicle with a Heineken's barrel body and wheels that look like beer bottle caps. It has lights, a rearview mirror and a bulb horn on the top.

Carbonated beverage makers Nu-Grape, Coca-Cola and Pepsi-Cola have all had relevant productmobiles.

A unique fleet of 20 straight delivery trucks has successfully done the advertising honors as rolling billboards for Lehigh Valley Farms' Abbotts Old Philadelphia premium, all-natural brand ice cream since 1983. These oversize carton replicas

of a regionally-known package on the smooth-side, aluminum-body vehicles enable the dairy to maximize its graphic impact. The front, sides and rear are decaled with durable, color-coordinated reflective film to insure safety and identification at night.

In the 1930s in Florida an orange juice vending truck had a model A Ford body shaped like a can. In 1969 Campbell Soup's V8 vegetable juice can-shaped roadster had a 350-horsepower engine from a Ford Mustang and V8 cans for hubcaps. Vegetable cocktail was dispensed from a tap located in the car's rear-mounted spare tire. A-1 Steak Sauce bottles went on the street as vehicles in 1999.

There have been several promotional vehicles built with bodies the shape of a

A successful transformation of a Model A Ford into an orange juice vending vehicle. The enticing attributes—pure, wholesome and ice cold—were prominently featured on the colorful unit which frequented venues where large crowds gathered. *(Courtesy Samuel LaRoue, Jr.)*

shoe or boot to advertise footwear or repair service.

A California shoe repair service has a brown Bootmobile for neighborhoods with a vanity license plate "Boot" on the 1972 Honda modified to resemble a short-topped boot using steel, chicken wire and fiberglass, powered by a motorcycle engine. Another shoemobile is operated by American Franchise Systems. A French manufacturer of Kickers shoes for children uses a plastic-bodied vehicle ten feet long and six feet tall built on a Peugeot chassis and used in Germany, shaped like a laced-up boot. Barnum and Great London Circus had in 1882 a pony-drawn float shaped like a shoe to symbolize the nursery rhyme "The Old Woman Who Lived in a Shoe."

Roller rink operator Butch Cleland used in 1980 his Skatecar, a two-seater convertible powered by a Volkswagen engine with a body the shape of a roller skate to advertise his establishment.

In the automotive field we find two very interesting examples.

The Mufflermobile was built by the Minghenelli brothers, who operate franchised Meineke Muffler shops in New Jersey. It is 16 feet long with an open cockpit. All body panels, doors, fenders and the cargo bed were taken from a mini-pickup truck. The outer body is 16-gauge steel panels, and an exhaust pipe is attached to the platform.

Bowman Industries, suppliers of auto sound systems, has used an exact scale model automobile based upon the design and specifications of its top-of-the-line auto stereo speaker system Model SK 4000 GL. This promotional SpeaCar was

There was no mistaking the intent of the Shoemobile in Los Angeles when it came to your neighborhood. The little import always attracted attention no matter how many times seen before. These types of vehicles have also been used in Europe to advertise shoes and boots for sale. *(Courtesy Quality Shoe Service)*

designed and custom-built in-house in 30 days in 1978.

Some symbolic productmobiles have featured a representative major aspect of the business such as a trademark or mascot, rather than a specific product itself.

Mountain Bell Telephone used a little car with a body mounted on it shaped like a telephone complete with a 100-pound, eight-foot-long red telephone receiver bolted on. BTI, a regional telecommunications firm in North Carolina, in 2000 advertised with a New Beetle 1.8T featuring a glass phone stuck through the sun roof.

The Pac Man Mobile emphasized the familiar profile of the video game hero.

This bright yellow custom street rod contained hand-formed top panels from a Volkswagen Beetle, fenders from a Peterbilt truck and a gold-plated Buick V-6 engine.

What would you expect to find at the International Bowling Museum and Hall of Fame in St. Louis, Missouri? Why, a 1920 Studebaker shaped like a bowling pin, of course, with tires called pin wheels. It was built by the late Frank Skrovan, a onetime Cleveland, Ohio, bowling alley proprietor.

Hub Mail Advertising Services, for pick-ups and deliveries, has used a panel truck painted to resemble an 11-foot-high red and blue mailbox, an apt symbol of the

Top: This Mufflermobile supports the services provided by the Meineke franchise shops in New Jersey. A pickup truck was converted to this form to draw attention to the business with the colorful logo on the side. *(Courtesy Scott Minghenelli). Bottom:* To celebrate one of the oldest indoor sports, this bowling pin car was built; it now rests in a St. Louis museum. *(International Bowling Museum and Hall of Fame, St. Louis, Missouri, USA)*

firm's printing, mailing and occupant addressing business.

Starting in 1960 route trucks for the Home Milk Producers Association were literally built like a home. Their distinctive silhouette featured a gabled and bracket-mounted shingle roof topped by a chimney.

If you see a bright yellow, custom-sculptured, peanut-shaped specialty vehicle with Mr. Peanut perched on top, it's Nabisco's Mr. Peanut Hotrod advertising

The jaunty yellow fellow saluting from the top of this advertising hot rod is the well known Planters trademark character, Mr. Peanut. In his unique vehicle he hangs out at car races and the like on his tour across the nation. Young people are particularly taken with such an approach. *(Courtesy Nabisco)*

Planters Peanuts. It has gone over 50,000 miles since 1999 on a tour visiting auto and truck races and schools and parades in over 35 cities. Construction is from a frame of GMC W-4 Series truck and it is 23 feet, six inches long, 12 feet, six inches high and eight feet wide, and weighs 10,000 pounds. Mr. Peanut himself is 12 feet, six inches high. The vehicle features zoomie pipes, exposed engine, authentic moon disc hubcaps and has a four-speed automatic transmission. Mr. Peanut Cam-A-Camera, located in his monocle, transmits his view onto his large screen TV. In 1927 Planters had a salted peanut Dodge with a Millspaugh and Irish body.

Recently several organizations have produced replicas of older model product-mobiles.

Russell Stover candies were originally made at home in a bungalow in Denver, Colorado, in 1923. For promotion a custom-built 1925 Dodge delivery truck was ordered with a small bungalow home on the chassis. It toured the Midwest in 1926 and featured a smoking chimney and flower boxes. This model has just recently been resurrected as a replica advertising vehicle.

A cottage industry is "a small scale business where a family works at home," and that is how Russell Stover Candies began. The original bungalow advertising car was replicated recently for promotional purposes. *(Russell Stover Candies)*

The Zippo Manufacturing Company first sent its windproof lighter Zippo car out to advertise in 1947. A record of 180,000 miles took it to all states. A recreation of the vehicle was made up in 1998, a custom replica on a 1947 Chrysler Saratoga New Yorker chassis. Two large lighters that open and close realistically stretch above the roofline of the converted four-door model, now a two-door business coupe. There are removable neon flames that are lifted out and set in the back seat for traveling. The car is 17 feet, 11 inches long, six feet, two inches wide and eight feet high with the lighter closed and 12 feet when opened, weighing 4,020 pounds. There is a five-foot by six-foot custom-made steel cab with 24 karat gold-plated lettering. It has acted as a pace car and now rests on permanent display at the firm's headquarters visitors' center in Bradford, Pennsylvania.

Uniquely shaped vehicles have been used very effectively in connection with television shows, moving pictures and TV commercials.

The caped crusader, Batman, crime-fighting hero of comic books, movies and television since 1939, rode in his jet-powered, fireproof Batmobile, a futuristic black, custom-made coupe based on the Lincoln Futura. The front is styled to look like the face of a bat, the hood scoop has a nose-like appearance, eyes on either side extend out to form ears, the grille cavity resembles the mouth, dual 84-inch bat fins are in the rear and four six-inch flared eyebrows and bulletproof wheel wells were designed as tire protectors.

Productmobiles have always been very popular in Europe, especially in Great Britain. Some of the most novel vehicles to come out of England between 1972 and 1974 were from the Outspan Or-

This custom replica of the original 1947 advertising car for Zippo Lighters was put together in 1998. The vehicle has become a top tourist attraction at the firm's headquarters, above. The whereabouts of the original are unknown. *(Courtesy Zippo Manufacturing Co.)*

ganization, orange importers. Six advertising versions of vehicles shaped like oranges have dimpled, fiberglass bodies. They are based on specially fabricated spaciform chassis of Austin Minis from British Leyland with wheelbases of only four feet which yield a length, breadth and height of seven feet, six inches. Some 200 pounds of ballast are built into the rear to prevent rolling forward under hard braking. The relentlessly orange theme sees orange wheels, orange-tinted windows, and orange leather segmented, padded roof, sides and seats for six. Speed is 30 miles per hour. The vehicles have been shown in Great Britain, France, Germany and South Africa. Outspan has also had promotional tours with eight-foot high oranges on Ford trucks aimed at wholesalers

and consumers. A model of the original 1970 vehicle is on exhibit at the National Motor Museum in England.

An outstanding example of an industrial productmobile is the Steelmobile. The Armco Drainage and Metal Products Division of the Armco Steel Corporation sent out in 1956 its custom-built vehicle on an 18-month, 50,000-mile tour of the United States and Canada. It reached major cities served by its 50 fabricating plants. Designed by Armco engineers, it required nine months to build. The elliptical body in the shape of a huge, corrugated drainage pipe such as the company provides for sewers and culverts was 35 feet long, eight feet wide, 12 feet, three inches high and weighed 22,000 pounds. Multi-plate, finely-finished, 12-gauge

England's Outspan Orange Organization produced some of the most novel round advertising vehicles in the 1970s. These vehicles really stopped traffic. A Japanese round ladybug car is powered by a pair of hamsters running on a treadmill. *(The National Motor Museum)*

In the early 1920s Swedish Viking Spark Plugs were "plugged" via this custom-made advertising vehicle devoted to racing plugs. Note the extra large radiator cap. The factory still exists today, turning out fine Swedish saw blades. *(Courtesy Roland Swalas)*

stainless steel was used and all seams waterproofed. Another product of Armco, Flex-Beam Guardrail, was used on the rubrail along the sides and the rear bumper. The electrically-operated door in the side doubled as a canopy and steps. The top sign lowered during travel. Inside were 16 different exhibits and a conference area. Trade shows were included on the itinerary, and 5,615 visitors were reached, including customers, prospects and engineering students.

One might easily assume that when more sophisticated media became available to advertisers, like radio, television and even the Internet, that these advertising vehicles would have faded into oblivion, but surprisingly enough they have

persisted right up to the present day. As a fascinating marketing phenomenon they prove once again the viability of the basic concept by surviving the test of time.

For example, Hershey Foods Corporation has sent its Kissmobiles on an annual tour since 1997 to advertise its chocolate confection. These 60-city, 50,000-mile trips reach consumers at supermarkets, warehouse clubs, colleges, hospitals, museums, parades, fairs and sporting events where samples are distributed. The vehicles are built on 1997 GMC W-4 truck chassis and are 25½ feet long, eight feet wide, 11½ feet tall and weigh 13,250 pounds. It took six months to design and build them with a body made of three giant, side-by-side Hershey Kisses.

This rolling drainpipe was designed by Armco Drainage and Metal Products as a demonstration unit to reach engineers, public officials, contractors and engineering students in 28 different colleges as it toured the United States and Canada. *(Armco Drainage and Metal Products, photograph by Henry Elrod)*

A multimedia center entertains visitors with games and contests. Top speed is 74 miles per hour, and the vehicle has fulfilled the role of a pace car. The project acts in the capacity of a fundraiser for the charitable organization Children's Miracle Network.

American Airlines in 2001, as a way to promote its Website, converted a 2001 Volkswagen New Beetle to resemble an airplane and took it on the road. The shiny silver exterior sports the airline's signature colors, the AA.com logo, airplane wings and tail.

Bodies shaped for religious and governmental applications are described in those respective chapters.

OTHER VEHICLES FOR CONSUMER ADVERTISING

Although we can be impressed with the diversity of probably well over 75 different major product categories normally involved with vehicles for consumer advertising, certain ones stand out clearly above the rest. These are foods and beverages; magazines, newspapers and books; automotive equipment; television networks; cars and trucks and beer and liquor. To a somewhat lesser extent we must include toys and games; radio stations; tobacco; hair care and cosmetics; over-the-counter medications and computers.

Activities emanating from these ve-

Chocolate lovers won't settle for anything less than samples, given out when Hershey's Kissmobile rolls into town. Yearly trips take it all over the country. *(Courtesy Hershey Foods Corp.)*

hicles are largely displays and exhibits, demonstrations, sampling, entertainment and contests. Anniversaries quite frequently precipitate a mobile venture and sports themes are very popular.

The vehicles reach their intended audiences at shopping centers, fairs, parades, charity events, grand openings, sports games, trade shows, parks and schools.

Many different kinds of exhibits draw crowds to advertising mobile units but not always favorably. A negative note was struck by the Scottish writer Thomas Carlyle who spoke disparagingly in 1843 of a hatter in the Strand of London who put a seven-foot-high hat on wheels to advertise his business on the streets.

The National Bank of Detroit has had a mobile money museum since 1968

with 12 different multimedia historical exhibits. It took three months to build and equip with the displays. It has visited over 108 schools and some 70,000 children and parents have seen it.

Calling them the world's largest tires, Goodyear Tire and Rubber exhibited in 1972 the 11½-foot, 7,000-pound giants mounted on special trailers for automotive shows, conventions and dealer showings.

Two 45-foot customized motor coaches set up as mobile television studios by C-SPAN have so far traveled nearly 200,000 miles since 1993. The intention is to educate both students and teachers about the public affairs cable television channel. The coaches have been in 49 states and 988 cities at 774 schools.

Thomas Kinkade, a California artist,

To build customer recognition of a package at the retail shelf level, Bromo-Seltzer has been advertised with this giant replica bottle on wheels. Emerson Drug used a White truck in the early 1920s to reach consumers with acid indigestion, upset stomachs, headaches and heartburn. *(American Truck Historical Society)*

has had his paintings displayed in a touring museum called Sharing the Light, a 38-foot retrofitted vehicle offered to the public beginning in 1998.

Bardahl takes its Miss Bardahl hydroplane out on a giant trailer for off-season personal appearances to promote its oil.

Many products and services lend themselves to demonstration as a requisite selling technique which can be taken right to the customer. Goodrich demonstrated its new light-truck pneumatic tires on a 1911 White canopy express truck on a tour.

The Peoples Gas Light and Coke Company in Chicago started in 1922 to send out home economists to give curbside cooking demonstrations from a special truck.

W.A. Sheaffer Pens were in a 1925 White bus outfitted as a rolling showroom.

In the early part of the twentieth century, Singer Manufacturing Company generated an interest in home sewing by trailer demonstrations by its dealers at county fairs. Later Westinghouse refrigerators were similarly promoted.

In 1967 Teleprompter CATV parked vans at the curb to demonstrate cable TV versus an ordinary antenna with salespeople stopping passersby.

A unique, old-fashioned railroad caboose on wheels fashioned on a Ford

Chicago housewives in the early 1920s were treated to a free curbside cooking school, courtesy of the Peoples Gas Light and Coke Company. Demonstrations were designed to build usage for the public utility at the grassroots level. Invitations to come to the store were also given from the mobile kitchen. *(Courtesy Peoples Gas Light and Coke Co.)*

Econoline chassis is used to show off Hammond organs as a demonstration showroom introduced in 1976.

Raid Max Insectmobile is a specially-constructed, high-tech Winnebago van designed in 1991 to house an insect zoo, diagnostic and interactive computer, video monitor, player, demonstration bait house and a product demonstration. Tours teach consumers how to control cockroaches with Raid Max at shopping centers for S.C. Johnson Wax.

Model railroad fans in the United States and Canada can see their favorite Lionel trains in a 46-foot custom trailer with 350 feet of track spread out over 256 square feet.

To advertise its power tool battery system, Black and Decker has used since 1998 a fleet of 21 custom-designed and refitted white Ford and Chevrolet truck showrooms. Since the back window areas are used for displays, rear vision from the driver's seat has been set up with special graphic imaging.

In 1999 Land's End catalog merchandisers sent out a black, 48-foot, expandable, 18-wheeler trailer dressing room. A computer took scanning measurements to help consumers choose clothes on the

Web that actually fit their individual body types. The 14-city U.S. and Canadian tour went 12,000 miles.

Swissair for 12 weeks in 1999 used a unique see-through mobile exhibit van with Plexiglas sides and roll-up rear door with steps, to introduce its new Customer Care Program in 15 U.S. gateway cities. Featured in the window was the new first-class sleeper seat in the diesel GMC cab chassis with a 14-foot by eight-foot display walk-through sampling area.

Where food products are concerned it is only logical to feature sampling.

Hills Brothers gave out samples in 1963 from its fleet of portable coffee shops at supermarkets.

In 1971 the RJR Foods chuck wagon offered samples of Chun King Skillet Dinners and coupons at shopping centers.

For hand-dipped sampling of its Dove ice cream bars, M&M/Mars began using in 1995 a custom 30-foot, 26,000-pound Big Dipper Truck with a ramp and an eight-foot-long walk-up window. A ten-by-12-foot Dove inflatable emerges from the roof.

Tying in with the PGA tour, DiGiorno Pizza tours its Rolling Clubhouse for sampling. over 300,000 pizzas have been dispensed from the 67-foot custom semi in 50 cities in 36 states. Visitors have also enjoyed golf practice, a lounge and discount coupons since 1997.

Movement and sound are two recognized key elements in getting attention. Quaker Oats developed this dramatic mobile demonstration of its products to symbolize its slogan "Foods Shot from Guns." A cannon at the rear of the touring car shot the puffed wheat or rice into the gazebo. *(Auburn Cord Duesenberg Museum)*

The Home Box Office (HBO) Kid Flicks Studio Tour uses this 34-foot mobile film studio to teach students the art of making movies, and encourages participation in its online film festival. Home Box Office is the television programming division of AOL–Time Warner Entertainment. *(Courtesy HBO)*

The number of people sampling A1 Steak Sauce from a Rolling Steak House had reached 1,042,985 at last count. Its fleet of mobile grills are 53-foot customized semi-trailers which resemble closely authentic working restaurants in every detail with huge replicas of A1 bottles. They have stopped at over 203 supermarkets in 40 cities since 1998.

The Eckrich Fun House van, 13,500 pounds, 22 feet long, which mirrors a 1930s cartoon house, hit the bricks in 1999 to promote its brand of meats. It is based on a W4 Isuzu chassis as a 12-foot tall cartoon dwelling with fiberglass bumpers, box windows and a smiley-face cab. Inside is the kitchen, with a four-foot by three-foot barbecue grill that slides out from the bottom of the vehicle to provide samples.

Campbell's Chunky Soup has been promoted since 1999 with tours featuring custom buses, trailers and Chevrolet Suburbans at football games, retail headquarters, supermarkets, mass merchandisers and college campuses combined with a hunger relief charity effort.

The Kraft Cookhouse is a 46-foot trailer kitchen offering food from custom serving windows prepared with over 30 branded items. The truck was developed to support the County Fair featuring Vince Gill.

Other products as well move when hands-on sampling is offered for maximum impact. Nintendo gets young people to try out its games in 26-foot mobile arcades with 38 sampling stations. A built-in hydraulic stage provides for hourly competitions. Sony had similar vehicles put on the road not long ago.

Entertainment will draw a crowd every time to a mobile unit.

Beginning in the 1940s with loud-speaker trucks playing music interspersed with commercials, subsequent efforts have seen movies invade the Philippines for such well-known names as Colgate-Palmolive, Pepsi-Cola, Plough, San Miguel Brewing and 7UP. Video vans in rural India have sold toothpaste.

It took three different firms in 1984 to produce a unique, 45-foot display van for Oldsmobile. Sculptures were added to a General body custom van built on a Dynaweld dropdeck chassis. Display ears were built on a removable aluminum framework supported by huge doors.

As part of an anniversary celebration a mobile unit adds a welcome element.

Billed as the world's largest touring grill, the Johnsonville Big Taste Grill was conceived to celebrate the firm's 50th anniversary in 1995 in a sampling promotion for bratwurst. The fully-customized semi-trailer log hauler included a reinforced carbon steel grill weighing 53,000 pounds. It was 45 feet long and six feet in diameter. On deck were propane fuel, a 100-gallon water storage tank, refrigeration unit, hot and cold running water and an aluminum walkway for the cooking crew. A pneumatic system opened and closed the grill lid. Popular demand led to second unit's being developed.

For the fiftieth anniversary of Tonka toy trucks (1947–1997) Hasbro invested in

This Oldsmobile 45-foot custom display van was taken to stock car races in the 1980s. The unique rooftop viewing stand was accessible for up to 50 people by aluminum stairs using the gooseneck section as a landing. The colorful vehicle graphics and signs never failed to draw huge crowds at well attended events. *(Courtesy Oldsmobile Division, General Motors Corp.)*

Anniversaries often generate mobile units. Johnsonville billed its fiftieth anniversary sampling as the world's largest touring grill to offer bratwurst. *(Courtesy Johnsonville Foods Co.)*

a 67-foot customized semi. It had exhibits of the toy line and games to attract people to over 170 retail stops at 40 cities in the United States and Canada.

A perennial problem facing advertisers with vehicles is constricted space. Expanded designs obviate this negative feature.

The New Jersey Telephone Company exhibited its services in a specially built 32-foot vehicle in 1956. The sides moved out on tracks, providing a fully anchored space 30 feet by 15 feet. An aluminum gangplank stairway folded out from the rear.

The Baltimore Gas and Electric Company fit a couple of kitchens and some other demonstrators into its aluminum vehicle in 1959 by designing in two wings, one on each side, that expanded to 14 feet. On location it became a 32-foot by 14-foot showroom on wheels. A hand crank slid out the wings and when they went back, the floor and roof telescoped. It was used to show homemakers its products and services.

Miller Brewing's Miller Sound Express offers neighborhoods free concerts from two specially-designed sound stage trucks which convert into a 32-foot stage in 90 minutes. It took four months to make and has traveled over 26,000 miles.

A problem with such vehicles is to dispense food samples from a mobile unit and still maintain space for exhibits. Sopexa, a French association of food product manufacturers, met this challenge in 1964 designing outside shadow-box displays, four on each side, of its buses going to France, Germany, Belgium, Switzerland and Sweden.

Joining several vehicles together is another clever way to achieve expanded exhibit space.

Several years ago General Motors scheduled three Parade of Progress road shows, organized with a caravan of eight huge red and white vans, custom-built by Fisher Body's Fleetwood plant. Each streamliner spanned a 223-inch wheelbase truck chassis. Canvas awnings joined six of the vans to form walk-through exhibits of future science and technology marvels. After the first tour the original vehicles were replaced by a dozen new Futureliner vans 33 feet long with 16-foot sides that opened to form exhibit areas or stages. Over a million miles took the tours to 251 towns in the United States, Canada, Mexico and Cuba, reaching 12.5 million people.

There are several different types of sponsoring organizations behind multiple cooperative advertising efforts involving vehicles. Noncompetitive advertisers have combined their efforts successfully on a shared basis in dual promotions in several instances.

In 1963 Mobile Media put 12 trailer showrooms in regional shopping centers for several sponsoring organizations.

A joint 1977 promotion for Coca-Cola, Levi Strauss denim outfits and Ford has taken place both in the United States and Canada involving customized vans called Denimachines.

To promote Reynolds Wrap aluminum foil, Reynolds Metals Company's blue and coral custom-made kitchens went out on a 67-foot truck with interactive, walk-through computer displays to 18 cities on the 50th anniversary of the foil in 1997. General Electric appliances were used exclusively.

The National Basketball Association Jam Van was designed in 1998 to offer four interactive games and exhibits oriented around a 67-foot, 68,000-pound customized truck which unfolds hydraulically to reveal 4,000 square feet of basketball entertainment. Sponsors are Adidas and Gatorade. Over two million visitors have attended nearly 300 stops.

Polaroid and Wal-Mart set out in 1999 on a joint road tour with a Max Mobile to demonstrate digital photography on the computer with interactive demonstrations. The 25-foot custom-made van

Tandem mobile operations with compatible noncompetitive products are logical. When Reynolds Aluminum Foil teamed up wtih General Electric Appliances, the custom-made traveling kitchen proved a success. Interactive computer displays were used in the nationwide tour. *(Courtesy Reynolds Metals Co.)*

Active participation was the watchword in the Jam Van of the National Basketball Association. Numerous promotional signs and logos were liberally displayed. *(Courtesy the National Basketball Association)*

had a ground platform stage and overhang awning. On top was a 15-foot-high inflatable Photomax Cockatoo logo. The unit has visited over 256 Wal-Marts. Polaroid vans have also toured Russia.

Lego Systems and Major League Soccer teamed up in 2000 to provide an interactive traveling show visiting 15 major sports venues. The 40-foot special-purpose truck has had as supporting sponsors MasterCard, Ortega Foods and Sunkist Growers.

The Home Depot store chain, the official NASCAR warehouse, united with Ridgid and Husky tools in 2000 to bring Tony Stewart's Trail Blazer Racing Rig to its stores. Visitors can sit inside the Winston Cup Pontiac Race Car simulator.

Canadian Westinghouse has used

mobile displays for its major appliances in concert with IGA–sponsored cooking schools in a 36-week tour of small towns and villages.

The Big Helpmobile is what Nickelodeon called its 34-foot Airstream equipped with interactive games and digital video technology. Visiting 100 different destinations, it aimed to encourage young people to fix up their neighborhoods. Co-sponsors included Burger King, the Boys and Girls Clubs of America and the YMCA.

The media are also represented in group efforts with sponsored vehicles coordinated by *American Heritage Magazine*, *Health*, *Sports Illustrated*, *Cooking Light*, Cahners Publishing and CHUB Radio.

There have been several attempts by

The more good sponsors the merrier is the motto for Lego Systems, Major League Soccer, Master Card, etc. Important sporting events all over the United States were visited with the interactive show. Colorful graphics drew large crowds. *(Courtesy Lego Systems)*

outside, independent firms to set up traveling road shows for a variety of relevant sponsors, going to college towns, sports events and shopping centers.

Some alternate approaches to a large, specialized truck have worked for imaginative advertisers.

The vehicle department of Anheuser-Busch, the St. Louis brewery, was maintained for many years in the early part of the twentieth century. It produced bus bodies, barn-shaped horse vans, refrigerator truck bodies, armored car bodies for banks and camping vehicles. August A. Busch, Sr., during World War I undertook a project on behalf of the government to develop a special inboard land cruiser which went both on land and water. It was intended as a reconnaissance vehicle for the military. By the time it went into production the war had ended in 1918. It then became a promotional vehicle for some of the Liberty Loan war bond drives, to tour soldiers and sailors, and for recruitment. After that it was devoted to promoting as

the Bevo Boat Car. During prohibition the drink Bevo, which had negligible alcohol content and tasted like beer, was produced. After Repeal in 1933 it was rechristened as the Budweiser car and taken on national tours, appearing at the Indianapolis Motor Speedway for the 500-mile race and was featured in a Billie Burke movie, *Gloria's Romance*. Four different versions were successfully produced. Nineteen feet long, they were mounted on Pierce Arrow chassis and powered by Continental Big Six motors, and had bell and snout front ends and screw propellers, rudders, anchors, harbor lights, mounting lines, flagstaffs, life preservers, guns and cameras. The driving compartment was railed in cockpit style, as was the rear seat for two or more passengers. Carried as auxiliary wheels were five Silvertown Goodrich cord tires. There was a spacious hold, leather upholstery, thick carpets, fine wood and a radio. Garish touches included brilliant metal mountings.

It is said to have taken six years to

The
All-Year-Round
Soft Drink

Bevo
THE BEVERAGE

In World War I, U.S. armed forces were driven around in the famous Bevo Boat Car of Anheuser-Busch. Originally intended as a military amphibious reconnaissance vehicle, it later toured the country to promote the soft drink Bevo and Budweiser Beer. It was made in-house on a Pierce Arrow chassis. *(Courtesy Anheuser-Busch Companies)*

build the Roach Coach, promotional car of Roach industries, makers of iron-on T-shirt transfers. The body is handmade of fiberglass and the chassis and engine are like the ones used in cars running at the Indianapolis 500 race. It has shiny chrome from grille to exhaust pipes and the gas tank is made from very light titanium. With a bug-eyed windshield, the car is painted Roach red.

The totally functional, multicolored, composite Anycar II is a 1929 Hudson which combines parts of 50 domestic and foreign car models dating from the 1930s to the 1970s. It was used by Manufacturers Hanover Trust to advertise retail automobile loans. Represented in the most unusual vehicle are Chrysler, General Motors, Ford, American Motors, Nash and imports.

Cars and pickup trucks with merged bodies so that they have two front ends facing in a different direction are favorite advertising gimmicks. They have been exploited by Tuff-Kote Dinol; Desert GMC, a Las Vegas dealer; Coca-Cola; Mello Yell'o; KRUB Radio; Fram/Autolite; an auto transport company and a national restaurant chain.

Manufacturers of cars and trucks enjoy a special advantage with the opportunity of producing their own vehicles for advertising and publicity.

Pace cars are modified production models used in such events as the annual Indianapolis 500 Race. Later on replicas are sold by dealers along with other special event and limited edition models. Concept cars are one-of-a-kind experimental prototypes featuring innovative options and alternate power sources, and are used at auto shows, parades and the

Top: Designer Gene Winfield is shown with his composite Anycar II that he put together for a promotion by the Manufacturers Hanover Trust. Not just for show, it could be driven. *(Courtesy Manufacturers Hanover Trust). Bottom:* This Ford Phaeton official pace car at the 23rd annual 1935 Indianapolis 500-Mile Race took on added significance because of its famous occupant, pioneer aviatrix Amelia Earhart. The race is said to be the biggest single-day sporting event in the world. *(Indianapolis Motor Speedway)*

Contrasts in size always attract attention, as did this 1906 Baby Reo shown with midgets and a giant. The Barnum and Bailey Circus provided a venue for such a promotion. The half-size novelty was converted to gasoline after using compressed air initially. Reo cars were made from 1905 to 1936. ("Reo" stands for Ransom E. Olds.) *(Detroit Public Library, National Automotive History Collection)*

like. Cutaways are exhibit cars designed to show the inner workings not normally apparent.

Miniature replicas like a half-size baby Reo built in 1906 were used in circus publicity and other events.

Contract Advertising

Consumer advertisers who want to supplement their own advertising vehicle programs or who prefer not to get directly involved with buying, renting, leasing or borrowing a vehicle, can look to several

other outside contract mobile sources. These firms offer moving media on a national, regional, state or local basis for promotional coverage in the United States and similar geographical options in other parts of the world.

Public transportation transit vehicles sell advertising outside on the front, back, sides and top and the inside. These included buses, subway cars, trolley cars, streetcars, cable cars, suburban commuter trains, etc. Television advertising on municipal buses has been tested in Orlando, Florida, Singapore and London. The closed circuit system offers news from wire services and weather. A so-called Merchandising Bus or Show Bus is a regular transit vehicle chartered and converted in and out with advertisements, driven to customer and prospect locations.

Most large cities in the United States and abroad allow taxi advertising: sides, trunk and top. Allover paint is sometimes available. The latest devices are animated electronic color video screens on top which change continuously and also show weather and stock market quotes. Depending on the time of day and location, the rotating ads flash block to block through a satellite feed and Internet link. Inside may be found leaflet racks and Taxigrams which are moving, lighted repetitive ad messages.

Intercity buses may allow ads on the sides and rear and also offer full wraps on both sides. Inside space is on ceilings and bulkheads.

Private trucks lease their space to independent firms which in turn rent it out to advertisers. Both local and highway fleet vehicles carry messages on the noses, side and rear doors. A few trucking companies sell their space directly.

Billboards are towed on flatbeds or specially-designed narrow custom vans in metropolitan areas for two-sided views. Rotating kiosks are a variation and public address systems are optional. In some cases the truck's grille and door can also carry ads.

In 2001 Ford Motor Company rolled out a novel two-ton, ten-foot-tall billboard on a trailer with a bird feeder covering the ad. When birds ate the seed, the exposed message introduced the 2002 next-generation Explorer.

Lighted, third-dimensional displays in the middle of a glass cube on trucks are also available.

Each racing car has available an average space of 55 square inches for advertising decals.

Volkswagen Beetles, Minis and SUVs have been favored for private car advertising in the United States, Japan and other nations. Firms contract with the vehicle owners for signs or in some cases complete car paint jobs or wraps with vinyl adhesives. Some drivers are provided with the ad car which they must wash at least every two weeks.

Other vehicles for advertising messages are farm tractors, Zambonis, forklift trucks and motorcycles with back billboards and saddlebags.

Vehicles for Industrial Advertising

While there have been many types of products and services represented in industrial mobile units sent out for exhibits and demonstrations, the highest numbers are found in machinery, particularly electrical and electronic; instruments; fabricated metal products; chemicals; transportation equipment and food products. Costly, complex capital equipment is dominant.

Industries which can also be listed to a somewhat lesser extent include primary metals; printing and publishing; rubber and plastic; and stone, clay, glass and concrete products.

Business to business mobile advertising is a worldwide proposition. In addition to the United States, units are on the road in Canada, Mexico, Great Britain, France, Belgium, Holland, Sweden, Czechoslovakia, Iran and Australia.

While intended primarily for advertising purposes these vehicles also serve significant secondary uses for training, marketing research and hospitality.

Back in 1912 in Canada a true pioneer effort was undertaken by Ontario Hydro. It took out a three-ton, 50-horsepower, gasoline-driven, Canadian-made

1904 Gramm truck to demonstrate electricity to farmers and their wives, touring as the Adam Beck Traveling Circus. (And this was before the word agribusiness was even a part of our business vocabulary.)

Another early custom-built, blue demonstration truck was used by Heidelberg for its printing presses in the 1920s and 1930s. Its distributors employed them for calls on printers and for exhibits here and abroad.

It is informative to recognize that advertisers have successfully adapted vehicles to many different situations to meet their selling objectives.

Stuart Warner, manufacturers of automotive instruments, desired the ultimate in its customized promotional visual display vehicle in 1969, which was based on a Dodge A-100 Tradesman series van body. Modifications included extending the front to form a full-width grille housing; tucking both the front and rear bumpers in tighter; flattening the wheel wells; welding and filling the original side and rear doors and cutting eight-foot panel doors to fold out of the reinforced side and creating a recessed, rectangular rear window.

Transporting particularly large products can present a formidable problem but Mobile Vision solved its dilemma several years ago by bringing its giant, 13-foot by 18-foot television set mounted on a truck to demonstrate the system's capability to prospective executives as it parked at the curb.

The Do All Company had to demonstrate machine tools, metal cutting machines and precision gauging equipment, rather large items that usually aren't taken directly to the customer. The answer: a specially fitted 40-foot Fruehauf trailer whose electrical power system was adapted to various circuits and other modifications made to accommodate the cumbersome items. This vehicle appeared in 1969 after three months of planning.

Expandable vans have been employed by several firms to give them more room, including Electronics for Imaging, makers of servers for digital copiers and printers in 1998; Worthington, air conditioning and heating; DuPont, plastic resins in 1972; Eastman Kodak, video film in 1967; and the Aluminum Company of America, primary metal products in 1973.

These expandable vehicles through various mechanisms can yield exterior sections on one or both sides giving two or three times the normal width for the exhibit area.

A most unusual design was incorporated into a 1973 vehicle with two floors for the United-Carr Group in Great Britain. Four European tours have been made to show products used in the automotive and appliance industries. The purpose-built unit, based on a Bedford coach chassis, was 36 feet long and eight feet wide. The roof of the upper deck was lowered on the road.

What do you do to get the attention of high up customers? Put your name on *top* of your advertising vehicle, of course. That is the strategy used by Hilti USA, makers of construction fastener systems, calling at construction sites with a custom cargo van; Budd Company, products for automotive and industrial markets; and Leon Office Machines, parked near highrise buildings.

Some advertisers have found that it has taken two units to achieve their marketing objectives. The Carborundum Company operated a 20-ton Abrasive Workshop for a 60-minute demonstration of grinding materials housed in two tractor-trailers joined together from 1954 to 1958. Lubrizon Corporation took two vehicles out together in its Performance Technology Caravan in 1983 advertising lubricants: a 48-foot display trailer and a 32-foot recreational van used as a conference center.

The expandable 40-foot Alcoa Trailblazer Theater Showcase boasts both a kitchen and restroom. It was designed to reach distributors and customers at warehouses. The custom-made truck opens up to nearly triple the enclosed width of eight feet. It seats 30 for audience presentations. *(Courtesy Aluminum Company of America)*

Building up a fleet of custom advertising vehicles has served Armstrong Cork well for its various divisions. One of the largest total number ever sent out simultaneously for a single line was its 22 showcases for resilient flooring materials in 1960, which were operated by wholesale distributors visiting retailers.

Some other advertisers who have agreed that if one is good, several are better include the Enterpac Division of Applied Power, 17 for hydraulic tools; IBM, 14 for typewriters and dictating equipment; Nibco, 14 for valves and fittings; Worcester Controls, 14 for ball and butterfly valves; Briggs, seven for plumbing ware; National Gypsum, seven for building products and wallboard; and GE, five for lamps.

It is very unusual to run into full-scale operational equipment taken out in a vehicle, but mobile manufacturing can take place. National Engineering in 1960 took a 40-foot trailer to foundries with a demonstration pilot plant to sell its machinery and equipment. International Paper Company has targeted its Roving Chicken 40-foot trailer at poultry processors to show off packaging systems since 1974.

Bringing large-scale models into the field on a vehicle requires some skill and planning. Cessna Aircraft displayed a mock-up of its Citation Jet Plane at airports and private firms on a custom 40-foot Model FB van trailer in 1972. A single axle air suspension was installed, and

At its one hundredth anniversary, Armstrong Cork sent out a fleet of 22 mobile showcases on resilient flooring. The custom 35-foot trailers were completely self-contained and featured displays and marketing aids in the comprehensive program. *(Courtesy Armstrong Cork). Bottom:* Visiting 80 foundries was this demonstration pilot plant of National Engineering. The trailer had a fold-out stage with the opening of 16-foot doors. Over 1,000 in 20 states were reached in the ten-ton vehicle's 30,000-mile tour. *(Courtesy National Engineering)*

the center of the sidewall, on the curbside, was modified into two sections. One segment swung upward to form a canopy, while the other section dropped to a level position to act as a walkway. A special side door was built on the curbside sidewall. Astra Jet Corporation trucked a full-size mock-up of its Galaxy Jet around North America and Europe in 1994. Pacific Mountain Express enlisted a Mighty Mite machinery-moving trailer to carry its scale model of the equipment it uses, an exact replica of its road rig in 1954.

Consumer goods depend rather heavily on entertainment to draw crowds, but their industrial counterparts find the ploy works equally well.

The 1974 Power Parade Caravan is what the Detroit Diesel Allison Division of General Motors called its mobile promotion for independent truckers. It traveled 10,000 miles to visit 28 different truck stops offering engines and automatic transmissions. The specially built vehicles included two 40-foot trucks with displays; a 28-foot computer unit; a transmission display vehicle with a built-in movie screen and driving simulators and a show unit for the country music stars.

Amenities for customer and prospect hospitality frequently involve some type of refreshments, but Symons Manufacturing Company, maker of concrete forming equipment, believes in going full bore with its combination mobile product display-meeting-dinner Form-A-Van. Contractors in the expandable unit are treated to a bar and a full-course dinner.

Sometimes advertisers are perceptive enough to uncover a need not being met. Rothmans of Pall Mall Canada used 11 Special Events Caravans in 1968 as free mobile headquarters for those putting on fairs, picnics, parades, carnivals, sports events and all types of community activities. They expedited administration and communication with broadcast facilities,

lounges, kitchens, public address systems, a slide-out stage and first aid and firefighting apparatus.

Another advertiser, Monroe Canada, makers of automotive shock absorbers, provides free, comprehensive mechanical services to auto racers. A 30-foot, 14-ton Max truck does the honors in a tour of major drag events.

One way to gain attention is with a bizarre vehicle. Miller Beer took its Monster Squad fleet of 11 fully-customized hearses out six weeks before Halloween for trade and retail calls. Each vehicle was equipped with a sound system, fog machine, neon running lights and hidden strobes.

A few advertisers have been fortunate enough to have products that can be built right into a vehicle as integral parts for truly working demonstrations. Specially built cars or vans have been used to focus on the use in the automotive industry of aluminum, copper, steel and zinc, sponsored both by individual primary metal firms and trade associations. Other products featured in demonstration vehicles are petroleum tanks and wood paneling.

United States Lines has used two vehicles made up of its 40-foot marine containers converted into mobile showrooms in 1972.

Demonstration heavy-duty trucks are common, used by Diamond Reo, International Harvester, Tatra, Navistar, Ford, White and other makers. This same technique is used infrequently on buses.

Various types of automotive equipment, parts and accessories are regularly installed on vehicles sent out as demonstrators. Seen frequently are engine and transmission coolers, batteries, engines, transmissions, spark plugs, air conditioners, tires, brakes, sound systems, lighting and police equipment.

Multiple mobile exhibits allow joint participation by noncompeting advertis-

In order to promote the use of stainless steel in passenger cars, Allegheny-Ludlum Steel Corporation produced (bottom to top) a 1936 Ford, 1960 Thunderbird and a 1967 Lincoln Continental with special steel bodies. These one-of-a-kind custom vehicles were used extensively for promotions at various automotive events. *(Courtesy Allegheny-Ludlum Industries)*

ers at reduced costs by sharing expenses in a cooperative caravan format.

These are put together by several different groups: independent firms, publishers of trade magazines, trade organizations and trucking companies. The U.S. Bureau of International Commerce fosters mobile trade fairs overseas. Markets frequently represented in multiple efforts are automotive; computers and electronics; appliances; public utilities; institutions; publishing; food products and healthcare.

Political Advertising Vehicles

In political campaigns candidates at all levels have traditionally looked to mo-

U.S. Brick covered a 1975 32-foot Airstream travel trailer with ornate oak trim and 500 square feet of one-half-inch thick bricks weighing 3,000 pounds. The refitted, customized recreational vehicle has been used as a trade show display in many spots. *(Courtesy United States Brick, Inc.)*

bile offices and advertising vehicles to reach potential voters to augment their door-to-door walking trips, bicycle tours and forays on trains and even boats.

William Jennings Bryan in 1896 was the first presidential candidate to campaign from an automobile during his first bid for the presidency. The Mueller Manufacturing Company provided the horseless carriage, one of only ten cars in the United States at the time.

In 1918 in Grove City, Pennsylvania, Dr. E.J. Fithian was running for governor on the Prohibition Ticket. He personally designed a custom 33-foot motor home built on the extended chassis of a 1917 Winton Big Six Touring Car, the General. It boasted an ornate rear platform with grillwork, railings and brass fittings like those on a Pullman car.

Politicians worldwide use a variety of vehicle types in looking for votes, but if

they were ranked in order of preference they would probably be recreational vehicles, buses, trucks and vans. Buses are used, of course, mostly in state and national elections. A very few opt for motorcycles, golf carts and even street sweepers to get attention and media coverage. Sound trucks blaring out messages on the streets through public address systems are very popular, especially outside the United States.

Shopping centers, parks and theaters are favorite stopping spots where crowds gather.

Politicians delight in christening their advertising vehicles with unofficial, fanciful names: Chariot of Divine Enlightenment (India), Battle Bus (South Africa), Straight Talk Express, Rhodesmobile, Yortymobile, Pattmobile, Griffenwagen and Fiegermobile.

When Mayor Christopher of San

Francisco ran for re-election, he used a locomotive-shaped car in 1959 with the slogan "He Gets Things Done."

About 40 crusading movie stars and celebrities, including Jane Fonda, traveled the California coast in a Greyhound bus in a Hollywood Clean Water Caravan for three days to register voters to support a toxic chemical and hazardous waste proposition on the ballot. It stopped at college campuses, among other places.

To encourage voter registration, the MTV network and Rock the Vote sent out in 1996 and again in 1999 the red, white and blue, 45-foot Choose or Lose Bus. Cross-country tours of 28,000 miles have signed up over 12,000 young people at colleges, shopping malls and concerts. An interactive kiosk offered a ten-question political poll and information about parties, platforms and issues.

In 2000 the Service Employees International Union operated there tractor-trailers. Inside volunteers telephoned on behalf of Democratic candidates in Pennsylvania, Michigan, and Missouri using a special computerized system.

Advocacy Advertising

It is quite logical for both aggressive individuals and passionate coalitions to take to the streets to choose a specialized vehicle. It can spearhead crusades in a deliberate effort to further a vital cause, raise funds, urge a boycott, recruit new followers, embarrass the opposition or just protest vehemently. What better way is there in a dramatic fashion to make an effective statement?

Many different kinds of issues are supported or rejected by activists and reformers, including social, political, medical, legislative, ecological, religious, patriotic and financial.

Virtually any type of vehicle has been successfully used locally, regionally, nationally or even internationally. Eight like-minded Britons took a trip to 19 different countries in two trucks to raise awareness of the hospice movement.

Not surprisingly the most violent, ongoing protests are leveled against local, state and national governments. Other major mobile adversarial topics are peace, product quality and prices, traffic safety, labor unrest, animal rights and abortion.

Vocal vehicle campaigns take place worldwide but probably the most frequent reported are in the United States, France, Spain, Poland and Great Britain.

Various militant devices are used in connection with the vehicles: special paint, banners, ribbons, wraps, loudspeakers, vanity license plates, static and audiovisual displays and handouts. Those protesting the planned phasing out by General Motors of the Oldsmobile brand advocate tying a black ribbon on one's vehicle. Sometimes vehicles are even destroyed to make a point, as against gas-guzzling cars.

The most dramatic move is a show of force in the form of a blockade or slowdown to confound traffic. Convoys and caravans have toured with as many as 3,000 participants. One man drove all the way across the country backwards to protest the government's energy policy.

Favorite demonstration stops are shopping centers, schools, fairs, carnivals, festivals, auto shows, parades and other community events.

Advocacy vehicles have generated some surprising names: Life Mobile (anti-abortion); Death Mobile (assisted suicide); Madd Mobile (Mothers Against Drunk Driving); Sludge Buster (water pollution); Tractorcade (farm protest); Divorcemobile (laws inimical to fathers); Peacemobile (anti–Vietnam War) and Justice Buggy (voting rights abuse).

Some of these significant efforts exhibit elaborate organization and considerable expenditures for special vehicles.

In 1970 and 1971 the Earth Liberation Front (ELF) toured on behalf of several social causes: ecology, birth control, women's liberation and education reform. The caravan consisted of a big red ELF bus, general store, book bus, advance bus, multimedia bus, resource bus, flatbed bus and a follow-up bus. Eleven young college students visited college campuses distributing pamphlets, putting on shows, seminars, concerts, town meetings and puppet shows as Survival Revivalists.

The Gripemobile 423Z led the Great American Complainathon, a 28-city odyssey completed in three months in 1993. It was a book promotion tour led by two authors gathering material for a sequel on men's and women's complaints about each other. The 1982 Chevrolet cargo van stopped at street corners, shopping malls, truck stops, bars, restaurants and other high-traffic areas where 7,500 were interviewed.

The American Association for Retired Persons Voter Express Bus was on the road in 1999 for a two-month tour for 4,000 miles to deal with legislation issues for older Americans to urge them to vote. In 24 cities visitors signed a special material wrapped around the vehicle.

In 1999 visiting 36 cities in two months the National Environmental Trust took its 25-foot, solar-powered Airstream Pollution Solution vehicle to educate the public about global warming. The Washington-based lobbying group demonstrated energy-saving devices such as an electric-powered bicycle.

The Pork-Buster patrol saw service in 1999 also, a ten-ton pink Fleetwood Discovery 37V motor home, 37½ feet long, 12 feet, one inch high and 102 inches wide, used by the Seniors Coalition lobby group to tour key states to identify and eliminate wasteful government spending and special-interest legislation. It featured an electronic slide-out living room and bedroom.

Unofficial Advertising Vehicles

Many passenger cars and trucks inadvertently turn into advertising vehicles because of the manufacturers, dealers, licensing authorities and the motorists themselves.

Car and truck makers normally place the name of the vehicle prominently on the outside somewhere (hood ornament, nameplate, etc.) and often too on the inside on the dashboard.

Dealers are famous for very subtly offering free license plate frames with their names on them. The same goes for spare tire covers. After servicing, they often put a paper floor mat ad in also.

Owners or leasers can advertise a consumer or industrial product or favorite social message with bumper stickers, decals, sun screens, antenna attachments, ribbons on rearview mirrors or door handles, hubcaps, rear-window lights and so on. Old-time western movie star Tom Mix had the tires of his Rolls-Royce embossed so as to leave "TM" imprinted all over the dirt roads of his day in Southern California.

State licensing bureaus like to put a provocative slogan and graphics on plates, usually symbolic of some attribute to attract tourists.

Trucks have extra opportunities for advertising in addition to the item lists for passenger cars: mud flaps or splash guards and wind deflectors, some of which are lighted.

Vintage cars and trucks are also used for promotions. Two customized 1966 Ford F-100 Good Humor ice cream trucks are in service now for advertising by Breyers Ice Cream. Millers Farms Dairy uses a 1929 Hupmobile in parades. Acoustical Specialty Products depends on a 1924 Ford Model T truck to tell its story. Stanley Publishing Company in Chicago has appropriately featured a 1919 Stanley

Some advocacy groups go to elaborate lengths to further their favorite cause. This garish pink 37-foot, five-inch Pork-Buster Patrol was a mobile command center. *(Courtesy Seniors Coalition)*

Steamer. A restored 1929 Model A Ford truck was used for advertising by Kruse Electrical Contractors up to 1974.

And famous owners can transform a vehicle. Take a plain, old 1965, 19-foot, 6,000-pound Rolls-Royce Phantom V limousine and use it for the Beatles tours. Call it the Beatlemobile and paint it by hand with psychedelic-patterned scroll-work, signs of the zodiac and floral de-

By virtue of association, this Rolls-Royce limousine became famous as the Beatlemobile. John Lennon, Paul McCartney, George Harrison and Ringo Starr used it in their 1960s concert tours. Taken at Chertsey, Surrey, England, May 26, 1967. *(Hulton/Getty Archive Photographs)*

signs created by a gypsy mystic working with the late John Lennon. It was subsequently loaned to the Rolling Stones, Bob Dylan and other friends. Was it a successful promotion as an adjunct to their persona? By virtue of its significant association and ornamentation it sold for $2,2990,000 at Sotheby's auction in New York City.

CHAPTER III

Training Vehicles

Putting wheels to training is an intriguing concept.

Mobile training may be defined as an instructional program oriented around a vehicle as its principal focus which is taken to learners.

This chapter covers mobile training by industrial organizations, educational institutions, membership organizations, foundations, multiple sponsors and commercial outside vendors. Training by governmental bodies and religious groups is described in their respective chapters.

Industrial Training

A very wide variety of organizations has been involved in industrial mobile training, but manufacturing firms and service providers are dominant. Other elements include wholesalers, retailers, public utilities, banks, insurance companies, real estate firms, agricultural interests, construction contractors and mines.

As production of the normal range of goods and services resumed after the end of World War II it became immediately apparent that mobile training as an instructional technique was of paramount importance for successful operation of some programs.

Mobile training activities expanded rapidly in the 1950s and 1960s, peaked in the 1970s heyday and began to phase out to a lower level gradually after that, with only sporadic programs necessitated by particular training objectives. Training yielded to technological advances in more sophisticated audiovisual techniques: teleconferencing, videoconferencing, distance learning on the Web, CD-Rom, etc.

Although most programs emanated from the personnel department or the marketing areas for sales training, some of the larger businesses now place training under separate human resources management and development functions.

Larger vehicles can accommodate from six to 30 students, averaging 15. (It has been determined that the optimum ratio between students and instructors is about 20 to 1.)

Four common situations which require industrial mobile training have been isolated:

- Mechanical or technical products with involved applications which need sales demonstrations, installation, maintenance and ongoing service
- Relatively frequent need to update employees, channel of distribution personnel and customers in skills regarding the aforementioned areas
- Employees, dealers, and distributors dispersed geographically in far-flung, remote locations
- Sales force in the field

Automotive Training

More mobile training has been carried out regularly in the automotive industry than in any other. This involves both the original equipment market and the replacement or aftermarket. Represented are vehicle and component manufacturers; wholesalers; retailers; truck fleets; bus operators; moving and storage firms; oil companies and manufacturers of service equipment.

Virtually all major domestic and foreign manufacturers of cars, trucks, farm tractors and recreational vehicles have used mobile units at one time or another for training service mechanics at their dealers and distributors. Prominent in this regard have been General Motors, Ford, Chrysler, American Motors, International Harvester and Mack. Foreign-based companies include British Leyland, Fiat, Mazda, Peugeot, Porsche-Audi, Rootes, Saab, Toyota, Volvo and Volkswagen.

In sheer numbers of vehicles General Motors has probably had more experience than any other manufacturer in this endeavor. Trained have been employees, dealers, distributors and customers. Topics offered cover such areas as mechanical service, used car reconditioning, auto body repair and safety. For its car divisions (Buick, Chevrolet, Oldsmobile, Pontiac and Cadillac) beginning in 1972 mechanic training was accomplished with a total of 122 specially-built, self-contained vans equipped with portable, pull-out workbenches and special rear screen film projection which dropped from the side, with swing-out diagnostic materials.

Automotive Components and Equipment

Principal suppliers to the automotive industry of such items as engines, bearings, transmissions, axles, clutches, brakes, carburetors, air conditioners, heaters, lighting, tires, batteries, spark plugs and gaskets all have depended on mobile service training for their various products.

Recognized as a pioneer in mobile training is the Champion Spark Plug Company. Beginning in 1952 over a million service technicians and related attendees participated in more than 30,000 clinics in the United States and Canada. Some 14 red, white and black, specially-built Dodge B380 vans were used in this effort. Average attendance was 35 in automotive dealerships, independent garages, VFW halls and other sites. At trade shows a van served as part of the exhibit, and one session was even held on a Navy aircraft carrier.

Such retail and wholesale automotive organizations as the National Automotive Parts Association (NAPA) in 1973, Midas in 1975 and the Autopro Division of Mid-Con in 1978 have all used mobile training to good effect.

Many of the larger truck fleets, bus operators and moving and storage companies train drivers in vehicles in classroom settings. Also included in some extended programs are dock workers, office clericals, salespeople, supervisors and shop men.

Oil companies and manufacturers of

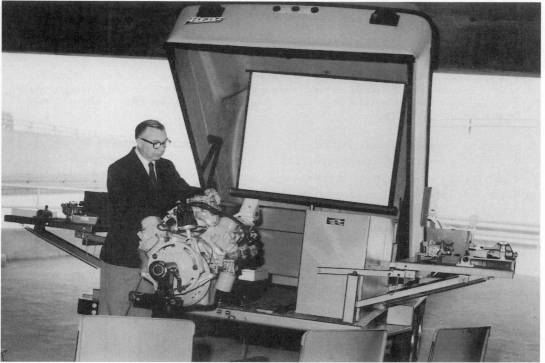

Top and bottom: The Pontiac Motor Division of General Motors has used a six-foot by eight-foot lightweight trailer with a fiberglass body and hinged top that opened to expose a fully-equipped workshop with two fold-out benches, a variety of test equipment and tools, 20 folding chairs, and a film projector and screen. Setup time was under 15 minutes for sessions trainng dealer mechanics. *(Courtesy Pontiac Motor Division of General Motors Corp.)*

The Transmission Division of the Dana Corporation used this custom-built 40-foot Spicer Power Train mobile classroom for mechanics and maintenance personnel. Field sales engineers put on the driveline application and service program. Seating capacity was 15 for jobbers, distributors and fleets. *(Courtesy Dana Corp.)*

service equipment, including Mobil, Texaco, Vickers, Ameranda Hess, Keygrip and Technical Rubber, have traditionally taken the mobile route to the field. Beginning in the late 1940s Texaco Canada launched one of the earliest programs for its service stations with courses on management and sales.

Non-Automotive Training

Outside of automotive mobile training there is a variety of other types of organizations involved with only a slight concentration apparent with manufacturers of machinery, equipment and supplies, instruments, chemicals and fabricated metal products.

Other mobile training is carried on for public utilities, construction contractors, mines, railroads, motels, banks and for glass products, wood products and beer. This training is pretty well confined to employees.

Two typical efforts are worth detailing.

Two 35-foot workshop-classroom Techmobiles were used between 1956 and 1962 by Heli-Coil in the United States and Canada for training and demonstrations for its own salespeople, distributors, customers and prospects. These laboratories on wheels covered the design, maintenance and repair of screw thread inserts and fasteners of interest to technicians and engineers.

Whirlpool, manufacturer of home

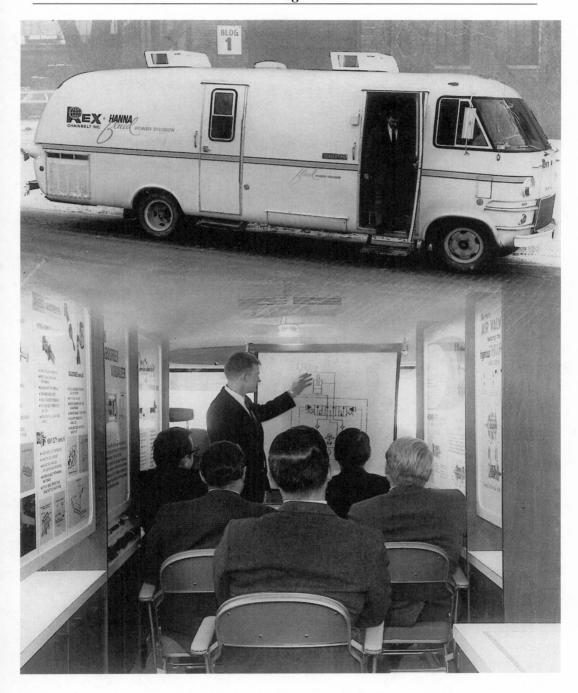

The Fluid Power Cruiser went on the road to train distributors and customers of the Hanna Fluid Power Division of Rex Chainbelt, Inc. With a student capacity of ten it was used for the complete line of pneumatic and hydraulic components in two-day sessions. A product sales group of nine operated the van. *(Courtesy Rex Chainbelt, Inc.)*

appliances, employed a traveling service training classroom from 1963 to 1965 designed by in-house engineers and built to specifications by no less than five construction and supply contractors. It contained a special tubular steel framing structure and a self-contained hydraulic system to operate six leveling jacks. The interior was walnut paneled. The tractor, a modified F-500 Ford, was equipped with special fuel tanks and brake mechanism, ICC lights and west coast mirrors.

Unusual Aspects and Features of Vehicles

Unique attributes set some mobile training programs apart from their more mundane counterparts: roominess, flexibility, integration of products into vehicles and sites.

Several firms have found the answer to more room in multiple units. Armstrong Cork's 1954 Merchandising Motorcade, a traveling school for 20,000 flooring dealers, consisted of two large, specially-designed truck-tractors joined together to form a completely equipped auditorium when set up.

Creative design has expanded the capacity of several vehicles, through configuration of the units themselves or through the use of auxiliary equipment. Worthington used expandable Climate Vans in 1957 for sales training on home and commercial air conditioning and heating.

They went out to 15 feet, two inches wide, nearly twice the normal width. They reached dealers, architects, builders, students, stockholders and the general public. Aluminum-maker Alcoa and the Magirus Deutz Division in Germany, truck manufacturers, employed similar vehicles in the 1970s.

Lone Star Industries, to reach its home care stores with necessary training, sent out simultaneously both a van and an auxiliary portable classroom holding 30, while National Building Centers used a large training truck and a 16-foot by 16-foot tent as an expedient for the overflow, both in the 1970s.

AT&T for its Bell System Associated Companies produced a 1970s Data on the Move training program for its service advisors. It butted end-to-end two 50-foot by 10-foot trailers with glass-paneled sliding doors, one for a classroom and the other for equipment. To prepare for the class it was required to place a metal floor piece between the two units, adjust a Velcro cloth air lock to cover the open space and put steps into position.

One of the most elaborate setups was that of Anheuser-Busch's mobile beer school, which visited over 90 cities and held 1,400 brewery classes for wholesalers, retailers and consumers in the United States and Puerto Rico in 1996. This design saw two 53-foot long trailers joined together to create a classroom seating 50 in 1,400 square feet with a 12-foot, 10-inch ceiling. It contained a galley, two restrooms and enjoyed an outside covered

Opposite, top: This 45-foot rig housed the testing equipment used in Detroit Diesel Allison's second annual Craftsman Guild Skill Contest, and was transported to ten different locations. Participants were diesel engine, transmission and parts specialists who represented 56 distributors in the United States and Canada. The division used station wagons for other training operations. *(Courtesy Detroit Diesel Allison Division, General Motors Corp.). Bottom:* This versatile 40-foot trailer, in addition to training 16 new driver-candidates at a time plus retraining employees, served as a demonstration unit at high schools, safety meetings and as a public and community relations vehicle at field locations. The Mason and Dixon Lines considered its converted freight hauler an integral element in its three-week training course. *(Courtesy Mason and Dixon Lines)*

Top: **Worthington's expandable Climate Vans had a pull-out section to allow adequate field sales training on its complete line of home and commercial air conditioning and heating products.** *(Courtesy Worthington Corp.).* *Bottom:* **Replacing a fleet of motorcoaches, these Anheuser-Busch trailers unfold and join to create a mobile training facility of unique proportions. Called the Suds Truck, it is said to be the largest traveling classroom ever built. It often parks at state fairs, and so far over 46,000 people have attended sessions.** *(Courtesy Anheuser-Busch Companies)*

patio area. Set-up and tear-down time was eight hours each.

Just how flexible can mobile training become?

Ask Northwest Pacific Bell Telephone for its ultimate answer in 1968: two 23-foot trailers to train installers, linemen and repairmen. The interlocking inner shells could be dismantled in four hours, allowing for intermixing of the courses and all their necessary equipment. Back in 1958 Fiat's four 11-ton training vans had

English caterer Gardner Merchant Trust House trained its industrial restaurant staffs in two articulated mobile units built specially on Vauxhall chassis to take a 12-ton load. The vehicles were styled at an aggressive forward angle with very large underfloor lockers. The body was extruded aluminum paneled with stainless steel and aluminum sheet. *(Courtesy Vauxhall Motors)*

sides that opened to the roof level to afford maximum illumination and ventilation while the rear opened downward as an entry ramp.

In order to save the cost of hotels and motels, living quarters for personnel traveling with mobile training units can be built right into the vehicle. Thermo King, makers of transport refrigeration, did this in 1972. It converted four 40-foot 1967 Crown highway post office buses into training facilities, each with living quarters for two men. Units were originally stripped and theater-type seating for 12 installed with insulated walls, birch paneling, acoustic ceiling, carpeting and special lighting. Each session for transport dealer mechanics on repairing electrical systems lasted a week in the tour in the United States and Canada.

By incorporating some of their own products into a training vehicle those setting up such a project not only save money but also enjoy a great opportunity to demonstrate their worth under operating conditions.

Montgomery Ward's four appliance repair vehicles were 40-foot customized school buses using its own floor tile and acoustical ceiling. These were taken in 1967 to its department and catalog stores to train 14 technicians at a time. There was a rear workshop and set-up time was only an hour.

Ekco Containers, maker of aluminum foil packaging, ordered this mobile packaging center to train its 700 distributors and their salespeople and as a showroom to go directly to big accounts. The 40-foot aluminum trailer seated 20, weighed three-quarters of a ton and was quickly converted into a walk-through product display area. *(Courtesy Ekco Containers)*

DAF, Holland-based heavy-duty truck manufacturer, in the 1970s toured its custom-made, 33-foot training trailers with its own model FT-2800 sleeper cab. It visited 21 British dealerships to train service engineers in two and three-day courses using a six-man classroom and workshop area. The cab was used to familiarize personnel with that series, new at that time.

Meyer Products in 1973 had an opportunity to install its snow and ice control equipment on its four-wheel-drive pickup truck which pulled the 34-foot trailer with food service facilities and crew quarters. It was used as a sales and service demonstrator at truck dealers, fleets, municipal service departments and trade schools.

It may seem odd to do training *inside* a factory with mobile units usually only associated with tours throughout the country, but it makes sense when you carefully consider the advantages of bringing the training to the work area rather than having employees travel over considerable distances to a central location.

Western Electric ordered in the 1970s four custom-built training vehicles for its vast Atlanta Works which cover 1.3 million square feet of shop area. When the trailer with its furniture and apparatus re-

In-factory training by Western Electric involves four custom trailers in the Atlanta, Georgia, facility. An operator uses a film projector in this illustration. *(Courtesy Western Electric)*

quired for training was moved to a site, installations meant only blocking up for stabilization and attaching a single electrical cable for power. One of the four was a unique double unit with a room in the center for projecting films into classrooms at the ends.

Another similar situation took place in the 1970s at Dow Chemical's home plant and office in Midland, Michigan. Its school on wheels was remodeled from a trailer used to transport cans. It measured 10 feet by 38 feet and accommodated 15 students at tables and 30 people with expanded seating at conferences.

Many organizations with exceptional training programs have exhibited great originality in developing valuable secondary uses for their vehicles, turning them into enhanced multi-purpose units. This often means sharing part of the training budget with one or more other departments which could turn out to be a definite financial advantage. Of course, close coordination is critical if responsibility is split.

The Maremont Muffler Division of Maremont Corporation extended the usefulness of its Salesmobiles, panel trucks for training service station personnel, by enlarging their scope by including display, installation laboratory and product quality presentations. The truck exteriors were finished in a close replica of the steel used in its alloy coated mufflers. More than double sales were reported in Chicago area outlets after this training in 1961.

Ekco Containers, makers of aluminum foil cartons, trained from 1962 to 1964 in a unit fabricated from a 40-foot, ¾-ton Clark truck with 20 seats. It reached distributor salespeople. When the seats were removed it could be quickly converted into a walk-through product display area and much valuable marketing research data resulted. The exterior was decorated to resemble the plant.

The Federation of Migros Cooperatives in Zurich, Switzerland, put in service in 1969 two mobile, raised-roof workshop vans for its Do It Yourself division, serving a dual purpose as training centers for salespeople at supermarkets and as display rooms for machines and tools at trade fairs and exhibits. They were phased out in 1975.

Wagner Electric, maker of automotive brakes and lighting, employed a 26-foot motor home to provide jobber service clinics but also used it very effectively in 1976 for sales calls on customers. The custom interior seated ten.

McQuay-Norris, automotive engine parts maker, found a unique method to use its fleet of service training vans intended for dealer clinics, to enhance its overall corporate image in the industry in 1976. The units were recognized as "Trucks of the Month" by *Signs of the Times* magazine because of the outstanding exterior graphic design, painted to resemble its packaging.

Global Van Lines used its training units to recruit new drivers with audiovisual presentations in the 1970s.

Caterpillar Tractor's custom-built Super Truck in 1977 doubled as both a service and sales training facility. The modified cab accommodated the instructor and six students for classes or the driver and six passengers during live demonstrations focusing on Caterpillar's engine, transmission and brake saver system.

Anheuser-Busch used its fleet of five 26-foot GM Kingsley motor coaches, intended primarily as training for wholesalers and retailers, for hospitality for consumers. Folding side awnings transformed the units to serve draught beer. They all contained full kitchens and bathrooms and were custom-painted in white, red and gold in 1979.

Daniel International Construction Company, a division of the Fluor Corporation, has been able to sell its craft and supervisory skills mobile training programs to other firms on the outside through a subsidiary, Dantrain, since the 1970s. This revenue generates welcome addi-

tional funds for its own training programs.

A most unusual combination van use was made by mobile veterinarian Dr. Keith Grove in 1985. He started teaching veterinary dentistry to area practitioners in the unit. His clinic on wheels is in Vero Beach, Florida, and has radiology as well as special dental equipment.

Organizations which share their training vehicles with others cannot only be characterized as magnanimous but smart in enhancing their public relations stance, opening up a whole range of audiences beyond those being trained.

Allied Van Lines in 1964 had a 35-foot furniture-moving training vehicle open to schools and service clubs.

The Spicer Division of Dana in 1965 used its 40-foot mobile classroom Power Train for mechanics and maintenance people on its transmissions, but the unit was also available for driver training by other organizations.

Altrans Canada Express in 1974 converted tandem line-haul trailers into training vehicles for drivers, dock workers, clericals, salespeople, supervisors and shop men. These were readily available, schedules permitting, free to other carriers, groups and safety organizations. A similar system was used by Thomas Nationwide Transport in Australia.

The Realco Division of Interway Corporation had a Blue Bird bus to train field personnel in its piggyback trailer leasing and service operations in 1974. It was available to customers, non-customers and virtually anyone in the industry.

Nissan offered its ten specially-equipped Dodge service training vans to colleges.

Engineering students and auto shop instructors enjoyed in 1978 the benefits of sharing the four MOPAR training vehicles that Chrysler set up for its Chrysler, Plymouth and Dodge dealer mechanics.

Restricted Training

Sometimes an opportunity arises whereby training can be given on a vehicle for a limited purpose if management is alert.

On a week's bus trip for its salespeople in 1959, the beer firm Blitz-Weinhard had them call on customers and prospects, and then on the road between cities the sales manager and an outside sales training consultant offered instruction. The company uses distributors and sells at markets, restaurants and bars.

All-O-Matic Industries, an automotive parts manufacturer, provided a free busing service in 1970 for commuting Spanish-speaking employees with instruction in English en route to and from the plant.

Procter and Gamble also used a bus for training when it transported a toilet goods division group in Cincinnati. District and division managers on the 46-passenger rented Silver Eagle Trailways bus saw a color, closed-circuit TV presentation in 1971.

Educational Institutions

There is a varied pattern in the use of vehicles for training by educational institutions.

Beloit College, Beloit, Wisconsin, started its Environ Van traveling educational project in 1970 to stimulate the study of the environment at the high school level. For three and a half months a team of undergraduates has taken five 20-foot Winnebago campers for lectures and field trips in the Great lakes region. Funding sources include foundations and the U.S. Department of Health, Education and Welfare.

The University of Michigan in Ann Arbor beginning in 1972 made its graduate level courses for engineering and business administration available to employees at the General Motors Proving Grounds in Milford, Michigan. Television broadcasts are received on monitors in two trailer classrooms equipped with a telephone talkback system.

The University of California at San Diego sponsored a free computer course for Blacks and Chicanos in 1975, brought to them in a truck once a week to outlying areas. A California Vocational Education grant helped support it. Other mobile courses from the institution have involved nursing education and home heating from the La Jolla campus.

North Carolina State University operated a Computer Awareness Laboratory, a converted bookmobile, for training at high schools in 1976-77. It was supported in part by a grant from the National Science Foundation.

Ohio's Bowling Green State University has carried out an outreach program for area schools with a 24-foot Winnebago van. Alive Puppet Players was developed by the Martha Gesling Weber Reading Center as a collaborator. The portable literacy classroom boasted computer counters and five cabinets. Graduate students have comprised the traveling troupe since 1999.

Professor Douglas Brinkley has toured the nation since 1991 annually for ten weeks and 12,000 miles in his natural-gas powered Magic bus. He wants the college students aboard to experience American history, literature and culture. A typical trip for this University of New Orleans tour is 80 stops in 40 states.

The Institute for Competitive Manufacturing at the College of Engineering, Department of Mechanical and Industrial Engineering, University of Illinois at Urbana-Champaign, has had a mobile lab to teach quality control management techniques to personnel in small area industries. Undergraduate student teams and faculty members are involved. Some state and federal funds support the project, which began in 1992.

The Ameritech Center for Business Solutions Lab normally meets at Walsh College in Troy, Michigan, but a mobile lab has supplemented these sessions since 1999. It brings computers and a facilitator to southwestern Michigan corporate clients.

There are several mobile training programs for mechanical and trade skills.

The University of Texas started the Mobile Automotive Specialist Training (MAST) program in 1945. It reaches mechanics by working with manufacturers, wholesalers, dealers and independent service shops, as well as schools.

Ferris State College, Big Rapids, Michigan, sent out in 1971 a classroom on wheels to spread tutoring to various northern Michigan communities. The goal: upgrade the skills of 250 automotive mechanics in 34 counties. A grant by the Upper Great Lakes Regional Commission supported the project.

Larry N. Stallings of the North Carolina State University in Raleigh designed in 1971 a self-help system, Community Action Extension, a tool shop and living quarters in one to teach trade skills. The aluminum trailer was intended to visit jobsites.

Advanced students in auto technology at Chaffey College, Alta Loma, California, began in 1972 to conduct service clinics at area junior and senior high schools, car dealers, shopping centers, auto shows and fairs. A specialized Ford van supported the lectures, films and demonstrations. There were some ten contributing sponsors, such as Sears.

Several other U.S. institutions have been active so far in mobile training projects: Colorado State University; Gulf Coast Community College; St. Clair County Community College; Tampa Technical College; Grambling State University; Louisiana Tech University and California State University.

Activity in Canada has seen several training projects. The faculty of Education at the University of Lethbridge in Alberta employed in 1970 a 65-foot Peterbilt trailer lab addressed to reading difficulties of children. Attendees have included children, high school students, teachers and parents; other departments also have access to the vehicle. A mobile unit went out from North Island College, Courtenay, B.C., in 1978 to extend distributive education with 20 courses for remote communities. The Printmobile is what the Emily Carr College of Arts in British Columbia called its mobile self-contained print shop in 1978, intended for eight students at a time. It has visited community art schools and museums with equipment for silk screening, relief, intaglio and lithography techniques.

Membership Organizations

Mobile training programs are quite common and are conducted by all sorts of membership organizations, such as labor unions and trade associations.

The Women's Advertising Club of Chicago, in order to teach Spanish-speaking Chicagoans in 1968 how advertising could help them shop more wisely, launched a two-month mobile classroom project. Called Operation Marketour, it had the cooperation of the Better Business Bureau and several food companies and related organizations.

The Choanoke Area Development Association found a converted house trailer a suitable vehicle to teach seasonal farm workers in North Carolina how to repair television sets as a second career in 1970. It accommodated eight students in two daily sessions. A related program by the National Urban League in 1988 saw it offer the COMPUTERwise project in a van for affiliated chapters working with Digital Equipment Corporation. The object: to help spur minority youth to consider college.

The Independent Garage Owners of North Carolina had a mobile training program for automobile mechanics from 1973 to 1975. These field clinics were held at member sites in remote areas using a van equipped with large diagnostic and service equipment.

The U.S. Wheat Association, financed by growers, the U.S. government and 92 countries where the American promotion campaigns were carried out, employed in 1981 a van to give lessons on how to be better bakers and stimulate foreign taste and demand for wheat, especially American. Vans traveled in China, the Philippines, Mexico and Indonesia.

The New York City YWCA has had a mobile audiovisual unit to serve teenagers and young women in their neighborhoods with classes and other group activities.

In the first six months of 2001 the Ohio Board of Regents coordinated an effort to get more Ohio high school students to go to college. They sent out the Ohio Success Express, formerly the bus of pro-football broadcaster John Madden. Juniors and sophomores had a rally, with video and talks by state and local leaders and local college representatives.

Automobile clubs in Michigan, California, Washington and other states have favored mobile training programs on highway safety, gasoline conservation, car care and mechanic skills.

There are several examples of organized labor mobile training efforts.

One of the most unusual union training programs was a Fruehauf-built portable classroom placed on a tour for the American Line Builders Apprenticeship Training Program in 1972. A standard Warehouseman van trailer had a unique fold-a-room which expanded 26 feet of the midsection from eight to 16 feet wide. The center compartment was fitted with three large plymetal doors which were individually lowered (and raised into the traveling position) to a horizontal position by an electrical winch system. When the doors were lowered, they descended upon a series of ratchet type jackscrews which were also individually adjustable to keep them level, even when parked on uneven terrain. These doors now became an extension of the vehicle floor. Once lowered, the additional floor section was covered with a series of aluminum and translucent Plexiglas panels. Over the trailer's coupler section an eight-foot by ten-foot room was created to house the lavatory.

Education on the Move is the name of the mobile training of the United Steelworkers of America District 6. The 27-foot rented van has given a labor relations course to 15,000 members in mining communities in isolated western and central Canada.

Foundation Training

A broad variety of foundations has found mobile training meets their needs.

The Frank E. Gannett Newspaper Foundation used a purpose-built, 40-foot by eight-foot van to teach new electronic journalism techniques to college students and faculty nationwide in 1974. It spent two weeks on each campus it visited. The vehicle had pull-out sides to make it 17 feet wide in use. Some 15 students at a time could be reached. It also was used at conventions and conferences.

The National Paraplegia Foundation began using in 1982 a Mobile Computer Skills Evaluation Unit in a van which teaches basic skills to people confined to wheelchairs at home in a 16-hour course.

An unusual "fold-a-room" in the center of the apprentice training trailer of the American Line Builders expanded 26 feet through a panel arrangement. On-the-job instruction was furnished to electrical workers in the field by this labor union facility. *(Courtesy Fruehauf Corporation, William E. Bradley, photographer)*

The Children's Better Health Institute Division of the Saturday Evening Post Society has operated a Health Mobile since 1989. It teaches CPR and the Heimlich Maneuver to third-graders and provides cholesterol testing and nutrition education.

The Freedom Forum, formerly the Gannett Foundation, gave a grant to the Center for Adult Reading and Enrichment in 1992 for its Learning Lab, a 30-foot-long motor coach with ten computers. Teachers use the lab to instruct in reading, mathematics, social studies and coping skills at temporary locations in Madison, Tennessee. A similar lab operates in the northeast part of the state.

The nonprofit California Community College Foundation's Institute for Multisensory Learning mobile lab provided computing multimedia training for faculty at community colleges, and K12 campuses. Over 35 major technological corporations were represented in the renovated recreational vehicle in 1998.

Also in 1998 the Community Memorial Foundation gave a grant to a literacy mobile schoolroom operated by the Sisters of St. Joseph of La Grange, Illinois. It's a refurbished used bookmobile for immigrants, including Hispanic, Vietnamese and others. They receive tutoring in basic English and language skills. Other funding comes with businesses and civic groups.

The California Community College Foundation's Institute for Multisensory Learning mobile lab, with the state capitol dome at Sacramento in the background. A refurbished recreational vehicle provided teacher training in the learning lab. Names of participating organizations such as MCI and Compaq were included on the side. *(Courtesy California Community College Foundation)*

Multiple Sponsors

Just as with many other types of mobile projects training sometimes requires two or more sponsors for a program to be launched.

Automotive Wholesalers of Oklahoma sponsors mobile mechanic training with cosponsors the Division of Extension of Oklahoma State University and the Oklahoma State Department of Vocational Education. Two such schools have been made available to automotive jobbers for night sessions since 1957.

In conjunction with the Federal Manpower Retraining Program, Echlin, maker of automotive electrical systems and carburetors, provided training for mechanics with 15 spaces in rolling classrooms. The fully-equipped vehicles offered courses set up by jobbers from 1967 to 1972.

The combined efforts of the Liberty Mutual Insurance Company and state insurance departments of local civic or governmental organizations made possible driving skills courses in 110 cities in 1973. Some 16 policyholder employees in the custom-built units met at a time in shopping centers, parking lots and other places.

A joint effort by Ford Motor Company and the United Auto Workers union produced a 48-foot trailer that opened into a fan shape with almost 1,000 square feet of display area and seating for 25. The objective: to boost education and foster personal growth among UAW–represented Ford workers. Over 35,000 were reached on its tour.

It required a cooperative group of five organizations to put together CyberEd, a mobile training program for public school children. Its main thrust was education regarding the so-called information superhighway and computer skills. Skillful graphics on the trailer symbolized the technical objective. *(Courtesy Tech Corp.)*

Six Classrooms on Wheels (COW) began operating in 1992 with preschool training in Las Vegas, Nevada. The nonprofit project has public funds and corporate sponsors. The renovated buses hold 18 children each as they meet in 23 area neighborhoods. Louise Helton, who created these facilities, has also launched Clinic on Wheels and Computer on Wheels. The programs are modeled after similar ones in Tennessee.

CyberEd was a bright yellow converted 18-wheeler, a touring truckload of technology. It carried computer and video-conferencing equipment to 400 high schools to reach principals, teachers, families and community leaders. Funding was by corporations and foundations. In five months in the 1990s it visited all U.S. urban and rural empowerment zones. Tech Corporation, a nonprofit technology vol-

unteer organization, administered the project.

Mobile training for entrepreneurs has been provided by a joint venture in Chicago involving the Women's Business Development Center, Dominick's Finer Foods Supermarkets and Bank One. The Wheels of Business vehicle in 1999 gave information on becoming self-employed for the benefit of low-income area communities on a weekly basis.

Commercial Outside Training Vendors

Some companies which offer training courses for different types of organizations use mobile training approaches.

The Huxley Institute for Modern Security in New York City is a franchise operation providing vocational and adult education subjects in a remodeled bus.

RSKCO's driver simulator is housed in back of a truck to train drivers of school buses, trucks and transit vehicles. It seats eight students at simulated dashboards and visits clients nationwide.

TecQuipment International Contracts, England, offers engineering education in a wide variety of subjects in mobile laboratories.

The Thiokol Educational Develop-ment Operations Division of Thiokol Chemical offers in its Transmodular Learning Systems for public schools vocational classrooms on wheels which are complete mobile shop units.

Vehicles are not by any means the only mobile training choices. To round out the full complement of land, water and air we have railway cars, commuter trains, ships, planes and even dirigibles in such service.

CHAPTER IV

Charity and Public Service Vehicles

Secular eleemosynary and public service organizations both in the United States and overseas regularly employ special vehicles with innovative approaches, mostly to augment government welfare programs. Charities serve their varied populations of the needy, suffering, poor and distressed in benevolent ways. The types of organizations involved include foundations, trade associations, professional societies, fraternal organizations, service clubs, educational and medical institutions, labor unions, settlement houses, ethnic groups, businesses and individual efforts.

Looking to them for help are such disparate groups as children, senior citizens, Native Americans, unwed mothers, single parents, abused individuals, prostitutes, migrant laborers, vagrants, displaced persons, refugees, ex-convicts, armed forces personnel, hospital patients, drivers and many others. Even animals come under their purview.

Mobile charity work has proven itself to be a real, expedient asset in providing on a continuing basis such goods and services as health care, meals, clothing, bulk food, day-care, shelter, employment counseling, transportation, vehicle repair, disaster relief and psychological counseling. Philanthropy on the move gets the job done.

The examples that follow exemplify both the diversity of the services offered and their sponsors. Certain states like Michigan, Ohio, Illinois and New York get frequent mentions since their populations reflect suffering from cyclical downturns in the economy, largely due to the types of industries present.

Charitable organizations with religious orientations like the Salvation Army are discussed in the chapter on religious vehicles and mobile governmental welfare efforts are described in detail in the chapter on governmental vehicles.

Health Care

Comprehensive, free health care is provided in many different places by a variety of local, regional, state, national and international organizations for children and youth, Native Americans, retirees and migrant laborers and the counterculture, as well as the general public. In addition there is a focus on such specific ailments as tuberculosis, lung trouble, substance abuse, sickle-cell anemia, kidney disorders and AIDS.

St. Vincent's Medical Center in Toledo, Ohio, has operated a Mobile Health Watch outreach program since 1982. When it first started out it was under the Mobile Medical Health Service of the Model Neighborhood Residents Association. Its Care-A-Van is used for health screening, education, emergencies, as a first aid station and resource center. Regularly it goes to churches, malls, senior centers, food stores, schools, health fairs, nutrition kitchens, homeless centers, migrant camps, businesses and hospitals within a 50-mile radius of Toledo, which includes southeastern Michigan. Benefiting particularly are Mexican migrant farm workers, Asian refugees and immigrants. The first specially equipped motor home was replaced with a 26-foot van in 1991 after logging more than 45,000 miles visiting 1,067 sites with the aid of 5,313 volunteers and participating in 143,861 screenings. The American Red Cross borrows it for special events, and cooperating with the program is television channel 13 WTVG. Since 1994 a seasonal migrant trailer has operated through St. Vincent's Medical College Hospital and the Farm Labor Organization Committee. The Henry County/Napoleon City Combined General Health District also operates a migrant health motor home.

In 1955 the Mount Clemens, Michigan, General Hospital fitted out a 40-foot truck with three examining rooms, bathroom, reception area and a storage room as the MCG Medical Outreach Clinic. It goes to four spots in Macomb County to hand out basic, comprehensive medical care to the poor, reaching 15 to 20 each session on a half-day schedule three days a week. One Sunday a month is devoted to migrant workers. Essentially it serves the homeless, working poor and Medicaid participants, stopping at soup kitchens, battered women's shelters and community health offices. Financial support is from grants and organizations like the Kiwanis International.

The Craig Medical Center Hospital in Denver, Colorado, has had a similar van since 1997.

Two semi trucks and trailers called Care-A-Vans toured the country in 1991 under the auspices of the American Osteopathic Association to celebrate the centennial of the profession. They provided health screening tests for those over 17 years old who had little or no health insurance or medical care. The vehicles were converted into medical clinics and those with serious illnesses were referred to a clinic or doctor who volunteered to help. The organization was founded in 1897 and is composed of physicians, surgeons and graduates of approved colleges of medicine which place special emphasis on the relationships among muscles, the skeleton and other body systems.

Project Concern International has had a van since 1973 in the Tennessee Upper Cumberland Mountains in nine counties bringing medical and dental services to rural villages. This multinational relief organization works with communities to ensure low-cost, basic health care for those most in need, particularly mothers and children.

In 1988 Planned Parenthood of New York City began operating Street Beat vans for prostitutes and drug addicts in the South Bronx. They provide health care in the form of free medical treatment and counseling, clean clothes, needle sterilization kits and sandwiches, among other services. The unit is a 31-foot recreational vehicle with an examination room, bathroom, shower and kitchen, operating five nights a week.

New York City Relief has served similar neighborhood unfortunates since 1989: the homeless, drug addicts and prostitutes. Its converted, specially equipped bus acts as a resource center with medical treatment, clothing, job aid, substance abuse rehabilitation, referrals, spiritual counseling and free Bibles along with hot chocolate. It boasts a first aid clinic, kitchen and computer room and is privately funded with the names of the corporate sponsors listed on the outside.

The National Urban League maintains blood pressure checking vans in large metropolitan areas. Established in 1919, it is a voluntary, nonpartisan community service agency of civic, professional, business, labor, and religious leaders with a staff of trained social workers and other professionals. Free blood pressure testing was offered in a special van to residents of Dearborn, Michigan, in 1976 by Union Prescription Centers.

Affiliates of the United Way of America maintain health vans for homeless projects in major cities. These are essentially fund-raising organizations established in 1918, popular known as community funds.

A major health maintenance organization, Comprehensive Health Services—The Wellness Plan, has mobile health screening vehicles.

There are several mobile health activities devoted to children and youths.

The Benevolent and Protective Order of Elks, a fraternal organization established in 1868, has a California-Hawaii chapter which uses a fleet of 47 Chevrolet station wagons with therapists who cover more than 800,000 miles a year to reach children living on isolated farms and ranches or in remote communities with no regular health care.

In the Riverdale section of the Bronx, New York, the National Association of Jewish Family Social, Children's and Health Services began to offer in 1973 services in a 27-foot-long recreational vehicle rap-room furnished with paneling, posters and pillows. It parks in shopping areas to reach teenagers in informal groups with counseling sessions on mental health problems. Discussed are drinking, drugs, car theft, gangs and other problems. It is privately financed, a nonsectarian organization of social workers, psychologists and psychiatrists who specialize in family therapy.

Health Adventure is a mural-covered 18-wheeler trailer traveling classroom for elementary school children, sponsored in 1984 by the Houston Academy of Medicine, Harris County Medical Society and the Shell Oil Company Foundation. It contains hands-on exhibits and health screenings. Typically it visits over a dozen Houston area schools yearly teaching physical fitness, nutrition, safety and personal health habits. It also visits fairs, museums and other special events. Exhibits in both English and Spanish are remodeled yearly. So far more than 46,000 students at 71 schools have been served.

Starting out in New York City in 1987, the Children's Health Fund expanded subsequently to 16 programs in ten states and the District of Columbia. In New York, using three custom-made, 33-foot blue vans, it supports pediatric health programs for children who are homeless, poor or who have no other access to medical care. There are examining rooms, corridors for weighing and waiting areas. Expanded services embrace teenage runaways, teen moms and their babies, immi-

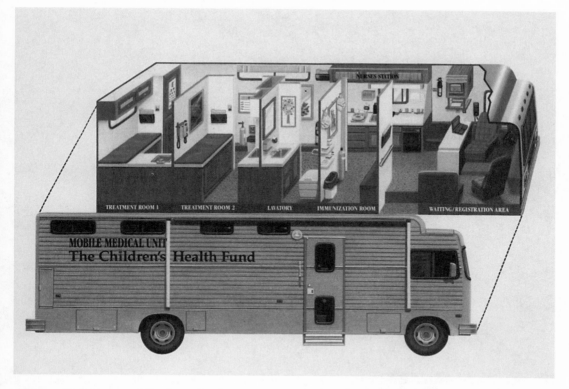

TREATMENT ROOM 1　　TREATMENT ROOM 2　　LAVATORY　　IMMUNIZATION ROOM　　WAITING/REGISTRATION AREA

NURSES STATION

MOBILE MEDICAL UNIT
The Children's Health Fund

Singer Paul Simon and Dr. Irwin Redlener organized the Children's Health Fund in New York City in 1987 for those without adequate care. A diagram of a typical facility is shown above. In 1998 a caravan of units destined for Mississippi and Arkansas traveled through seven states. *(Courtesy Children's Health Fund)*

grants in rural areas and disaster victims.

It took two sponsors in 1995 to launch Pediatric Mobile Team: Children's Hospital of Michigan and the Junior League of Detroit. Visits are made to four community sites for a half-day session every other week. The International Association of Junior Leagues, established in 1921, works to develop the potential of women, promoting volunteerism and improving communities as a nonprofit action and leadership organization.

In Denver a mobile health van for children is operated individually by Dr. Larry Wolk.

Native Americans also benefit from mobile health services. A 33-foot mobile ear care clinic, sponsored by the University of Washington since 1971, aids the 28,000 Native Americans in reservations in Montana, Wyoming and New Mexico. The Unit has equipment and facilities comparable to a modern urban medical center, including an examination room, and a sound-attenuated audiological suite.

Retirees have not been overlooked either.

The Medi Van Project in Broward County, Florida, was started for senior citizens in 1986. It offers medical services and prescriptions and visits 22 neighborhoods. Two 32-foot converted 1981 Cruise-Aire recreational vehicles have been made possible by the involvement of the Florida Department of Health and Rehabilitation Services, Elderly Interest Fund and the Hollywood Memorial Hospital Auxiliary.

Filling the gap left by the retrenchment of state and national welfare programs are such facilities as the LensCrafters Foundation "Give the Gift of Sight" mobile unit. It offers free eye examinations to children. Cooperating sponsors of the service include Lions Clubs International, Luxotica Group and Alcon Laboratories. *(Courtesy LensCrafters)*

Each unit has two examining rooms, diagnostic equipment, EKG machines, nurses' station, pharmacy and a waiting room. A separate mammogram vehicle often accompanies the vans.

Two groups, migrants and members of counterculture communes, because of special circumstances, often lack adequate health care. Educational institutions have stepped up to these challenges. Southern Colorado State College operates a migrant health van out of Pueblo and the University of California School of Nursing provides communes with medical information in a camper truck, the Traveling Medicine Show, through reading matter, films and slides.

SPECIFIC AILMENTS AND TESTS

Most of the mobile health care units devoted to a specific disease or ailment began operating in the 1970s. These efforts reflect a relative response to various scourges coming on the scene worldwide.

After their use for 30 years or more, the National Tuberculosis and Respiratory Diseases Association in 1970 no longer recommended mobile chest X-rays for general use, although they were still in operation locally in some special situations. They had been supported by groups like Kiwanis in 28 states.

Today the lung emphasis is on asthma, healthy indoor air, the effects of smoking and secondhand smoke. The American Lung Association of Southeast

Local chapters of the National Tuberculosis and Respiratory Disease Association used mobile chest X-rays from vehicles like the Riverside County Breathmobile (above) up to the 1970s. *(Courtesy Riverside County Tuberculosis and Respiratory Diseases Association)*

Florida in 1997 introduced the 30-foot Lung Mobile motor home funded by a Quantum Foundation grant. It is a high-tech education center on wheels visiting schools, senior and community centers, churches and health fairs with computer programs and interactive displays.

To combat alcohol and drug abuse with counseling and referrals at least three different organizations were involved with mobile units in the 1970s: Teen Alcohol and Drug Education, the Jaycees civic service organization of the U.S. Junior Chamber of Commerce and the Addiction Rehabilitation Coordinating Organization.

The Sickle-Cell Anemia Disease Association of America, organized in 1971,

coordinates mobile test clinic efforts to fight the disease in local communities. These Sicklemobiles bring free information, detection and counseling services in cooperation with area hospitals. Pepsi-Cola and Champale Malt Beverages have aided the financing.

The American Cancer Society chapters have used vans since the 1970s to take cervical cancer screening and education to women in their local communities in low income areas. These are typically 60-foot custom-built house trailers. Established in 1913, the Society is a national, community-based volunteer health organization dedicated to eliminating cancer as a major health problem by prevention, saving lives and diminishing suffering

This Lungmobile features displays showing the effects of tobacco as a disease-causing agent. *(Courtesy the American Lung Association of Southeast Florida)*

by research, education, advocacy and service.

In California educational cancer Moviemobiles are taken to neighborhood centers. These buses are self-contained outdoor theaters for such hard-to-reach audiences as Mexican-American migrants, as well as middle-class residential sections.

In 1997 the American Cancer Society's 34-foot NicoVan was put on the road to help smokers to quit. Co-sponsors were SmithKline Beecham, gum and patch makers; it has visited over 20 cities.

In the 1970s the National Kidney Foundation and its local units became active with mobile laboratories to give free kidney disease detection tests, particularly to elementary school children. Another customized van is used as a transport vehicle for donated kidney transplants and educational materials. Funding is supported by states and local daily newspapers and business groups. Since 1950 the Foun-

dation has supported research, patient services, professional and public education, organ and tissue donor programs and community services.

Several different groups have used mobile units to combat AIDS.

Since 1987 nonprofit Alternatives for Girls in Detroit, Michigan, has operated a van street outreach program for girls and young women, mostly prostitutes: 6,600 girls and their families have been served so far. Information dispensed covers HIV, drugs, domestic abuse protection, and so on. Given out are condoms, bleach kits for needles, sandwiches, juice and referrals to other related agencies. Support is by federal block grant funds, the Michigan Aids Fund, Kroger and Oprah Winfrey.

The Midwest AIDS Prevention Project uses a 1969 Volkswagen bus for condom distribution and health promotions in Michigan.

The Newark, New Jersey, Red Cross

The American Cancer Society's NicoVan helps those who want to try to give up the tobacco habit. *(Courtesy American Cancer Society)*

Community Health Service began in 1989 to use buses and vans to combat HIV, handing out condoms, bleach kits, bilingual literature and referrals, concentrating on welfare hotels.

Since 1990 in New York City the Life Style Caravan has been sponsored by Lifestyle Condoms. It serves streetwalkers with AIDS testing, education, free condoms, food coupons and counseling. Dr. Joyce Wallace, who operates the vehicle, previously used a car, testing in the back seat. The late Arlene Carmen had a van on 8th Avenue offering evening counseling, coffee and cake to street prostitutes in the 1990s. In Detroit mobile units of the Early Intervention Project give AIDS tests and the Life Points Agency provides needle exchange programs from a van. In Spokane, Washington, health workers in Winnebagos hand out condoms, clean needles and cookies to prostitutes.

The Saturday Evening Post Society, growing out of the Benjamin Franklin Literary and Medical Society, produced five mobile units in the 1980s whose names describe their use: Heartmobile, Mammobile, AIDSmobile, Momma Mobile and Children's Better Health Mobile. They feature testing for their respective diseases and education.

Other service clubs, hospitals and health practitioners and societies sponsor mobile units addressed to stroke, speech and hearing difficulties, arthritis, vision problems and vaccinations for communicable diseases.

In addition to the purely medical emphases just described there are several other mobile health units used for related purposes.

The American Red Cross uses bloodmobiles to collect donations at schools, churches, government agencies, factories, shopping centers and hospitals. It serves members of the armed forces with Clubmobiles and veterans and their families, aids disaster victims and assists other Red Cross societies in times of emergency, all with mobile units.

Two groups regularly provide special transportation for patients to doctors and distant hospitals, as well as outings. The Shriners, a fraternal and charitable organization use customized motor coaches; the Angel Bus volunteers use luxury coaches and recreational vehicles.

In Brooklyn, Crown Heights, East Harlem and Cypress Hills, New York, volunteer ambulances in 50-foot trailers are operated.

The Michigan Osteopathic Medical Center operates a bookmobile service manned by volunteers.

The Toledo, Ohio, Hospital Auxiliary has a Health Bearmobile van which it

Top: To prevent breast cancer, the Saturday Evening Post Society uses its Mammobile for patient screening and to distribute education. Free mammograms have been offered in several different states in an attempt to create an awareness of the need for early detection, with stops at churches, governmental offices and other sites. *(Reprinted with permission of The Saturday Evening Post © 1988 BFL&MS, Inc.).* *Bottom:* The Canadian National Institute for the Blind calls its mobile program "Technibus." Because of Canada's large French-speaking population it initiated a bilingual approach on its seventy-fifth anniversary. The technology exhibit was designed to educate the public with equipment and displays. Some 23 different groups supported the bus. *(Courtesy Canadian National Institute for the Blind)*

Children flock to the Crest Toothpaste mobile dental clinic wherever it parks. *(Courtesy Crest Toothpaste)*

uses for promotional purposes at community events such as festivals or games.

DENTAL CARE

Several different kinds of organizations bring free dental care on wheels: nonprofit Children's Dental Health Service, since 1971 in Rochester, New York; University of Michigan School of Dentistry, since 1973 in Ypsilanti and Willow run for children and migrants; Tooth-Mobile in Michigan by Mobile Dentists since 1997; Health Clinics Interaction in Toledo, Ohio, for indigents; and Christine's Smile for children in 20 cities that host the Senior PGA tour.

Two specialized dental programs use vans: The National Foundation of Dentistry for the Homebound (1974) and the Michigan Academy of Dentistry for the Handicapped (1979).

The Crest Toothpaste Mobile Dental Clinic started in 1996 to give free oral check-ups to children through Dr. John Miller, an Indianapolis, Indiana, dentist who travels the Indy Lights series racing circuit with the vehicle.

FOREIGN HEALTH CARE

Mobile health care in foreign countries has been active at least since the 1940s in England, Africa, Sweden, South and Central America, India and Thailand.

The American Field Hospital Corps, formerly the American Volunteer Ambulance Corps, is an organization of American citizens which provides through private donations relief for civilian war victims in Europe. It constructed a mobile field hospital in England in 1941 made up of 36 separate units including 17 specially designed trucks and eight trailers, housing a laboratory, X-ray, sterilizing, medical and surgical supply, kitchen, lavatory and shower, refrigeration, steam, power, water, machine shop and cargo. Relevant trailers are directly connected to the operating tent by special weatherproof connectors. The complete hospital can be erected on location and in full operation within ten hours.

Several organizations operate in two or more countries. The Cooperative for American Relief Everywhere (CARE) is an international disaster and aid development organization operating in Latin America, Africa and Asia. It has mobile health clinics and eye hospitals on wheels. The Thomas A. Dooley Foundation In-

termed is a nonprofit, private volunteer organization which assists Third World countries in the development of medical care systems through self-help projects in disease prevention, health education, personnel development and research and medical aid for refugees. It has provided medical trailers to Nicaragua and Honduras.

Since the 1970s the African-American Labor Center has placed major emphasis on mobile health clinics in helping independent nations who face enormous problems in the creation of their new economies. It also develops projects on workers' education, vocational training and housing. In order to extend health care, entertainment and education film shows and talks to such countries as Ghana, Tunisia and Mali, it sends mobile clinics in cooperation with local trade unions.

Over 40 different mobile dental and eye health clinics have been operated by New York–based CARE. Above is a remote village in India showing a unit staffed and maintained by the Bombay Mothers Welfare Society. *(Courtesy CARE)*

Since 1957 the African Medical and Research Foundation in Nairobi, Kenya, has operated throughout remote parts of eastern and southern Africa. It is supported by governmental and non-government aid agencies and private doctors. Its Kibwezi Mobile outreach clinics operated from Land Rovers offer immunizations for nomadic and pastoral peoples.

Lions Clubs International sponsors eye clinic vans in Kenya monthly on a four-district circuit. SightFirst is part of a global initiative.

Also active with mobile medical programs in Africa are UNICEF, Health Clinics International and Health Teams International. The latter also offers dental care.

Completing the overseas picture are mobile programs in Sweden by Dr. Gustaf Adolf Axelsson in Goleborg; in Chile by Rotary International; in Central America by Partners of the Americas; in India by Colgate Toothpaste for dental care; and in Thailand by the Population and Community Development Association, offering free vasectomies.

Other Charitable Activities

Besides health care other charitable work is focused on children, unemployed, retirees, homeless, disaster victims and veterans.

Charitable helps for children have taken many different mobile approaches.

Organized in 1966, Reading is Fundamental (RIF) began to offer millions of books to disadvantaged children through bookmobiles. Implementing the program are volunteers, groups composed of community leaders, educators, librarians, parents and service club members who sponsor local grass roots reading motivation programs serving 3,750,000 children nationwide.

Every Halloween since 1974 the O'Neil Moving and Storage Company of Santa Ana, California, has set up a 35-foot-long moving van as a haunted house for area youngsters. It is complete with a gabled window and picket fence–enclosed tumbleweed yard. About 6,000 enjoy the program annually including hospital patients, retarded pupils and the handicapped. The firm also sponsors a mobile Christmas van.

The Boys and Girls Clubs of America take Funmobiles out in various cities to offer games to the neighborhoods. This 1906-founded youth development organization is composed of a network of more than 2,000 neighborhood-based facilities offering services to more than three million disadvantage youths.

Since the 1990s the Ohio Family Resource Car-A-Van has provided a toy lending library taken to mobile home courts and libraries.

Since 1968 in Houston-Texas, the Sam Houston Area Council of the Boy Scouts of America has operated a Scoutmobile to extend Latin-American youth service programs to forgotten young people: ghetto children in broken homes, low-income families, dropouts, isolated rural poverty pockets and migrant workers. Meetings are held in and around a trailer by volunteers who accompany district scout executives. The unit was funded by the Sear Roebuck Foundation.

The Dearborn, Michigan, Gabriel Richard Center set up in 1972 its Omnibus drop-in center for students of Henry Ford Community College and the Dearborn Campus of the University of Michigan. It is a 40-foot, 49-passenger GMC diesel bus which also offers programs and drug education for parents.

Because of the ongoing conflict in Northern Ireland in 1971 three playbuses began to be used in Belfast to ease the fears of children. These old British double-deckers were refitted to visit neighborhoods twice a week under the guidance of the Voluntary Service Bureau, which was started in 1965.

The unemployed habitually need help in getting back in the work-force, and several different groups have used mobile programs in this area.

The Greenville, South Carolina, Technical Education Center operates a Careermobile, and Tampa Technical College in Florida offers a mobile automation center.

Project Daymaker is sponsored by salons and local distributors involved with Aveda environmental beauty products. The custom-designed, 34-foot Winnebago motor home is devoted to needy, unemployed women who are given free hairdos and personal hygiene education since 1992.

In 1999 Mervyn's California department stores sent out a mobile facility, the Community Closet, to provide work clothes to former welfare-recipient women now employed. The custom-built, 53-foot rig has visited ten states and outfitted over 1,000. It spends ten days at each locale, offering job interviewing tips also.

Retirees and senior citizens come in for their share of help.

Independence for Life is a community outreach program of transportation for the elderly by the Michigan National Bank Foundation started in 1985. Over 250 vans and small buses have been involved with 77 nonprofit agencies in 70 communities cooperating. Detroit-based Help Elderly Maintain Independence and Dignity sponsors a monthly bus service for grocery shopping by low-income senior citizen homeowners. Hull House in Chicago delivers warm meals for shut-ins.

A good appearance helps to find success on a job, and that's what Mervyn's California Department Stores mobile Community Closet provided to former welfare recipients now working. The large yellow truck offered new clothes, dressing rooms and stylists. Each client received $350 worth of clothes as the program outfitted 32 a day. (Courtesy Mervyn's California Department Stores)

Detroit's homeless benefit from the Operation Get Down Car-A-Van mobile canteen program, a 350-foot white motor home. Also dispensed are clothing, hygiene articles and housing and job referrals. The Master Transportation Corporation has coordinated an area transportation program to take the homeless to warming shelters and workers to suburban jobs.

Disaster victims require aid *right now* and that is exactly what Water Pik provided to flood victims in Des Moines, Iowa, in 1993: traveling shower trucks were immediately dispatched.

Three Lucas County, Ohio, amateur radio groups have equipped a van as a mobile radio communications center for use in weather emergencies, major fires and disasters. The refurbished bookmobile serves as a central radio command post and contains sleeping quarters for eight, kitchen and restroom. Corporations and foundations fund the project.

All war veterans with service-connected disabilities look to the Disabled American Veterans, established in 1920. It sends out six motor homes nationally as a free field service with a benefits expert in each to assist with government regulations at local chapters. In 1974 the Purple Heart Veterans Rehabilitation Services used a 41-foot La Crosse trailer as a vocational skills testing center in California.

Mobile units expedite the distribution of meals and bulk food. Many organizations donate their trucks on a one-time basis to carry not only food but also relief supplies in times of disaster.

The Enesco Division of Stanhome used a 53-foot specially designed traveling museum for its display of its Precious Moments collectibles to celebrate its twentieth anniversary in 1998. Adorned inside and out, the vehicle made a 20,000-mile nationwide tour. Inside displays featured special pieces, original artwork and videos shown at 200 locations in the United States and Canada. One mission of the project was to collect 60,000 pounds of food for the Second Harvest hunger-relief food bank umbrella network distributing to 40,000 local charities.

Campbell Soup has sent out a Soup-mobile on a ten-city tour to warm up outdoor workers and needy people during the coldest months of the year.

In the 1980s McKenna's Wagon was a rolling soup kitchen in Washington, D.C. A favorite but embarrassing spot was Lafayette Park, right across the street from the White House. The old van was operated by Veronica Maz and named after a Roman Catholic priest.

The makers of Little Caesar's Pizza decided in 1985 to operate a self-contained Love Kitchen, an 18-wheeler tractor-trailer pizza restaurant for underprivileged children, senior citizens, soup kitchens and homeless shelters across the United States and Canada. The project has the status of a nonprofit foundation. Rival Pizza Hut has a similar vehicle which serves hot meals at disasters such as hurricanes.

Millionaire Richard Galloway has operated a mobile soup kitchen in New York City for the homeless since 1989. He uses a converted bus to serve 2,000 hot meals a month. He and his staff of volunteers also use computers to counsel clients and make referrals to other aid.

Two trailer "instant Hull Houses" went on the street in Chicago as settlement houses in 1964, run by the Chicago Federation of Settlement and Neighborhood Centers. Six staff workers form the crew in each small house trailer to meet the needs of neighborhoods rapidly changing due to urban renewal upheaval. The services include a day care nursery for children, community center for literacy classes and youth and adult clubs. Kitchens provide lunches for children of working mothers.

Little Caesar's mobile charity restaurant serves food donated by local franchisers. Since 1985 it has reached over 600,000 recipients from its tractor-trailer, which boasts complete self-contained kitchen facilities. *(Courtesy Little Caesars Pizza)*

Better Business Bureaus in Detroit, Denver, Washington, D.C., New York City, St. Louis and other cities since 1968 have used mobile offices to reach low income inner city consumers. They offer free, confidential counseling and advisory services on problems in a wide range. The units are vans, buses and mobile homes sent to libraries, supermarkets, churches, welfare centers, block clubs and housing projects. They particularly benefit citizens who seldom seek professional legal counsel for a redress of grievances.

Animals

Animal activists look out for the four-footed population with mobile services.

Dale Shields, known as the Pelican Man, has sent out ten vehicles in his fleet to pick up injured birds and bring them to his Bird Sanctuary in Little City Island in Sarasota Bay along Florida's Gulf Coast. Since 1988 he has been a licensed wildlife rehabilitation authority. His hospital treats an average of 7,000 birds a year. Ten veterinarians donate their skills to support 250 volunteers.

To help injured animals, humane societies throughout the country operate medically-equipped Dodge vans, purchased by contributions from local citizens who are often inspired by newspaper campaigns.

In 1998 the Animal Planet Rescue vehicle, an 80-foot blue trailer, visited shopping centers nationwide, sponsored by the American Humane Association and the Animal Planet cable television channel. Its mission was to find and treat domestic pets and wild animals injured in natural disasters. The big truck had a veterinary clinic, four-wheel drive ambulance, rescue rafts, water tanks, portable corral and residential facilities. Since 1877 the Association has represented agencies and individuals seeking to prevent cruelty to children and animals. In Washington State Mark McGuire has a 75-foot animal rescue truck in operation.

The American Society for the Prevention of Cruelty to Animals operates Petmobile traveling adoption vans funded by the Astor Foundation. They usually contain about 15 homeless dogs and cats and are parked in shopping centers in New York, Florida and other states. Since 1866 the Society has sought to enforce all laws for the protection of animals; promote appreciation for lost, stray or unwanted animals and operate a veterinary hospital and a major low-cost spay-neuter clinic.

The University of Pennsylvania has a veterinary hospital bloodmobile which it sends to animal clinics or kennels for donations for transfusions for injured canines.

Fund-Raising

Raising money for worthy causes has often looked to mobile facilities to implement projects.

In 1948 Jack Benny the comedian promoted his television show by having a covered wagon travel across the country collecting money for the March of Dimes, carrying a safe with a million pennies in it which he was donating to the drive. Then in 1952 the March of Dimes field service unit was a display trailer with removable side panels showing polio treatment equipment. It has been characterized as the largest ambulance in the world, 45 feet long. The truck-trailer weighed ten tons. It was specially built for the National Foundation for Infantile Paralysis and appeared in California communities as a public information and education service. The March of Dimes Birth Defects National Foundation was established in 1938. It was first started by President Franklin D. Roosevelt as the National Foundation for Infantile Paralysis to promote prevention by focusing on maternal and child health issues.

In 1968 Hendries Ice Cream had a traveling baseball exhibit trailer, the Carl Yastrzemski All-Star Gallery, containing the Triple Crown winner trophies on behalf of the Jimmy Fund, a regional crusade against cancer in Boston. It toured six New England states soliciting contributions.

Three traveling units described fully in the chapter on advertising vehicles have been involved in raising funds: The Hershey Kissmobile is used for the Children's Miracle Network; the Oscar Mayer Wienermobile is used for the Second Harvest National Food Bank Network to battle domestic hunger and Toys for Tots, and the Eckrich Fun House gives to each state's Second Harvest food banks.

A 1997 Kraft Foods' Maxwell House Coffee promotion focused on a custom-made country cafe on wheels for its Build a Home America program on behalf of Habitat for Humanity. At each cafe stop coffee was served and home exhibits shown at every home on the tour. The project reached 37 cities in 60,000 miles.

Laidlaw Education Services, which transports children to and from school, has also collected money for the Children's Miracle Network with a school bus exhibit. The Network is a national, year-round effort dedicated to helping hospitalized kids through corporate sponsors, television stations and newspaper campaigns.

The Maxwell House restaurant on wheels offered refreshments both to volunteers and the public, as well as relevant exhibits. Parking at such spots as supermarkets, it actively solicited more volunteers for the housing organization, Habitat for Humanity. *(Courtesy Kraft Foods)*

In 1993 Wilfred Keagy started out with his trailer petting zoo which supports fund-raising efforts of churches and service clubs for hunger relief, such as the Heifer Project. He displays it at fairs.

Southern Michigan Area Regional Transportation, Media One Cable, WNIC-FM and Borders Books and Music have joined in Michigan touring a Book Bus to collected donated new or used children's books for needy and low-income children.

Novel stunts involving vehicles have been used effectively for soliciting money.

Former Milwaukee Bucks coach Don Nelson, to raise money for farmers, set out on a seven-day, 200-mile trek aboard a tractor.

In events across the country women have driven BMW cars on special routes to raise money for breast cancer research. The official pace car moves from place to place.

At Michigan Technological University in Houghton students hit with sledge-hammers a car painted to resemble a police cruiser to help raise the funds for a new arts and humanities center.

Operators of transit mix trucks often put institutional ads on them for support of local municipal projects like orchestras, teams or celebrations.

Public Service

Public service mobile units offer continuing benefits in such areas as exhibits, museums, entertainment, information and road aid.

Exhibits

Public mobile exhibits cover a variety of topics and sponsors.

Rembrandt Peal's famous 1820 painting *The Court of Death* toured the Eastern United States during that year rolled up in an 11-foot, six inch by 23-foot, five-inch carrier in a covered wagon.

Gifts from France in reconverted museum trailers toured North Carolina under the auspices of the State Department of Archives and History, visiting 523 schools in 57 counties and setting up in central town locations for the public. All told, 233,494 saw the exhibits during 1949–50.

In Chicago the nonprofit Milk Industry Foundation mobile unit, an Airstream trailer, has visited area schools to show how milk is produced in various exhibits. About 60,000 children have visited it yearly since 1955. The Foundation started in 1908 composed of processors of fluid milk and manufacturers of milk by-products.

The Michigan State Medical Society in 1966–70 sent out a 50-foot Marlette custom-built Healthmobile trailer with 24 decorated exhibits, photos and models covering 100 years of medical history in Michigan. It was taken to shopping centers, the state capital and other stops for students, parents, teachers, government employees and health officials.

The Heavy Specialized Carriers Conference of the American Trucking Associations arranged with the National Aeronautics and Space Administration (NASA) to transport the Apollo 11 space command module Columbia display in 1970–71 to all state capitals. Nearly three

Many people in the United States had an opportunity to view the Apollo 11 space command module Columbia, thanks to this specially-built trailer. *(Courtesy Heavy Specialized Carriers Conference, American Trucking Associations)*

million viewed the exhibits in the wide-load, 14,000-mile tour. The vehicle, a Challenger Air-Ride Low-Boy Talbert, was a custom-designed, 40-foot-long and 14-foot-wide trailer, which opened to 20 feet. It traveled 5,250 miles by sea to Honolulu and Juneau.

Since 1970 Gene Reaves of Plymouth, Michigan, has displayed what he calls the world's largest autograph collection in a trailer. It has 20,000 signatures and weighs 250 pounds.

In 1972 a patriotic touring show went out: America on the Move, a 40-foot, star-spangled red, white and blue special Gindy trailer. Housed were exhibits and interactive materials on American history, keeping America clean and drug abuse. It was intended primarily for trade union members and the general public. It completed a nine-month, 33-city tour of the United States and Canada. The International Brotherhood of Teamsters Union which sponsored it was organized in 1903 for workers, retirees and other members in transportation, construction, factories, offices, hospitals, public agencies, movies, convention centers, and many other kinds of workplaces.

A host of cooperating agencies used mobile exhibits during the 1976 U.S. Bicentennial Celebration to show historic displays and documents on national tours. Trailers and vans were used by trucking interests, museums, educational institutions, societies and commercial sponsors.

A particularly innovative vehicle was used in the mobile Bicentennial Exhibition of Minnesota Art and Architecture, sponsored by the University of Minnesota Art Gallery and the Minnesota Society of Architects, with the cooperation of the Minnesota Motor Transport Association. The 40 displays traveled in a 42-foot Fruehauf van. Folding walls became their own packing cases in the 20-city statewide tour.

The Chicago Historical Society has a traveling forge field workshop exhibit oriented around the Civil War, with blacksmithing for field artillery.

Bugs-On-Wheels is the traveling exhibit of the Lansing, Michigan–based Young Entomologists' Society, which on its visits provides free lecture programs.

Exhibits involving two or more organizations are not uncommon.

A collaborative project involving the Shanti Foundation for Peace, the Chicago Children's Museum and the Chicago Transit Authority put the Getting Along Peace Bus on the streets in 1995. The traveling exhibition features children's art and posters in peace themes painted on the bus sides.

The Detroit Institute of Arts Truck Art Project in 1997 involved three 48-foot semi-trailers decorated with original art created by young students from Southwest Detroit. Murals traveled the highways and were exhibited at festivals and art museums. The project was supported by the Detroit Institute of Arts, General Electric Automotive and the El Arte Alliance.

Under the auspices of the Detroit Heidelberg Community Street Art Project, artist Tyree Guyton has taken his Rosa Parks bus decorated with polka dots on the road as part of his exhibit and lecture tours. It is a former city vehicle from 1955, the year Parks made civil rights history when she was arrested for not moving to the back of the bus in Montgomery, Alabama.

A refinished antique bus was sent to the United States and Canada by the Society for French American Cultural Services and Education Aid as an exhibit sponsored by the Youth Tribunal and the Association for Development of Help to Students in 1970.

In preparation for the 1988 Olympic Games in Calgary, Canada, a 65-foot tractor-trailer went out with sports displays and a simulated bobsled ride. The modified vehicle was loaned by the Alberta Trucking Association; the major sponsor of the program was Labatt Brewery.

Museums

Mobile museum projects have taken place in several states and specialized individual museums have had national tours conducted.

In 1964 the blue and white Artmobile outfitted as a gallery was presented as a gift to the Founders Society of the Detroit Institute of Arts by the Chrysler Corporation. It was a specially built, 42-foot converted moving van designed to encourage membership in the Society, the museum's sustaining organization, and to expose fine art to outstate residents. The swing walls were lined with pegboard and the ceiling studded with swiveling spotlights. The interior display was supplemented by ten floodlit exterior display panels. A fee was asked of each city visited. After three years it was discontinued. Traverse City, Michigan, has had an Artruck van, a former bookmobile, purchased and maintained by local art teachers and educators to bring art to area schools.

The Virginia Museum of Fine Arts has toured four Art Mobiles throughout

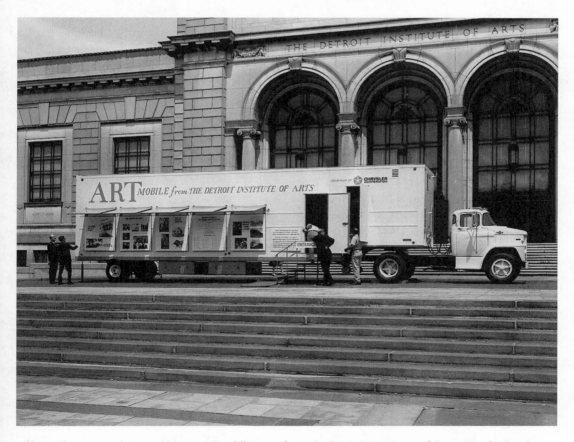

Several museums have used artmobiles. This one from the Detroit Institute of Arts visited schools and civic centers. Chrysler donated the vehicle. *(Courtesy of the Detroit Institute of the Arts, Joseph Klima, Jr., photographer)*

The Cavalcade of Trucking exhibit in a state-of-the-art trailer celebrated 50 years for the industry. The vehicle was equipped with a computer and all of the latest techniques and developments. *(Courtesy American Trucking Associations)*

the state since 1967. Custom-designed wide-load Fruehauf trailers, they were at the time considered among the largest in the world. Flaps on the sides opened automatically to reveal information panels and awnings and display signs went around the top. Steps and platforms all unfolded automatically. It took 30 minutes to prepare the 42½-foot long, nine-foot wide vehicles, which visited 19 cities as well as colleges and universities.

The Friends of the Middle Border Museum in South Dakota have used a Historymobile with the South Dakota State History Society featuring the theme Dakotarama. This was a Title III project.

Other such mobile projects have been carried out using vans, trailers, buses and recreational vehicles by the American Museum of Natural History in New York; the Chicago Children's Museum; Newseum (news media) in Arlington, Virginia; the Museum of New Mexico; the Susquehanna Art Museum in Harrisburg, Pennsylvania; the Natural History Museum in Louisiana, and the Detroit Historical Museum.

Since 1964 four traveling museums operated by Don Bryne have visited about 150 Florida schools yearly with specimens of snakes, insects, marine life, rocks, minerals, fossils and birds. Education lectures have also been featured.

Fruehauf, White Truck and Volvo co-sponsored the Cavalcade of Trucking mobile museum through the American Trucking Associations Foundation in the 1980s. The year-long, 25,000-mile tour went to 139 cities with 300,000 viewers. In a 48-foot display van trucking programs were presented with five dioramas, pictures, displays and memorabilia. A total of 42 manufacturers donated components.

The International Towing and Recovery Hall of Fame and Museum organized by Friends of Towing operated a 45-foot converted used furniture trailer of exhibits, artifacts and photos in 1990.

Joe Janshen runs a mobile museum devoted to memories of rural radio, which he has taken to antique shows and festivals since 1993. It features 1930s and 1940s stations, particularly WLS in Chicago.

Entertainment

Traveling entertainment goes way back in history.

During the Great Depression, the Shell Oil Christmas Show, four red and yellow trucks, were converted from year to year into Noah's Ark, an iceberg or a spaceship. One side opened up to become a miniature stage for an original 30-minute show of puppets, or a magician. They toured the West Coast for a month at schools and played to over one-half a million children, logging 13,000 miles and staging a total of 689 performances in 395 cities.

In Baltimore the Children's Theater Association has used a Showmobile since 1963 to put on mobile performances. The vehicle is a converted trailer from Warner Fruehauf. Renovations included installing side doors and a platform and steps which hook together to extend the playing area in front.

In 1964 Beech Nut Life Savers sponsored a portable stage built on a trailer for New York's free Shakespeare Festival in 60 performances in 33 neighborhood parks. It also provided lighting and sound trucks. Other funding came from foundation grants and private contributions.

The Jazzmobile in New York City started out in 1965 as a parade float and a flatbed truck and is now two conjoined trailer bandstands with white grillwork hitched to a pickup truck. It visits over 100 neighborhoods with free evening concerts each summer. It is operated by a nonprofit organization supported by grants, and also makes out-of-state appearances, drawing crowds of over 5,000. The project is affiliated with the Harlem Cultural Council.

R.J. Reynolds Industries sponsored a customized 57-foot Fruehauf workhorse low-boy furniture van as a theater on wheels in 1982. Jazz Is was sent out on a 20-city tour equipped with a 25-foot-wide fold-down stage, dressing rooms and equipment areas. It was a production of the North Carolina School of the Arts.

The Barnyard Express is a traveling pet farm, a 16-foot barn on wheels that carries animals, fence, stage and sound system. Shows are put on for 25 minutes for children at festivals.

In England a Superbus community center on wheels was intended in 1983 as a neighborhood playbus for children in the form of a converted double-decker. It was used as a toy library, craft workshop and youth club by such groups as the Sheffield Council. The upper deck was a play area and the lower part contained a kitchen, washing and seating area.

Various types of mobile units give the public information on such topics as history, safety, security, ethnic heritage, home improvement, ecology, physical challenges and gasoline economy.

The Detroit Urban League in the 1960s sent out three Fruehauf Toolmobiles as neighborhood repair centers for houses donated by the Detroit Edison Company, Fruehauf Trailer and General Motors.

The Mediabus, a van with a television set in it showing closed circuit video tape programs, was sent out in 1972 to street corners and block parties in the Lower East Side of New York City by nonprofit Community Action Newsreel Foundation, a division of the Young Filmmakers. Audiences were largely Hispanic, Black and Chinese.

National Bank of Detroit has sponsored Project Help, a mobile Operation Identification program in 1974. Engraving pencils and stickers to warn off would-be thieves were distributed in a 27-foot GMC Trans Mode motor home which contained 4000 square feet of exhibit space of anti-theft devices and techniques. It made a six-month tour of Detroit area locations.

To extend the scope of the outdoor education program at the Grand River, Ontario, Canada, Conservation Authority, a Dodge Maxivan was equipped in 1978 with complete laboratory facilities, library and additional storage areas. In addition to serving community groups it could be converted to an exhibit for other outdoor displays.

The Champion Spark Plug Company sent out traveling testing laboratories twice, once in 1967–68 and again in 1975–80. This second survey series was the most ambitious, involving ultimately 20,000 vehicles. The main test facility consisted of five special mobile units: a trailer-mounted chassis dynamometer; a data collection center; a support vehicle; a diagnostic van and a portable generator. This was considered the most comprehensive examination of motorists' maintenance habits and their effect on gasoline consumption and excessive emissions ever undertaken by a non-governmental source. Tests took place in shopping centers in 30 U.S. and Canadian cities, three Mexican cities and ten European cities in England, Italy, Spain, Belgium and Germany. Free tests were conducted both before and after tune-ups and volunteer motorists were given written reports and recommendations for corrections. Special mobile tests also covered motorcycles and boats. All tests were observed and certified by officials of the U.S. Auto Club, and data gathered were compared to results from earlier studies and

provided to governmental agencies for their use in formulating policies.

Gulf Oil also used seven vans in shopping centers to test car engine emissions with analyzers nationally in 1975.

In the year 2000 Chevrolet sent out a fleet of 51 customized Venture minivans as a child car seat checkup in a Safe Kids Campaign in every state and the District of Columbia. This was a safety information project as a free public service to vehicle owners of all makes and models.

The Canadian National Institute for the Blind, a voluntary, nonprofit agency, had a wheelchair-accessible 1993 Technibus which went on a seven-month tour with high and low technology displays. Some 23 organizations supported the effort to educate the public. The traveling exhibit was part of a seventy-fifth birthday celebration for the Institute, visiting 175 communities in behalf of services to the blind, deaf-blind and visually impaired people.

Road Aid

Beginning in the 1970s in several major metropolitan areas freeway courtesy patrols were set up as emergency road aid to help stranded motorists who experience mechanical trouble, run out of gas or get in accidents. The vehicles are equipped to handle minor repairs free in most cases with a few organizations accepting token fees for parts or gasoline. They are now operating in Rhode Island, Massachusetts, New York, Michigan, Colorado, Ohio, Pennsylvania, California and Florida. Sponsors include automobile clubs, oil companies, drug store chains, dairies, automobile manufacturers and dealers, radio stations, trucking firms, financial institutions and chambers of commerce.

Chapter V

Religious Vehicles

An infinite variety of vehicles and conveyances is used in "mobile ministry" on land. These units are variously referred to as portable pulpits, holy rollers, traveling tabernacles, religion on the road, God-mobiles, gospels on wheels, prayermobiles, perambulatory pulpits, ministries in motion and other terms of greater or lesser reverence.

The list does not quite make it from A to Z, but it does embrace a range from A to W: all-terrain vehicles, ambulances, bicycles, buggies, buckboards, buses, cable cars, carriages, carts, chariots, covered wagons, cycle-cars, dog trains/sleds, fire trucks, go-karts, golf carts, hammocks, house cars, jinrikshas, komatiks, lavers, limousines, mini-mokes, mobile homes, motor bikes, motorcycles, motor homes, motor scooters, moving vans, palanquins, parade floats, passenger cars, pedicabs, prairie schooners, racing cars, rocking chairs, samlars, semi-trailers, sledges, sleighs, snowmobiles, station wagons, street cars, taxis, three-wheelers, tongas, tractors, trailers, trolleys, trucks, unicycles, vans, wheelbarrows, wagons and wheelchairs.

As to incidence of usage, trucks pre-dominate, followed by vans, buses, passenger cars, semi-trailers and recreational vehicles. The other units listed above are used relatively infrequently, mostly overseas.

The concept of mobile ministry is certainly far from new: "…prepare the way for the Lord; make straight in the wilderness a highway for our God" (Isaiah 40:3) NIV.

It must be admitted at the outset that some groups take a rather negative approach to mobility. Religious cultists in Manila in the Philippines in 1992 deflated tires on scores of buses and cars during the evening rush hour. According to spokesman Honora Dimaglia, "Air is from God. This is the solution to the crisis in our country. Flat tires are the key to salvation. It is God's will." Some 32 people were arrested.

Another rather sour note when it comes to vehicles has been registered by Bishop Joseph Wenger of the Old Order Mennonites. He believes that automobiles should not be used for either occupational transportation or coming to worship. His group in opposition is mostly in southwestern Pennsylvania. Bishop Moses

Central American refugees from various countries were given sanctuary in the mid–1980s in several U.S. churches, such as St. Rita's Catholic Church in Detroit (above) and the University Baptist Church in Seattle, Washington. Supporting the work was a multifaith effort called the National Sanctuary Freedom Train, which traveled by van. *(Reprinted with permission from* The Detroit News; *photograph by Edwin C. Lombardo)*

Horning has established a somewhat more liberal wing. His followers use automobiles, but only for necessary purposes. The car must be black and without frivolous trim. Most of the members cover their chrome with black paint. The Amish do not drive cars or ride bicycles, but they do now roller-skate to augment their horse-and-buggy transportation.

On the whole, though, the great preponderance of religious workers recognize vehicles as a very valuable boon, as evidenced by the wide variety of applications made of them: aid and relief; health care; mobile unit services; clergy transportation; street ministry; evangelism; missions; Sunday School and youth work; public display; audiovisual presentations; literature distribution; motorcycle ministry; and weddings and pilgrimages.

Aid and Relief

Both continuing aid programs and emergency relief efforts constitute major mobile ministry activities, providing food, clothing and various other types of community services.

Recipients include the general public, prostitutes, armed services personnel, refugees and others. Under the umbrella term "general public" are listed the homeless, poor, welfare recipients, unemployed, street people, and underprivileged children.

Individuals and families in need are served by a very wide variety of organizations employing various mobile units in their programs. Provided is a typical hands-on approach to physical needs along with spiritual values.

FOOD AND CLOTHING

Mobile soup kitchens are a real boon to the hungry who lack transportation to fixed base locations.

The Salvation Army operates mobile soup kitchen vans. On the east side of Detroit, its red-beaconed Bed and Bread Club trucks have been provided since 1989. Every day they serve food to about 800 at 20 stops on a four-hour trip.

Russian Orthodox Rev. Thomas Flower is a so-called vagabond priest in San Francisco's seedy Tenderloin area. His mobile soup kitchen is in a Volkswagen van in which he also sleeps.

Street People in Need Today, Newport Beach, California, was originated by Our Lady Queen of Angels Church. Over 130 volunteers provide homeless and poverty-stricken people with regular meals, clean clothes, blankets, first aid and hygiene supplies and emergency shelter. The van distributes nearly 700 meals a week on the street.

In Toledo, Ohio, the St. Paul Community Center van ministering to the riverfront homeless is a continuing outreach program. The focus is on the 80 or more known mentally ill among this group. Since 1992 they have received sandwiches, coffee and referral services. (It is estimated that 30 percent of the U.S. homeless suffer from mental illness.) Three case managers have contacted a total of 210 different individuals so far.

The Convoy of Hope, an international, transdenominational, humanitarian organization, offers refreshments, food and toys to the poor and needy through outreach activities in red, white and blue trucks.

Other cities such as Albuquerque, New Mexico, where four religious missions have combined forces, operate similar mobile kitchens.

Turning to overseas projects, in Paris, France, it is estimated that soup vans feed at least 300 nightly.

Water is a precious commodity, often taken for granted. In Angola, for example, Southern Baptist missionaries have to truck it in drums for residents.

The Hare Krishna's Food for Life program operated in Yugoslavia in 1992 for the poor and underprivileged. Children were given sweets and cookies at schools. Also served were old persons' homes, hospitals, refugee centers and the handicapped.

The Maine Seacoast Missionary Society, Bar harbor, has used its Recyclemobiles to serve the needy in remote settlements in coastal Washington County. Stocked are used clothing, household goods and blankets for distribution in school yards and grocery store parking lots. The vehicle is a refitted school bus driven by a United Church of Christ minister.

COMMUNITY SERVICES

Special vehicles help furnish a wide range of social services in addition to those already listed, including day care for children and adults; field trips; transportation to jobs, churches and prisons; and education.

The Young Women's Christian Association uses an Action Van, a self-contained camper trailer, for children's cooking classes and meetings for parents and teachers. It also operates Funmobile vans for children with games and sports equipment.

In 1984 the 38-block Ravendale section of Detroit saw Eddie Edwards set up a Christian ministry to rehabilitate the area. One neighborhood group on Wade Street uses a donated van to provide shuttle service for the handicapped, elderly and youth.

A yellow minibus holding 15 is used by the Rev. Rick Sebastian of Holt, Michigan, to take homeless men to church at the Cornerstone Assembly of God. He picks them up in Lansing and they get a $5 bill and lunch.

A key part of the Christian Appalachian Project is a School on Wheels satellite program started in 1992. These two old buses, affectionately known as the Little Red School Buses with desks, tables and a computer, help those in the rural South to learn to read and earn general equivalency diplomas. In five counties thousands have participated. Tutors are volunteers who conduct community classes or visit individual homes.

DISASTERS AND EMERGENCIES

Relief is provided by a large number of denominations, parachurch groups and independent organizations for all sorts of victims of natural and man-made problems.

Aimee Semple McPherson of the International Church of the Foursquare Gospel sent her mobile units to aid earthquake victims in Santa Barbara, California, in 1925 and again to Long Beach in 1934.

The General Conference of Seventh-day Adventists is very active in disaster relief in cooperation with the American Red Cross and the Voluntary Organization Active in Disasters. The Adventists operate distribution vans with food and water, clothing, bedding and linens, emergency electricity and communications equipment.

The Salvation Army forms caravans

for relief supplies. When Hurricane Andrew struck Florida in 1992, large convoys went to the Miami area. The Army also operates emergency walk-in canteen vans which feed people cafeteria-style at all types of disasters and emergency sites.

OVERSEAS

Examples of emergency vehicle help are also found outside the United States in abundance.

Since 1988 Pastors for Peace, in connection with the Inter-Religious Foundation for Community Organization, has sent out truck convoys in development aid. Recipients include Nicaragua, El Salvador, Guatemala and Cuba. Delivered are trucks, wheelchairs, bicycles, medical and school supplies, office equipment, emergency food rations, farm equipment, generators, tools, seeds, cash and Bibles. Up to 44 or so trucks form a caravan which travels initially along various routes through the United States organizing for aid collections, educational presentations and press conferences. As many as 100 cities get involved. The group is ecumenical and includes both clergy and laity, such as war veterans in concerned churches.

PROSTITUTES

Some agencies offer mobile assistance to girls and women who have ended up making a dubious and dangerous living as prostitutes.

The Rev. Marvin Crow operates the International Christian Center in Garland, Texas, which provides a mobile chapel to offer prayer and counseling to persons in crisis. The van is equipped with police, fire and ambulance scanners. It roams the streets, waiting for a call from 8 A.M. to midnight. His ministry is independent and charismatic.

Howard Moody, Baptist pastor of the

Judson Memorial Church in Greenwich Village in New York City, has a ministry for prostitutes, alcoholics and drug addicts. He cruises the streets in a green and white minibus from 11 P.M. to 5 A.M. to provide counseling and refreshments. In 1980 he acquired his converted National Rental Car vehicle after beginning in 1976 in a battered sedan. Some of the 20 to 30 people contacted nightly drop in two or three times.

Robert F. "Bob" Harrington, known as the Chaplain of Bourbon Street in New Orleans, has employed a motor home in his ministry in and around the infamous thoroughfare as he counseled prostitutes, runaways and others who need help.

In a recent Democratic national convention in New York city a minister cruised city streets offering aid, rest and coffee to prostitutes from a customized van.

ARMED SERVICES PERSONNEL

Doughboys in World War I in France considered themselves fortunate to enjoy the services of the Salvation Army trucks as they appeared at advanced military bases.

Health Care

Medical and dental vans and trailers of Project Concern have operated in East Tennessee and California since 1968. This international, medical-dental, nonprofit relief organization is active in South Vietnam, Hong Kong, Mexico, Ethiopia, Indonesia and Guatemala and is expanding. Over 500,000 persons have been served to date.

The Seventh-day Adventist Church has been operating 38-foot semi-trailer medical and dental units in the United States and abroad since 1971. This is a community service medical evangelism program in 800 inner-city locations and 400 small towns and villages. Health vans typically have four rooms with a reception area, eye screening clinic, blood chemistry lab and dental operatory. Sites include shopping centers, office complexes, college campuses, fairs, supermarkets and discount stores. Instructional health leaflets are given out, free blood pressure taken and eight medical tests, inspirational literature and counseling offered. Visits are made on a regular basis and greeters contact passersby. The staff includes lab technicians, nurses and trained lay people. About 100 can be processed a day. Vehicles are also involved in disaster relief, welfare programs, vegetarian cooking schools and Bible study. So far the Southwestern Union Conference has screened or treated over 100,000, with services worth over $14 million, working out of Burleson, Texas.

In Chicago the Northside Ecumenical Night Ministry has been operating since 1989 with a roving white, six-wheel, 33-foot Health Outreach Hopbus after starting out in a motor home. It goes out four nights a week for six hours, 8 P.M. until 2 A.M., 52 weeks a year. The staff consists of a doctor, nurse, outreach minister and volunteers. Provided are medical treatment, hospitality, health education, food, counseling and referrals. On an average 40 homeless teenage patients are contacted at three scheduled stops each night on the North Side, Lakeview and uptown neighborhoods. The Rev. Tom Behrens, ordained in the United Church of Christ, is the executive director of the nonprofit outreach organization.

Since 1991 the Maumee Valley Presbytery in Findlay, Ohio, has had its own health van. Formerly it used one borrowed from St. Vincent's Hospital in Toledo. The vehicle serves migrant farm communities in Ohio and Southeastern Michigan with screenings and education programs. Churches sponsor health fairs in the summer with Presbyterian church member volunteers and a doctor on duty.

James L. Gebhart, Southern Baptist missionary in the Rio Grande City, Texas, area, works with Mexican-Americans who have come for dental care. He operates the Concern for People trailer clinic in his ranch ministry with the help of area volunteer dentists. No fees are charged.

The Dream Center, Los Angeles, has a mobile medical unit and it also does drug rehabilitation, job skills classes and Bible study.

Outside the United States several groups are active.

Hap and Dorothy Parsons of McAllen, Texas, conduct a dental bus ministry to Mexico along the Texas border, particularly in Rio Bravo where they maintain a clinic. The vehicle is operated as a complete dental clinic on wheels. They distribute Bibles and tracts and conduct services, and Dorothy conducts Bible and craft classes, acting as members of Missionary Dentists, an interdenominational, specialized service agency of evangelical tradition engaged in medical work, evangelism and providing medical supplies and equipment.

The Dooley Foundation/Intermed in its health care ministry in Laos in Southeast Asia and Nepal in Northern India has been involved in a variety of vehicles. These include mobile clinics, Jeep Drawn medical trailers, X-ray vans and trucks, all used in remote jungle villages in the dry season.

Since 1970 the Convention of Philippine Baptist Churches has provided a mobile clinic for medical, dental and family planning care for the rural poor. It operates out of the Emmanuel Hospital in Rakos City.

The American Baptist Churches USA Foreign Mission Society has served leprosy patients among the Telugu people with a mobile clinic. A doctor and an evangelist make up the team in Andhra, India, and it has also provided a van with an ambulance body for the Nellore district of South India for family planning and other community health outreach programs for women in satellite villages.

Heralding Christ Jesus' Blessings radio station operated mobile clinics in Quito, Ecuador, in the 1980s.

Pacific Missionary Aviation offers mobile eye clinics, health and nutritional education and mobile dentistry in the Philippines and Micronesia.

The World Radio Missionary Fellowship operates mobile clinics in South America.

Samaritan's Purse has eight mobile medical vehicles operated by its World Medical Mission division in Mogadishu and other cities. They are staffed by volunteer doctors and nurses from North America. It has treated over 35,000 people since 1977. Billy Graham's son Franklin heads the organization.

Christians in Action medical teams use vans in Guatemala in Central America.

Amistad operates alcohol recovery in Mexico with ambulances to pick up Indian patients. Mexican Medical also uses mobile medical clinics in remote areas of the country.

AMG International, a nondenominational sending agency of Baptist tradition, maintains 11 mobile clinics in India. Since 1975 the vans have been used to facilitate treatment of leprosy patients.

Mobile Ministry Services

When Aimee Semple McPherson headed the International Church of the Foursquare Gospel in California she had two Gospel cars, a 1912 black Packard seven-seat touring car and a 1918 Oldsmobile touring car. On the sides were religious messages like "Prepare to Meet Your God," "Jesus Saves," "Where Will You Spend Eternity?," "Jesus Is Coming Soon" and "Get Ready." She played a small organ and preached from the back seat using a megaphone, handed out tracts and handbills and gave invitations to her meetings. In her world travels she recounted having been transported by a junk, river schooner, elephant, camel, bullock cart, donkey, tonga, dandy chair, ferry, motorcycle and horse and buggy.

In order to reach communities inaccessible by the railroad, the Catholic Church Extension Society of the United States of America sent out two motor chapels. These were employed chiefly in missionary work among Mexican settlers in little Texas towns too scattered to build and support a church.

The first, the 18½-foot-long St. Peter, was custom-built in 1913 and placed on an Alco truck chassis. The back behind the cab opened out to form a floor and walls of a sanctuary and to reveal a built-in altar. Eight cathedral windows with a cross in each one in the center imparted a church atmosphere. The center section served as living quarters and storage. When needed for protection against the elements a 20-foot by 50-foot gable roof, khaki tent with seven and a half foot walls was stretched over the entire vehicle. Two Oblate Fathers accompanied the chapel. The first mass was celebrated at El Salado, Texas, near Brownsville. Besides the regular religious services, illustrated lectures on Catholic doctrine and Bible subjects were given.

In the 1920s the second vehicle, St.

The American Locomotive Company in Chicago built this mobile chapel. Two of these vehicles augmented two railway chapels already in service by the Catholic Church Extension Society of the USA. *(Extension Magazine)*

The Baptist Crawford Memorial Chapel Car No. 1, also known as Carro Capilla Mexicano, towed a trailer with a tent, chairs and an organ. It was dedicated in 1922 and was part of a fleet, all built on White bus chassis and sent out by the Home Mission Society. P.J. Villanueva was the colporteur missionary assigned. *(From the Archives of the American Baptist Historical Society—Valley Forge, Pennsylvania 19482)*

Joseph, was designed as a small house trailer.

The Catholic Diocese of Richmond, Virginia, operated a large coach in the mid–1950s. It had a Gerstenslager body mounted on an International chassis. There was an altar in the rear with speakers mounted on the doors.

Out Lady of the Miraculous Medal motor chapel was used in Catholic motor ministry in Raleigh, North Carolina. This sumptuous coach had an altar that could be rigged for outside services or used inside with pews. It also had a Gerstenslager body.

The four-wheel, 20-foot trailer chapel of the North Carolina Missionary Fathers is called Madonna of the Highways, and was put in service in 1948. It contains an altar, pulpit, confessional, stations of the cross, PA system and equipment for movies, radio and video presentations. The trailer was a special mission-

ary project of the North Carolina Catholic Laymen's Association. It is towed by a Mercury sedan with a special transmission. Prior to the dedication it was on exhibition outside the Hotel Pennsylvania in New York City.

Since 1969 Father William F. Collins of Our Lady of Victories Rectory, Landisville, New Jersey, has traveled around his 2,400-square-mile parish using a church on wheels. Known affectionately as Father Bill, he ministers especially to the thousands of migrant farm workers of vegetable-growing Southern New Jersey, many of them Spanish-speaking from Puerto Rico or Cuba. His Winnebago motor home was provided by the Diocese of Camden.

Right after the end of World War I, the Rev. Branford Clarke of New York City built a tiny, traveling chapel on a Ford Model T touring car chassis. It had stained glass windows, a pulpit, a small organ and

The Rev. Branford Clarke looks like he meant business and his "business" was religion. *(From the Collections of Henry Ford Museum and Greenfield Village)*

a collapsible steeple to be folded down when parking in a garage. Going out from his Pillar of Fire Church in Brooklyn, he covered the city with what he called his perambulatory pulpit. Mrs. Clarke played the organ from the back seat.

The Second Hungarian Baptist Church of Detroit, Michigan, had a chapel car which went out in 1932. The Rev. Albert Petre was the pastor and Joseph Nagy who was a member and a carpenter built it. Cut off at the cab on the back and with the top left open it had benches as a converted 1928 Hudson with a pulpit and portable organ. Once a week during the summer church members would go out and park it on a street and conduct an evangelistic service with preaching, music and poetry. Religious tracts and Bibles

were distributed. Followed by other church members, the vehicle went out as far as Flint, Michigan, and Toledo, Ohio. As a result there were reported conversions of people who became faithful church members. After a few years, however, interest waned, and the church turned its efforts toward a radio ministry.

St. Paul's Wayside Cathedral opened October 1, 1937, as a trailer church under the diocese of the Southern Ohio Protestant Episcopal Church. It was built by the Aerocar Company. The exterior was gray with a silver roof, removable altar, organ, amplification unit and sound moving picture apparatus. It seated 25.

During World War II three mobile wayside chapels near the A-Bomb research site at Paducah, Kentucky, acted as a liai-

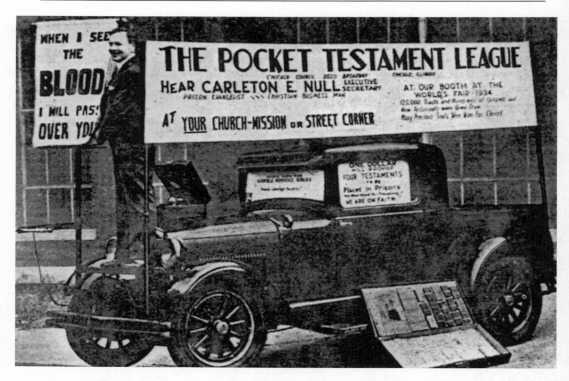

The Pocket Testament League used this car with a pickup box in 1935 in the depth of the Depression. It could stop anywhere that people were passing and be ready for a street meeting in five minutes. Pastor Carleton E. Null visited over eight states with it. Note the preaching platform on the front and phonograph on the hood. *(Courtesy Pocket Testament League)*

son between trailerite workers and the city churches. They were operated for 65 trailer courts. Sponsoring churches included Methodist, Evangelical and Reformed, and Lutheran. The staff was made up of eight full-time workers: pastor, director, parish workers and office secretary. Equipment included an amplifier, record player for outdoor services, visual education items, portable organ and a chancel with a pulpit lectern. A regular weekly schedule took the chapels to several other locations. The project was under the authority of the Paducah Defense Services Committee, composed of 16 people appointed by four interdenominational organizations in the county.

From 1947 to 1955 Ray and Darlene Brubaker coordinated from St. Petersburg, Florida, the ministry program of five Cathedral Caravans. These were streamlined, aluminum trailers which operated in over 15 different states in the Southeast, Midwest and South. They were towed by neon-lighted station wagons which were detached to circle the areas visited to broadcast invitations to the meetings over loudspeakers. The front of the unit was built like a living room where counseling took place. The rear was specially designed to form a platform which pulled out from below on hinges to make an illuminated stage, which folded up to close the entrance. The back raised to form a canopy. In addition to the public address system there was a movie projector, generator, midget piano and 25 folding chairs. The program offered sermons, gospel movies, music, magic, felt-o-graphs, chalk-talks and passed out tracts. Points visited in-

Taking religion to the people was obviously the slogan of the Second Hungarian Baptist Church of Detroit. Its unique chapel car drew large crowds as the photograph clearly indicates. A sizable ethnic population existed in the area in the Depression years when it was actively used; it also made trips to nearby cities. *(From the Archives of the American Baptist Historical Society, Valley Forge, Pennsylvania 19482)*

cluded chain gang camps, apartments, housing projects, amusement parks, playgrounds, picnic grounds, street corners, baseball parks, vacant lots, churches, parking lots, fairs, school grounds, migrant labor camps for Jamaicans, factories, carnivals, mobile home parks and Army bases. County fairs proved to be the most successful venues. Local police permission was always secured in advance.

Kenny Joseph in Japan used a tour wagon called the Cathedral Caravanette, affiliated with Japan Youth for Christ, in 1951–53.

The Chapel of the Highways is a small converted white mobile home operated by the Rev. Jimmy Cope, known as the Radio Gospel Singer, a traveling nondenominational missionary. He has roamed in trailers, house cars and trucks in his work. The chapel was originally built in

1950 by the Rev. C.G. Collins. The Reverend Cope parks at Native American reservations, roadside parks and other sites and conducts services, plays gospel records (the steeple is equipped for hi-fi sound) and distributes tracts and Bibles. At the side of the vehicle a section raises by hydraulic jacks and a six-foot platform lets down. A portable Bible stand is put in place. Behind the altar there is a scene of the Garden of Gethsemane. The interior has stained glass windows, fluorescent lights and a bench. The Reverend Cope travels with his nephew, Buddy Dickerson.

The Rev. Theodore Allison, called the Mobile Minister, serves mobile home residents near Grants, New Mexico, representing the Board of National Missions of the United Presbyterian Church USA. In 1960 he set up the Westminster Chapel, a special mobile home chassis 35 feet by

Note the rear preaching platform and illuminated stage of this Cathedral Caravan vehicle. *(Courtesy Cathedral Caravan)*

eight feet, functioning as a worship center. There are Sunday worship services held, and Mrs. Allison conducts Christian education classes for children, a girls' 4-H club, a home extension club for women, PTA and Vacation Bible School. Similar operations are found in the Northeast, Kentucky and New Jersey.

In the mid–1970s many unmarried student Hare Krishna devotees traveled around the United States and Canada as preaching parties in converted Greyhound buses. They put on week-long festivals featuring chanting, instrumental music, vegetarian feasts and lectures. Books passed out described Krishna consciousness for college campuses. Each bus was transformed into a temple, allowing the travelers to worship deities of Krishna and to introduce the worship to others.

The Rev. Theodore Menter, Lu-

theran pastor for the Center for Christian Service in Woodhaven, Michigan, started operating from a trailer headquarters in 1974. It served as a worship, meeting and counseling site.

A long, light blue, gooseneck, fifth-wheel trailer behind a camper has been used since 1976 by the Trans-Pecos Big Bend Ministry of the Episcopal Diocese of the Rio Grande. The vehicle is carpeted throughout and accommodates 18 people in folding chairs. The Rev. Bob Burton, Archdeacon, and his wife Phyllis serve an isolated desert parish of 200, mostly ranchers, scattered over 30,000 square miles in West Texas. The Reverend Burton uses a CB radio to invite people to services. So far the Burtons have logged over 75,000 miles.

The Lubavitch Youth Organization of Greater Detroit in 1969 used a Suka

On the outside of this Chabad House on Wheels are ten paintings of significant religious observances. The 1978 motor home's travels are reminiscent of those of circuit riders. The Chabad movement was formed over 200 years ago in Russia. *(Courtesy Lubavitch Orthodox Jews)*

Mobile to commemorate the most important of the three Jewish festivals as the nine-day holiday of thanksgiving variously referred to as the Festival or Feast of the Lord, Vintage, Booths, or other names. It was a beautiful walnut-paneled prayer booth or tabernacle mounted on a Dodge pickup truck. Drivers throughout the city and suburbs stopped at public institutions, schools, hospitals, shopping centers and nursing homes. This traveling holiday wagon was equipped with loudspeakers and visitors were presented with appropriate literature, palm leaves and rare citron fruit. The whole purpose was to acquaint Jews with laws of the observance.

From 1976 to 1990 the Chabad House on Wheels, or Mitzvah Mobile, a custom-designed, 32-foot, brown and white Winnebago motor home, was operated throughout Michigan by a group of bilingual Lubavitch orthodox Jews from Farmington Hills. It was part library, part synagogue with a kosher kitchen. A loudspeaker played Jewish music from a cassette/recorder player. It seated 25 and could sleep five. The young driver was Yitschok Lipszyo, known as the Roving Rabbi. Women also drove it. Stops were made in small towns, shopping centers and college campuses where religious services were performed, food was donated to the needy, counseling offered and literature distributed. The unit was donated

This Trail of Hope six-wheeler mobile chapel promises 250,000 Arizona Native Americans health, happiness and heaven. The often forgotten group on reservations is served faithfully by the Arizona Conference of Seventh-day Adventists. The vehicle, equipped with a satellite dish and a computer, is used for services, seminars, Bible study, Sabbath School, health education and family counseling. *(Courtesy Arizona Conference of Seventh-day Adventists)*

by Marvin Tarnoff, a Buick and RV dealer. Chabad-Lubavitch International had 24 centers at major universities in the United States and Canada, and is a nonprofit organization of 500,000 with over 1,500 centers in 40 countries worldwide. (Chabad is an acronym for Hebrew words for wisdom, knowledge and understanding.)

In 1976 the Rev. D.L. Garrard, Phoenix, Arizona, used a 25-foot trailer rig made to look like a miniature house of worship. He conducted services for migrant farm workers at their roadside camps. The white and green Gospel of the Highways was complete with stained glass windows. A pickup truck hauled it. A side swung down to serve as a pulpit platform after the hinged roof was raised manually or by a 12-volt motor. Behind the pulpit

was an organ, seats for a choir and storage space for 100 chairs. When lowered to the ground by jacks, it resembled a small country church.

When the Catholic Church near Tug Ford River in Kentucky was flooded and destroyed, the parishioners acquired a double-wide mobile home and converted it to hold temporary services.

Mobile unit services outside the United States are found in England, Ireland, Africa, Peru and other places.

In 1942 a three-ton, six-by-four AEC Marshal bridging vehicle was converted by the Royal Army Ordnance Corps in the North African Desert into the Motor Church of St. George. Bridge cradles were removed and on the chassis a wooden, caravan-type structure was built and suitably

The multiuse Churchmobile serves a widely scattered congregation in County Kildare, Republic of Ireland. The mobile Gothic is operated by the only rural Baptist gathering in Ireland, established in 1882. *(Courtesy Baptist Church of Brannockstown)*

decorated. It functioned as an office and quarters for the mobile padre.

A Churchmobile is operated by the Rev. Robert Dunlop of the Baptist church, Brannockstown Village, Kilkallen, County Kildare, Republic of Ireland. A converted bus, the chapel on wheels was built in Dublin in 1972. It has a pulpit and seats 40. It is used for services and meetings and to display and sell Bibles, records and religious literature over a wide area.

The Rev. Teddy Boston of Cadby Parish, Leicestershire, England, uses as a pulpit a big nine-ton steam tractor, Fiery Elias.

Ministries for truckers abound.

Transport for Christ International, a pioneering effort, was established in 1951 by the Rev. James Keys to minister to truck drivers and trucking company employees in the United States and Canada. An operation was begun in Australia in

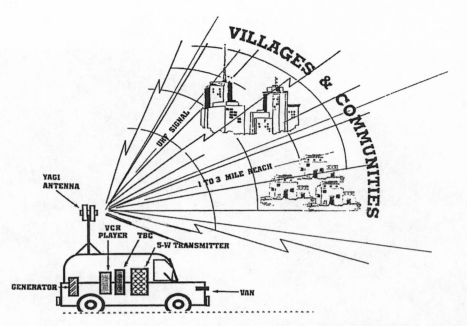

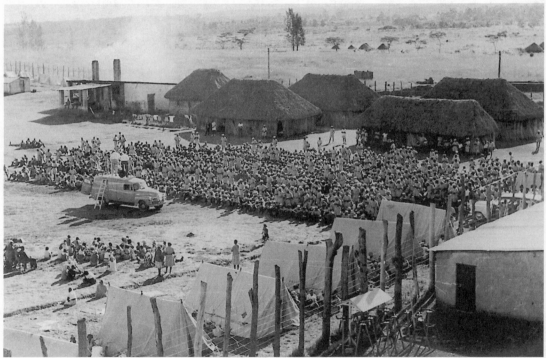

Top: The Society for International Ministries is setting up a ministry built around a mobile UHF television broadcasting mini station in Lima, Peru. It would dramatically expand the range and magnitude of Christian outreach. *(Courtesy SIM). Bottom:* This mass meeting of hundreds of military personnel took place in Kenya, East Africa, in the 1950s. It is typical of the efforts of the non-denominational Pocket Testament League, which depends on mobile sound units in 16 countries equipped with speaker platforms and loud speaker systems to spread the Christian gospel. It also uses minivans extensively. Its 105 evangelists are largely nationals. *(Courtesy Pocket Testament League)*

Faced with many worldly temptations on the road, truck drivers turn to the mobile chapels of Transport for Christ International. A typical chapel at Denver, Pennsylvania, is shown above. *(Courtesy Transport for Christ International)*

1976 which is currently inactive. At one time there were as many as three mobile units on the road. Now 16 are parked permanently at truck stops, 12 in the United States, three in Canada and one in Moscow. The 55-foot, red, white and blue 18-wheelers have a large white cross on top; the organization's name is also on the mud flaps. There is walnut paneling, carpeted floors, drapes, tinted glass chapel windows, a chandelier and living and sleeping quarters for three, complete with restrooms and cooking and eating facilities with an air conditioner, generator and propane tank. A typical unit accommodates 40 on benches, padded chairs or pews. In addition to the PA system there is an organ, electric piano, projector and screen. Mobile units require that an advance man travel ahead to set up the schedule and organize safety meetings. Stops occur at such sites as truck stops, terminals, warehouses, motels, restaurants, churches and truck rallies. Mileage per unit can average 30,000 miles a year. There are ten regions with monthly meetings at local chapters. The 30 staff chaplains are ordained clergy in uniform aided by licensed minister evangelists. Permanent truck stop locations operate 24 hours a day with up to 19 services daily. The 30-minute meetings emphasize safety and a gospel message, with music, films and discussions. Bibles and *Highway* magazine are distributed. Each year an average of 3,000 truckers visit each chapel and the overall program results in over 1,000 men and women becoming Christians. In the planning stages is an expanded truck distribution of Bibles, Christian literature and workshop materials for schools in the former USSR, and a ministry to truck drivers. The trucks are used at fairs, parades, rallies and rodeos.

The Rev. John Ritchey is the Assembly of God chaplain assigned to the trucking ministry. He drives an 18-wheeler chapel complete with hardwood pews, a donation box and CB radio. The red-carpeted truck holds 27. It is a Ford tractor with a Great Dane trailer decorated with two amber crosses on the front and inspirational messages on the back. His wife accompanies him from rest stop to rest stop nationwide.

The Rev. Sam Rust II since 1973 has driven a light brown 18-wheeler converted Great Dane furniture moving van with a diesel Autocar cab in his ministry to truckers through the Assembly of God in the eastern part of the United States and Canada. His Headlight in Trucking, Inc., has traveled over 10,000 miles a year. The unit has wood paneling, carpet, eight polished pews, an altar, kneeling rail, CB AM-FM radio, tape player, stereo sound system, air conditioning and gas heat. There is room for 27 worshipers plus a bed, shower and a kitchenette. On a typical recent three-month swing with his rolling chapel, the Reverend Rust contacted some 600 at truck stops, freight yards, loading terminals and rest stops.

Since 1975 the Rev. Jimmy Snow, known as the Preacher Man, has driven a giant mobile chapel promoting safety at truck stops.

In 1976 when Chaplain Jim Keys left the helm of Transport for Christ, an organization he founded, he and his father started a new organization, the Association of Christian Truckers. Like their predecessors, converted 40-foot mobile chapel semi-trailers are a feature in the highway ministry at truck stops.

"I never met a trucker who didn't believe in God!" So states the Rev. Dan T. Robinson, truck-driver evangelist who operates out of Clearwater, Florida. His motor van is the Circuit Rider. He is the principal missionary for the nondenomi-national Over the Road Evangelism. "Keep on Trucking for Jesus" is his slogan.

Truckstop Ministries, Inc., is a nondenominational, nonprofit, evangelical outreach network program placing truck chapels at truck stops. There are at least 25 so far, of which four are mobile units. Most are located at the TV lounges: State locations include Ohio, Oregon, Georgia, the Carolinas, Florida, Louisiana, Missouri, Arizona, Texas, New Mexico, Indiana and Alabama. The Rev. Joseph H. Hunter, a veteran trucker, founded Truckstop Ministries in March 1981. He still is known by his old CB moniker, Holy Roller. The Rev. Dan Ferrell is his associate. The 70 volunteer chaplains and laymen are from local churches in the areas involved. The 40-foot trailer chapels are modified furniture trucks. Each contains a cathedral ceiling, rough-hewn lectern, orange chairs to seat 18, air conditioning and a small counseling room. There is a red cross on the door and the mud flaps say "Jesus Is Lord." Most truck stops furnish electricity. Each of those attending a service is given a Bible after the one-hour Sunday meeting. A supply of Christian literature is always available. Promotions include flyers handed out and menu ads. Funding is by churches, trucking industry interests and individuals.

Ed Vandermeer since 1982 has operated a 77-passenger bus converted into a chapel. He functions as a highway chaplain on Sundays at Michigan truck stops and gives out 3,000 Bibles yearly.

The Guiding Light Mobile Chapel, a 40-foot converted tractor trailer rig, is operated for truckers by the Rev. Norman Ebersole of Annville, Pennsylvania. It has pews to seat 30, a pulpit and yellow stained glass windows. In the windshield of the cab is a large, lighted white cross. The Reverend Ebersole is on the road 26 weeks a year, trading off two-week shifts with fellow evangelist Harry Coken of Mechanicsburg, Pennsylvania. The Reverend Ebersole travels about 12,000 miles a year as he covers 75 truck stops and 140 trucking companies.

The Truckers Truck, Inc., a nonprofit anti-drug organization, operates two rolling red, white and blue video tractor trailers in the United States. Highway safety awareness is stressed at schools, truck stops, fairs, trade shows and other special events. In addition to its electronic equipment, each trailer has wood-paneled, soundproofed walls, carpeting, indirect lighting, heating, air conditioning and its own power. Included are an office and videotape library. On the sides are lettered 100,000 names of drivers, truckers' families and friends of truckers. The rigs are also available to transport emergency items to disaster areas.

Joe Katancik is a commissioned chaplain working out of Seattle, Washington. He covers 11 states and Western Canada with his truck trailer chapel.

Darrell Tielkemeier operates the Chapel of the Open Road, a 32-foot trailer parked in the back of a service station on Interstate 90 west of Chicago. The former trucker has persuaded at least 15 truckers to become Christians at last count and he has counseled many more.

Glen Cope heads up Truckers Christian Chapel Ministries of Dayton, Ohio.

The distaff side is well represented by the Rev. Heather Murray Elkins, known as the Truck Stop Preacher. Her parish is a 14-acre truck stop in New Jersey. She was ordained a United Methodist minister. In Texas, Sister Tackett, age 70, has operated her trailer since her husband died, holding truck stop revivals with her Spirit of the Open Road.

Jerry Don Brown has used a Trailways bus in his Truckers for Christ ministry program. His wife Carol is active in the work also.

A billboard tribute to the late Parson Bill (William Payne) of Omaha, Nebraska, has been erected on Interstate 80 southwest of the city by Trinity Church Interdenominational. He was an ordained minister of the congregation who preached while trucking. He called his ministry Just for Jammers; it included radio broadcasts in addition to CB messages in a work tied to Transport for Christ.

Other related groups include Gospel Roads, Highway Melodies, Jesus for Trucking, Truckers for Jesus, God's Trucking Ministry and the Association of Christian Truckers.

CLERGY TRANSPORTATION

As vehicles became available to the clergy, they lent both speed and efficiency to their "making the rounds."

From 1946 to 1955 the Nebraska Annual Conference of the United Methodist Church conducted a mobile mission ministry. Four pastors used a camper pulled by a ¾-ton pickup truck and a 1958 panel truck. Using sandhill trails, highways and unimproved ranch roads, they covered thousands of square miles in isolated, sparsely populated rural areas. Equipment included CB radios, portable pulpits and baptismal fonts and an AV lending library. It was not uncommon for one to travel 225 miles on a Sunday; the average was 30,000 miles a year. In one 15-month period 958 visits were made. Dozens of new churches were inspired and others revived.

Pope John Paul II rides in a custom-made, bulletproof Popemobile for visibility yet maximum security when he is in a motorcade in a crowd. The vehicles, by General Motors, Ford, Mercedes Benz and Range Rover, are converted pickup trucks with a platform and a railing added. There is a clear, laminated bubble top mounted on the chassis. They have been used in the United States, Canada, En-

Since attempts on the Pontiff's life security has been tightened for his public appearances. Crowded motorcades find him now in one of his custom-made Popemobiles. He is shown above waving to an eager crowd in 1991 in Esztergom, Hungary. *(Courtesy Gene Hogberg,* **The Plain Truth***)*

gland, Scotland, Poland, Hungary and Croatia, among other nations.

The Rev. James A. Zellner and his family have traveled in a ten-foot trailer. He is a Methodist preacher in Slocomb, Alabama. With his wife and five children along he has served a circuit of six widely scattered rural churches. He built the vehicle by himself during World War II. A jackstand provided a firm foundation, with a portable shower on the side. Inside was a pair of double-decker beds, office and storage area. The trailer was used in a variety of ways: for Boy Scout camping, Sunday school, revival meetings, Vacation Bible School and nursery. Outside attachments allowed the Zellners to take along playground equipment and toys for small children. All sorts of events involving food revolved around the unit: fish fries, barbe-

cues, candy pulls, peanut boils and popcorn parties.

From 1974 to 1979 American Baptist Churches USA Travelcade vans went out from Valley Forge, Pennsylvania, all over the country. This was a colporteur system with a four- or five-person team which held week-long workshops in the various regions.

In foreign countries conditions sometimes call for different types of nontraditional transportation.

Native priests in South Africa travel hundreds of miles every month on motorcycles to visit parishes and missions in their sprawling dioceses, such as the Umzimkula Diocese. The late Catholic priest John Kaiser used a motorcycle in Kenya.

The former Lord Bishop of Norwich, England, the Rt. Rev. Maurice Wood, sent his brigade of 500 vicars out on sky-blue Honda motorcycles to cover their 760 parishes. Some held services in as many as five churches on Sunday. The cost of automobiles was regarded as prohibitive for the budget.

STREET MINISTRY

Mobile units have been used for a good many years to reach people on the street or at public gatherings.

In the 1930s the Pocket Testament League used a car with a pickup box which could stop anywhere that people were passing and be ready to do a street meeting in five minutes. It had a platform on the front where the evangelist could stand and a phonograph on the hood. An open case displayed small Bibles or Testaments. Using this vehicle, Carlton Null's travels took him from Chicago, to Iowa, Missouri, Arkansas, Oklahoma, Texas, California and Washington.

Pastor Chet Schmear, illustrator/evangelist, uses his van for street ministry at parks and beaches. As a focus for his messages he sets up a portable sketchboard and uses a watercolor paint kit for gospel illustrations. He belongs to the Independent Fundamental Churches of America.

In the 1960s and 1970s the Jesus People movement used psychedelic vans and enormous red school buses in their street ministry with a bumper sticker which read "Honk If You Love Jesus." Traveling teams of counterculture commune Christians went all over witnessing, holding concerts at churches and parking lots with their rock groups and passing out literature at youth rallies.

As far back as the 1950s Jewish speakers climbed atop parked cars in busy Paris market squares and exhorted passersby to follow the Law.

A fleet of synagogues on wheels, known as Mitzvah Mobiles or Mitzvah

Tanks, with an electric menorah on top have been used by the Lubavitcher Hasidim Movement since 1974. Loudspeakers play joyous folk tunes and an oven is used to make potato pancakes. They park on the street or in malls to explain orthodox rites, holidays and the use of sacred religious articles of the 500,000 member worldwide body of Eastern European extraction. Cities involved include New York, Philadelphia, Milwaukee, Detroit, Toledo, Miami Beach and Los Angeles, with activity abroad in Canada, Australia and Israel. The vehicles are staffed by students from New York City's Chabad Rabbinical School. In Toledo, Ohio, the Chabad House used a Dreidel House mobile unit to depict a pictorial story of Chanukah, the eight-day festival of lights.

Jewish evangelist Esther Jungreis operates her heritage van with a loudspeaker in New York City, and also is a newspaper columnist and has a television program. She is a Long Island, New York, orthodox Jewish revivalist bent on summoning secularized Jews back to their faith.

In 1967 Dr. Billy Graham spoke to a crowd from on top of a parked car in the Soho district of London, England.

The Hare Krishnas in England operated a converted semi-truck mobile temple in the early 1980s. It was soundproofed, air conditioned and centrally heated, and included a stereo system, a kitchen and the very best interior decorations. The latter included more than $7,000 worth of gold leaf plus six drapes from India. Devotees played musical instruments to attract potential recruits from among passersby.

In 1959 the Episcopal Motorama was a project operated in cooperation with the Missionary Diocese of North Dakota. A small city bus was converted and renovated into a traveling exhibit which toured North Dakota, stopping at county seats, county fairs, shopping centers, public

The Hare Krishnas spared no expense to outfit their converted trailer temple for use in England. *(Copyright* **Back to Godhead,** *July 1987. Used by permission.)*

events and other prearranged locations. The purpose was to acquaint people with the Episcopal Church and its work. A team of clergymen accompanied it to answer questions and distribute literature. It marked the 100th anniversary of the Episcopal Church in the area. Included was material on church history.

EVANGELISTS

Early evangelists used wagons. One of these was C. Taylor, who traveled with his son Charlie. Sayings on the sides of the wagon were "Search the Scriptures" and "Preach the Word." Another was Elder Gardner and his wife, who traveled in a wagon in the early 1900s in Illinois, Wisconsin and Minnesota. He was an evangelical minister with a portable pump organ.

American Baptist John Roach Stratton was a militant fundamentalist minister from Calvary Baptist church in New York City. He used a portable pulpit mounted on the hood of a passenger car in his public debates.

Ministers of the Israelite House of David canvassed the United States in a Model T Ford in 1907.

Neb Thompson's Packard preaching car was operated in Southern California in the 1930s. There were numerous Scriptures on the vehicle and a preacher platform on the rear.

L.I. Bryant, Atlanta, Georgia, was a traveling Black evangelist in the 1930s, using a vehicle inscribed with Scriptures.

In 1945 Dr. Billy Graham visited over 47 states in autos furnished by car dealers. In his crusades he made effective use of

Neb Thompson's impressive white Packard used for mobile evangelistic work was photographed by Dick Whittington, a Los Angeles photographer. *("Dick" Whittington Collection, courtesy of the Huntington Library, San Marino, California)*

buses in Operation Andrew. Churches chartered buses and members received a free ride if they brought one or more unchurched friends with them to the meeting. In 1959 in Sydney, Australia, 40 buses came from Newcastle, 100 miles to the north.

Evangelist Cecil Todd of Revival Fires Ministry, who was very active in the 1950s, called his 22 automobiles Gospel Chariots. With a semi-truck, trailer and tent meetings he was responsible for starting 18 new congregations and saving 10,000 in his crusades.

The late Fred Hicks, who worked as a sign painter, traveled the United States for over 40 years preaching his faith in jails, on the street, and from the back of a mobile pulpit, a former newspaper delivery truck. He wore out six different vehicles owing to his heavy travel.

After Jim and Tammy Faye Bakker, founders of the PTL Ministry and Heritage U.S.A. Christian theme park, were first married in 1961, they spent the next five years in a trailer as traveling preachers for the Assembly of God Church.

In 1967 the Christian Foundation sent a bus into Hollywood, California, daily from its Saugus headquarters to gather people for nightly services. The group has since moved to Alma, Arkansas.

In October 1970 Stephen Gaskin and several hundred followers joined in a cross-country tour known as the Caravan. In four months they covered the nation, gathering converts for the farm commune near Summertown, Tennessee.

The Holy Spirit Association for the Unification of World Christianity sent out workers in 1972 on a 22-city tour of the United States in two buses. The mobile squads gave lectures at local churches and talked to college and high school students.

More bus teams operated throughout Europe.

Evangelist Charles Peterson preaches the Gospel from his camper at highway rest stops, aided by his wife and two daughters. Messages are transmitted by speakers or CB radio. He has so far traveled throughout the United States, Canada, Mexico and Central America.

When he was an 11-year-old evangelist, Windsor, Ontario's, Little Michael always took up a collection in his service for a 50-foot Gospel Hall of Fame trailer for shopping center converts. Michael Hugh Lord, Jr., specialized in healing services. In one year alone he traveled over 100,000 miles and in a five-year period he claimed 75,000 converts. The Faith Church of Denver, Colorado, ordained him when he was only eight. His father was also an ordained minister.

Beginning in 1992 Christians in Action International Ministries began using a 20-passenger diesel bus to take students training for the ministry out in Sao Paulo, Brazil, for practice evangelism trips. The bus has 21 seats and a dormitory.

The Reverend Jimmy Swaggart has always used trucks in his traveling crusades.

MISSIONARIES

How could missionaries ever operate without mobile ministry vehicles? The uses to which they are put are varied indeed.

Beginning in 1912 the American Baptists provided a fleet of automobiles for their colporteur missionaries in the United States and Latin America. D.K. Wood operated the first vehicle in Southern California. Auto number two was assigned to W.F. Newton serving in Connecticut. It was equipped with a folding Estey pump organ. The Elijah Terry Memorial Car, a Model A Ford, was dedicated in the memory of an early Baptist missionary in the Dakota Territory. The New Jersey Evangel Car was used by colporteur Neil C. Berg.

The American Tract Society also distributed through colporteur automobiles in the United States.

Station wagons called Harvesters are used by the Home Mission Council of North America to take health, recreation, education and worship services to migrants in fields and camps.

Fred and Bettye Boldt operated out of a station wagon with a public address system on top in the West Virginia mountains in the 1950s.

The American Baptists have offered five memorial chapel or Gospel cars for work in the field. These provided living quarters for the missionaries. Later there were even a few trailers of the early Airstream type that were used in the West. In the 1920s the Brockway, built on a White bus chassis, was used in Arizona by the Rev. Thomas D. Leyba and the Rev. and Mrs. John L. Losh. In California and Mexico it was the Crawford with P.J. Villanueva. It towed a trailer with a large tent, 100 chairs for meetings and an organ. The opened back door formed a platform for preaching. Inside was a combination sitting room and bedroom, dining room, kitchen, rest room and closet.

The Rev. Mary Murray-Sherman, known affectionately as the Church Lady, conducted trailer chapel ministries for over eight years in Michigan on the western outskirts of Detroit in the 1940s. Her small church on wheels was furnished as a meeting room to hold up to 60 people for services, Sunday School and Vacation Bible School. She lived in it and regularly visited government housing projects, 17 trailer camps and the like within a 25-mile radius. She is credited with teaching 400 children, conducting nine Vacation Bible Schools, contacting a total of 125,000 people and converting at least 400, and also organizing the Joy Road Baptist Chapel.

In 1970 Dr. Irwin A. Moon of the Moody Institute of Science division of the Moody Bible Institute introduced a concept called Operation Mobile Ministry, a trailer designed to solve many of the problems missionaries face in foreign fields. Versatility was the key. The unit was designed to be used effectively for classes, conferences, medical or dental work, literature displays, family relaxation, as a recording studio or library and for college campus outreach. The 31-foot Streamline trailer had a gasoline-driven power plant, a 44½-gallon gas tank, a 2,500-watt generator and an awning. It contained a hide-a-bed sofa, a water filter purification system, forced air heating, air conditioning, bathtub, shower, toilet, refrigerator-freezer, high-pile carpet, central vacuum system, PA system and multilingual AV equipment. The organization offered it and a Ford camper pickup truck to the missionary who evidenced the greatest promise in mobile evangelism in the foreign service. It was displayed for a year across the United States at missionary and Bible conferences, training schools and churches. Some 64 countries sent in applications from 162 missionaries and national workers. Stephen A. Hunter of the World Radio Missionary Fellowship, Quito, Ecuador, had the winning entry. He planned to use the unit in intensive evangelism throughout all of South America with different teams: musicians, chalk artists, evangelists and Bible teachers. This was to be on a rotating basis to keep the vehicle in full-time service.

The Osborn Foundation International has provided over 100 mobile evangelism units for the unreached in remote areas of the world. These four-wheel drive vehicles are in use in South Africa, the Philippines, Honduras, Nicaragua and other nations. The organization emphasizes deliverance or healing evangelism.

The Rev. Charles Roddy, a Colum-ban Father missionary in Japan, uses his Jeep as a pulpit to preach the Gospel to youths on street corners. There are now 70 Fathers working in four Japanese dioceses.

Roger Craig of Eureka, Montana, travels with a camper and boat up into northern Canada, giving out Bibles and tracts.

As a base for their missionary activities in the 1960s, two women from the Christian Church and Disciples of Christ pulled a 21-foot-long trailer with their panel truck, the Reluctant Draggin, in Mexico.

SUNDAY SCHOOL AND YOUTH WORK

Express wagons, scooters, bicycles, trucks, travel trailers, station wagons, motor homes, vans and buses have all become integral elements in mobile youth programs in the United States and abroad.

The Go Ye Chapel, a truck converted to the Gospel, has been operated by Charles Faust, New York City, with the Church of Christ and the Christian Church. He used this in 1969 to bring the 25-member singing group Sing Out for Christ to the thirtieth North American Christian Convention.

Wandering Wheels Ministry at Taylor University, Upland, Indiana, uses several different types of vehicles in its work with youth. Bicycle tours are organized regularly in the United States and abroad. The organization's three custom Possum Buses are luxury motor coaches which sleep 35 each in a mobile retreat to encourage a greater interest in God. Since 1971 the buses have traveled from Indiana to such destinations as the Great Smoky Mountains; Florida; Michigan and Colorado ski resorts; New England; Nova Scotia; and the Grand Canyon. The diesel buses serve church youth groups, school

The Witchmobile was set up as a traveling exhibit with displays oriented toward the youth culture. On the left is the Rev. Hershel Smith, with evangelist the Rev. Morris Cerullo. *(Courtesy World Evangelism)*

groups, senior citizens and families. A kitchen and lounge are included plus an elaborate stereo system.

Since 1972 Father George's Rolling Rectory has been operated by the Rev. George Mitchell, assistant pastor of the Roman Catholic Church of the Holy Spirit, New Hyde Park, Long Island, New York. The 17-foot travel trailer is used on trips with the parish teenage boys. Sometimes at public campgrounds as many as 30 campers come to the trailer when the Reverend Mitchell celebrates Mass, usually at a makeshift altar consisting of logs and boards gathered nearby.

In 1972 charismatic evangelist, the Rev. Morris Cerullo of World Evangelism, Inc., rented an educational Witchmobile and put it on the road. This 20-foot unique trailer, towed by a motor home, warned of the dangers of occult involvement and narcotics. More than 100 items were contained in the traveling display on satanism, sorcery, astrology, and other occult topics. Hershel Smith, founder of Teen Power, operated the exhibit in a U.S. tour of the largest 45 cities and Canada. Sites visited included church parking lots, college campuses, shopping centers, camps, conferences, hotels and convention centers. Viewers were given a free, 28-page tabloid newspaper. Coordinated with its schedule were crusades, tent revivals and rallies emphasizing deliverance or healing evangelism.

Smaller children are not forgotten either.

The Pocket Testament League put Ben Witherell in Florida in the 1970s to witness to children with his truck using film and other media. The Seerley Creek Christian Church of Indianapolis, Indiana, sent out in 1993 a purple and green, 66-foot passenger school bus converted

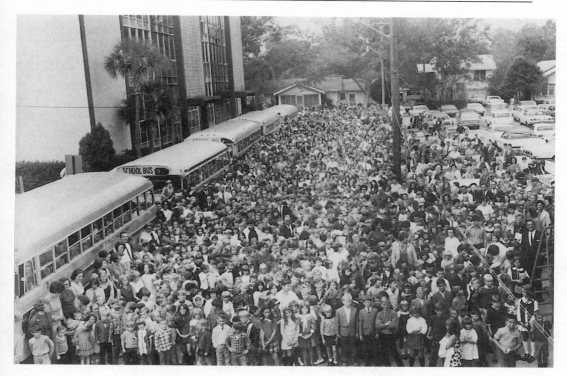

Trinity Baptist Church, Jacksonville, Florida, has operated a fleet of 60 buses and averages 3,700 in Sunday School in summer. Attendance was 2,105 when this picture was taken several years ago. The highest figure so far: 3,980. One of six assistant pastors is also the bus director. Such ministry is featured in large, fundamentalist, evangelical Baptist churches. *(Courtesy Trinity Baptist Church)*

into a mobile chapel as a summer outreach program for 800 children. The same nine sites were visited for nine weeks in June, July and August. Puppets, games and stories were featured. Increased attendance at church attributed to the program led to its being an annual project.

PUBLIC DISPLAY

Vehicles are used to promote religious messages in a wide variety of advertising applications.

Since the early 1970s several commercial over-the-road trucking companies have had religious themes painted on the sides and rear doors of their rigs. These include Pre-Fab Transit Co., Farmer City, Illinois; K & S Leasing, Sidney, Ohio; TJ's Fleet Service Inc., Lincoln Park, Michi-

gan; Cole's Express, Bangor, Maine; Centralia Cartage Co., Centralia, Illinois; Interstate Van Lines, Springfield, Virginia; and Beulah Land Trucking out of Georgia. Typical inspirational messages on the common carrier trucks concentrate on admonitions to attend church, with appropriate accompanying graphics of houses of worship, Jesus and so on. IML Freight, Salt Lake City, Utah, had one of its trailers decorated by the 12th Ward Youth Group of the Church of Jesus Christ of Latter-day Saints, Bountiful, Utah.

A truck side is employed to promote the Church of God in Christ Highway Revival in Chicago. On the city's south and west sides there are said to be more little storefront, fundamentalist churches, mostly Black, than in any other city in the country.

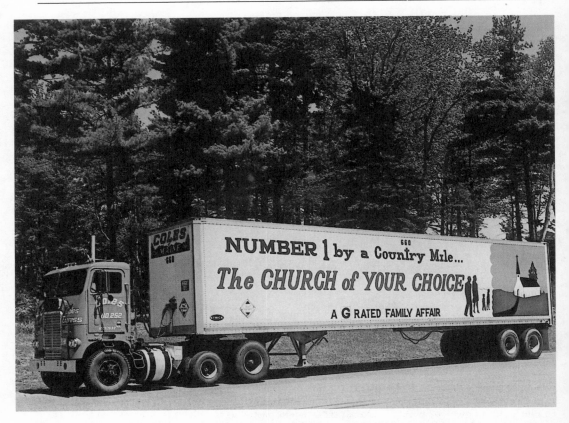

This truck from Cole's Express, a Bangor, Maine, common carrier, urges passing motorists to consider attending Sunday services. *(Courtesy Cole's Express)*

Church buses, parked or moving, have obvious secondary advertising value, especially when used in parades or similar public events.

The International Society for Krishna Consciousness holds annual summer festivals and parades worldwide. The two-mile parades are led by a horse-drawn chariot in the Festival of the Lord Jagannath. Wooden chariots pulled through the streets by thick hawsers are 50 feet high, weigh six tons, have 16 wheels and are lavishly decorated, hand-carved and flower-bedecked. Red, yellow and green silk canopies tower over them. Fully decorated, 45-foot floats are included which depict various themes of the Vedic tradition plus many classical Indian dance performers. The event draws crowds of up to 100,000 or more in cities like Toronto and New York. The parade in some cities moves to an exhibit area showing the philosophy and culture where an 11-course, free feast is offered to as many as 20,000 or more. This celebration dates back at least 800 years and takes place in various U.S. and Canadian cities, as well as in South America, Europe, Australia and India.

Opposite: Parades in major cities of the world are attended by the thousands at spectacular Hare Krishna events. This New York City festival is typical. They are frequently followed by exhibits and a free feast for all. The International Society for Krishna Consciousness is one of the more recent religious groups to emerge in America since 1965. *(Copyright* **Back to Godhead**, *Vol. 16 No. 8. Used by permission.)*

This Israelite House of David float appeared in the 1939 Blossom Parade in Benton Harbor, Michigan. *(Courtesy Clare E. Adkin, Jr.)*

The Israelite House of David participated in Benton Harbor, Michigan, events. In the 1908 Labor Day Parade, the Purcells and Mooneys, ministry operators, rode in a decorated car. In 1939 a prize-winning float was designed by Frank Rosetta featuring hydrostone statuary.

Evangelist Aimee Semple McPherson was in the 1916 St. Petersburg, Florida, Mardi Gras Parade and had prize-winning floats in four Pasadena, California, Tournament of Roses New Year parades. These were miniature Angelus Temples, replicas made of roses, carnations and other flowers on a flatbed truck.

Sound trucks are part of many religious promotional programs. When he was a Catholic seminarian, Father Ralph W. Beiting was part of a group in the 1960s who visited small towns in the South with loudspeaker messages at courthouses and filling stations. Bullhorns and loudspeakers are still used today by the

Christian Appalachian Project which he subsequently founded. Trucks with a public address system were used around San Diego, California, in the early 1980s by evangelists to try to influence those at wild summer beach parties. All were urged to read the Bible. Efforts were concentrated around Fiesta Island in Mission Bay.

During the Korean War in 1952 Jack Wyrtzen and Glenn Wagner of World of Life Fellowship contacted 250,000 Korean troops with a sound truck. They distributed Pocket Testament League Gospels of John.

In India vans broadcast Hindu religious messages in the streets.

Billy Sunday pioneered trolley advertising in Spokane, Washington, in the early 1900s. Aimee Semple McPherson advertised on streetcars in San Jose, California, in 1921. In 1992 the Danish Bible Society published the first Bible translation in the Danish language in more than

250 years. The first interconfessional version has seven different editions. Among other media, bus advertising featured the slogan "The Bible Is for Everyone and Also for You." Jews for Jesus in San Francisco, California, commandeered one of the famous cable cars and converted it into a temporary Messiah Mobile.

L.H. Gandy drives around Georgia in his Jesus Truck which he adorns with original religious paintings and scripture quotations. W.C. Rice of Prattsville, Alabama, has driven his Cross Car since 1973. He preaches, gives testimony and uses white crosses and crucifixes on his property and house.

The man simply known as Tex in Burlington, Iowa, drives an old beat-up pickup truck covered with painted religious messages and stickers. A chalkboard that hangs off the back end offers a new message daily. There is a cross hanging in the cab. Tex lives in the vehicle.

The congregation Mishakan Israel has placed an electric menorah or candelabra on the roof of a car as part of its religious celebrations in Oak Park, Michigan.

In 1985 the High Flight Foundation set up its Mobile Space Museum, a semi-trailer, to display items from the Apollo 15 space mission. It emphasized the spiritual effect such trips have on lunar astronauts. Included were color photographs, films, exhibits and models.

AUDIOVISUAL

Mobile audiovisual presentations are used extensively in evangelical programs, training efforts and music and drama approaches. They are common especially in remote areas where fixed facilities for presenting programs are lacking.

The Pocket Testament League has used film and video minivans and sound trucks around the world for many years.

The trucks have a platform on top for speakers to afford maximum visibility in large crowds. Their programs include preaching, literature distribution and films. Continents visited include Western Europe, Africa, South America and Asia.

The Billy Graham film *Two-a-Penny* was distributed in Japan by film trucks in 1968.

The Evangelical Alliance Mission uses two rear screen projection audiovisual vans in Venezuela in outdoor meetings. These are constructed on Ford chassis with Cummins Diesel engines. Half of one side is hinged upward to form a roof over a fold-out platform used for services, music or drama. Christian book and Bible display racks line the platform on three sides. There is also a set of bunk beds. A sound truck covers the surrounding streets an hour or so before the meetings. Stops are from three to six days with a different program every night.

Open Air Campaigners employ film vans in India, Jamaica, Paraguay, Australia and other countries for use by national evangelist teams. The group was founded in 1892 in Australia. The vehicles form a preaching platform at campgrounds, plazas, villages, campuses and beaches. They use sketch board illustrated messages illuminated by black light, usually with local church participation. Open Air Campaigners is an interdenominational support agency of evangelical tradition.

The Society for International Ministries USA has been using Cinevan ministry since 1952 in Peru and Ghana in West Africa. These mobile cinemas draw an audience for each showing in excess of 5,000. Teams visit prisons, army camps, church conferences and secondary schools. SIM is setting up a ministry built around a mobile TV broadcasting mini-station in Lima, Peru. Videos are very practical in this setting.

Part of the Operation Mobile Ministry Project already described was a self-contained, all-weather projection system. This was an outdoor type, rear screen projection system called Mobilux. Designed to fit on top of most vehicles, it is six feet by eight feet and is intended chiefly for outreach programs in primitive jungles.

Other film ministries include the Bible Club Movement (formerly BCM International) with a trailer in Sweden, and the Africa Inland Church, Kenya, East Africa, which uses film vans.

Mission Aviation Fellowship has developed a special film screen which can be seen from either side.

The Drive-In Ministries network has several traveling Christian screen units in the United States: the Magnificent Movie Machine, the Grand Van and the Movie Cube, among others. The vehicles travel to a variety of locations, from motorcycle races to urban neighborhoods, showing films and distributing evangelistic information. One of the units, a converted potato chip truck, has a portable screen on the side.

In 1944 Joy Ridderhof of Gospel Recordings took a ten-month recording trip in a station wagon in Mexico and Central America to pick up messages in 35 new languages and dialects. She was accompanied by Ann Sherwood.

A Skill on Wheels van was owned by the United Methodist Church. In the 1970s staff members took it to small churches to assist in training local religious education teachers. Equipment included videotape and print materials.

LITERATURE DISTRIBUTION

Distributing Christian literature via mobile units is a natural whether in a bookmobile, a simple display on a car hood or even a tract rack hooked over a window.

The opening scene in the Barbra Streisand movie *Yentl* showed a bookseller going through the countryside in an old wagon crying out "Sacred books for men—picture books for women," setting the theme for the story to follow.

In the late 1920s H.E. Hesseltine built six house car bookmobiles on one-ton truck chassis to cover the Southwest, particularly Oklahoma and Texas. He represented the American Bible society. One whole side of the vehicles opened up to make a large awning and revealed a series of bookshelves. They were hinged to tip either way for his indoor or outdoor store. The roof was sheet metal. He lived in the units and drove the equivalent of five times across the country.

Two Ye Olde London Buses were used to sell bibles, books, records and tapes from 1975 to 1979 in rural Eastern Oregon and Washington. Ron and Diane Forberg took the red double-deckers to logging towns and other small, isolated coastal communities with populations under 20,000. More than 100,000 visitors were attracted to the rebuilt and renovated Leyland diesel vehicles. Stops included courthouse squares, colleges, convention centers, fairs, festivals and churches. Stays averaged one to five days and total miles traveled reached 100,000. Amenities aboard included heat, air conditioning, carpet and taped music. The buses were usually open ten to six and operated on a regular circuit to visit a given location once ever two or three months. The nondenominational effort included books in Spanish.

The United Synagogue of America in cooperation with Temple B'nai Israel and the University of Toledo Hillel Student Association has operated an ATID bookmobile since 1980.

Brother Robert of the Society of St. Paul operates the Alba House Catholic Bookstore in Dearborn, Michigan. On

Top: In the early 1900s the New York Bible Society distributed Christian literature, Scriptures and Bibles in taxis, with items in many different languages. The Society's slogan was "One Book for all people." *(American Bible Society Archives)*. *Bottom:* "Here's the Bible Man" is how H.R. Hesseltine (right) referred to himself in the 1920s as he traveled in the Southwest. He gave away Bibles in all languages to those who could not afford to buy them. At the left is the Rev. J.J. Morgan, Society secretary. *(American Bible Society Archives)*

Ron Forberg and his father purchased three 24-foot, eight-ton London double-decker buses and brought them to the United States for Christian literature distribution. The upper deck lounge was used for counseling. *(Courtesy Ron Forberg)*

weekends he takes out a mini-bookstore to churches and other places throughout the Midwest.

There is no other organization that can boast that it has used any more different vehicles than the American Bible Society. It has used express wagons in the Southern United States; pushcarts and sleds in various locations; wheelchairs in Brazil; oxcarts in Paraguay; goat-drawn wagons in New York City; and, around the world, carts, bicycles, cycle-cars, vans, trucks and cars.

In New York City the New York Bible Society trucks were loaded with Scriptures for its Family-to-Family distribution campaign. The slogan was "One Book for All People." In the early 1920s it installed racks in taxis and at cigar counters to distribute free Bible booklets in several languages.

Active since 1941, the Christian Literature Crusade has bookmobiles in Austria, the West Indies, Brazil, Colombia, Uruguay, Venezuela, New Zealand, Pakistan and the Philippines. It is evangelical, interdenominational and inter-mission and uses colporteurs door-to-door, and stalls and book tables at fairs and markets.

An evangelical bookmobile and mobile church was used by the Lutherans in Japan in missionary work from 1951 to 1963. It contained two fold-down bunks, a food preparation area, pulpit, altar, portable organ, movie projector, gas generator and 500 books. An auxiliary tailgate was used as a platform for movies, preaching, flannelgraphs, slides and Japanese paper plays. Missionary Rev. Andrew B. Ellis operated it in rural Southern Japan, mostly around Kumamuto Prefecture and the southern island of Kyushu. It is given credit for establishing a number of churches in small towns. Mass meetings on school playgrounds drew over 1,000 people. The Rev. Carl F. Kaltreider originated the idea with Pastor Ellis.

Glad Tidings Literature Distribution of Guntor, South India, is operated by the Rev. and Mrs. William Scott, missionaries of the American Baptist Churches USA Foreign Mission Society. Two colporteurs distribute literature among the Telegu people using three-wheeled rickshaws.

The Hare Krishnas in Bombay, India, operate a traveling Bhaktivedanta Book Trust library bus in India and Nepal. It was originally activated in 1977 and ran to 1979 and then started up again in 1991 to distribute books to major educational institutions, public and private libraries and the general public. With the bus parked in crowded city streets, volumes are given out in English and every major Indian language. From June to December 1991, it was used to distribute 4,000 copies of books.

A truck was used to deliver 100,000 Russian New Testaments to Moscow in 1989. It was part of the Target One Million program of Open Doors with Brother Andrew. Brother Andrew, an unordained Dutchman and former army commando in Indonesia, took his Volkswagen Beetle stuffed with Bibles and tracts across the borders of Czechoslovakia. Open Doors is a nondenominational support agency of evangelical tradition engaged in Bible distribution, audio recordings and distribution, broadcasting, mission information services, literature distribution and training.

The Pocket Testament League operated its panel sound truck in front of the large Helsinki, Finland, railroad station during a Communist-sponsored youth festival in the 1960s. It distributed over 110,000 Gospels and New Testaments in 22 different languages. It is an interdenominational sending agency of Christian/Plymouth Brethren tradition engaged in evangelism, Bible distribution, broadcasting, church planting, support of national workers and training.

The secretary of the National Bible Society of Scotland used a Bible and Gospel book van for touring the country to sell Scriptures in the early 1950s.

The Venezuela Bible Society has operated since 1989 a large Bible Bus. In addition to Bible and Scripture distribution, Christian videos and films are shown. The couple who run it live in a trailer towed behind. It is used primarily in villages and appeals especially to children.

The Bible Society of Rwanda uses vehicles to distribute its Christian literature.

Four Pocket Testament League distributor vans have traveled England, Scotland, Wales and Ireland serving bookshops. This was the wholesale division of Operation Mobilization. The driver, Howard Hall, a Canadian, now manages the Dublin, Ireland, bookshop. Operation Mobilization is an interdenominational sending agency of evangelical tradition engaged in missionary orientation, Bible distribution, church planting, evangelism and literature.

MOTORCYCLE MINISTRY

A truly unique approach to religion is what might well be called motorcycle ministry, perhaps even an oxymoron, the antithesis of a typical "Hell's Angels" image as the world many times perceives.

"I'm a businessman who happens to ride a bike and my business is Christianity." With these few words maverick minister Rev. Robert Hershberger sums up his unconventional philosophy as director and founding pastor of the Missionary Church of Bikers International. He adds, "I'm a

man of the cloth, only I come in a different wrapper," as he refers to his all-black leather outfit. Since 1983 his highway parish has kept him on the road five months out of the year in the United States and Canada, racking up an average of 50,000 miles annually. He was ordained through the Universal Church of the Brotherhood in 1976 and calls himself a nondenominational circuit rider for God.

Motorcycle minister Herb Shreve, a former Baptist pastor, founded the Christian Motorcycle Association in 1975. He and another erstwhile Baptist minister, Tom Pitman, who rides his Gospel Goose, conduct Christian rallies, preach at secular rallies and sponsor rides, blessings, crusades and conferences, mostly using church parking lots as sites. Their meetings draw as many as 1,200 members. This nondenominational, nonprofit organization has representation in all states as well as Canada, Europe, New Zealand and South America, and boasts 4,200 members with 335 chapters in North America alone. They wear jeans and Levi jackets, and have made their slogan "Riding for the Son Into All the World."

Dino Rodrigues is minister of the Church of the Free Highway, which has 300 motorcyclist members and 38 ordained ministers in six states. His home base is the Rovers Motorcycle Club, Oakland, California.

Set Free Christian Fellowship was started in 1982 by Hispanic pastor Phil Aguilar. His family participates in his ministry and he wears biker clothing and rides a Harley-Davidson. The congregation of 5,000 from homes and ranches near Anaheim, California, has 300 in communal living. Those particularly welcomed are drug addicts, homeless and needy. The work is supported by Trinity Broadcasting Network.

Jerry Dill of Britton, Michigan, founded Circuit Riders Motorcycle Club, which is made up of motorcycling ministers. There are 150 members throughout the United States, including a retired Catholic nun over 70.

Pastor Jimmy Wilhelmsen in the 1970s was engaged in King's Kids Christian Motorcycle Ministry in Detroit, Michigan. He has led churchgoing cyclist members while riding his Harley cycle and wearing a leather jacket with a big cross and the word "Pastor" on the back on extensive tours.

In the 1970s in Orange County, California, an entire motorcycle club was converted and is now a band of disciples on wheels.

Other groups include International Christian Bikers Association; Bikers for Christ; Full-Gospel Motorcycle Association International; Righteous Riders; Tribe of Judah; the Spirit Riders; Chariots for Christ; and Resurrection Riders.

Erv and Dorothy Smith ride Suzukis in their ministry and have taken extension courses from Moody Bible Institute.

Bill Mays has a Full gospel trailer attached to his Honda HAJJ motorcycle containing jumper cables, cookies for children and religious tracts.

Barry Mayson, former head of the South Carolina chapter of the Hell's Angels, has become a preacher and has run a Christian youth center with Bible classes for teenagers in Plano, Texas, since 1984. He rides a 1978 Harley-Davidson and his

Opposite, top: **A good, strong public address message alerted peole that the National Bible Society of Scotland bookmobile had arrived on its countrywide tour.** *(American Bible Society Archives).* **Bottom: The Pocket Testament League operated this panel sound truck in front of the large Helsinki, Finland, railroad station during a Communist-sponsored youth festival in the 1960s. This effort resulted in distributing over 110,000 Gospels and New Testaments in 22 different languages.** *(Courtesy Pocket Testament League)* wife Fran helps him in their ministry. His jacket patch reads "I Love Jesus."

Elmo Tahran, pastor of the Bloomfield Hills, Michigan, Baptist Church, has an unusual nickname: Motorcycle Preacher. The denim-clad minister is part of a group of cycle owners called the Baptist Bombers or Tahran's Disciples. He owns a Kawasaki trail bike and rides in Northern Michigan mostly with 30 or more of his 250-member congregation.

Lutheran pastor and certified social worker Rev. James B. White probably never realized he would end up riding a motorcycle when he decided to become chaplain for the Detroit Police Department in 1974. Assigned to the Motor Traffic Section, he underwent intensive training before soloing on his 800 Harley-Davidson. A former research chemist, he

is now retired and pastor emeritus of Calvary Lutheran Church, Southfield, Michigan.

Since 1976 the White Mountain Riders Motorcycle Club of New Hampshire has organized an annual blessing of the motorcycles at the Shrine of Our Lady of Grace operated by the Oblates of Mary Immaculate, Colebrook, New Hampshire.

WEDDINGS

William H. Montgomery, a Black minister, has parked his marriage chapel on wheels in St. Louis, Missouri, in the city hall parking lot. He used the 19-foot Winnebago with taped music and dried flowers on his lunch break from his city hall job.

The Rev. Charles Neal, Texas, oper-

In deference to their religious beliefs, Islamic pilgrimages travel to Mecca on special buses like this one without a roof. *(Courtesy Wayne International Division, Indian Head Co.)*

ates a rolling Abiding Love wedding chapel van. He usually tries to park in on the street near courthouses and to intercept the couples coming out with their new licenses.

The list of conveyances used in mobile matrimony is truly unbelievable in these nontraditional nuptials, and includes automobiles, airplanes, all-terrain vehicles, aerial tramways, balloon gondolas, buses, cable cars, canoes, carriages, boats, fire trucks, garbage trucks, horses and wagons, buggies, helicopters, limousines, moving vans, motorcycles, motor homes, parade floats, pickup trucks, roller skates, submarines, streetcars, trucks, trailers, trains, trolley cars, vans and unicycles.

PILGRIMAGES

When Islamic pilgrims travel to Mecca in Saudi Arabia, their religious beliefs require that they not ride under a roof. Therefore specially-modified, U.S.–made prayer buses are provided which have no roofs. The roofs are easily bolted back for later commercial use. As many as 2,000 vehicles are involved in the trip to the most important shrine in the Moslem world. The vehicles seat up to 48 passengers and contain special luggage racks, 40-gallon water tanks, an inside electric cooler for drinking water and special water spigots outside so that the passengers can wash their feet before praying. Other amenities include reclining seats, window curtains, heavy-duty cooling system, fans and AM-FM radios.

Orthodox Jews have segregated prayer, separating the sexes on buses by a curtain hung from the ceiling down the aisle.

CHAPTER VI

Functional Vehicles

There are many categories of special use vehicles which are performing unique, on-the-spot functions normally fulfilled at fixed base facilities.

The major breakdowns are manufacturing; agriculture; fishing; power; mechanical testing; marketing research; personnel activities; transportation; communications; waste disposal and recycling; emergency response; offices; meeting rooms; warehouses; retail areas; and amenities.

Other unusual functions are recognized as domiciles and garages; food preparation; physical fitness and sports; special needs for patients, handicapped and security; and sculptures.

Manufacturing

Manufacturing, fabricating and processing on wheels a diverse range of products may seem like an unusual phenomenon but in many cases it is expedient to operate for a variety of reasons on a mobile basis. For example, some road-building contractors operate portable blacksmith shops to make tools for the employees right on the job.

Back in New England in the "old days" portable steam sawmills were horse drawn. Today sawmills on wheels appear in such vehicles as converted school buses, whose extra durable unitized floor structure lends itself to such use. The process involves stripping out all the seats, cutting through a sidewall and adding hinges to create a convenient opening for feeding in logs. For power an outer wheel rim is added to the rear drive wheel, a large exterior flywheel is attached to the saw and a drive belt connects the two.

White ash is the wood used in the 31-foot Adirondack Batmobile trailer used to custom-make major-league baseball bats sold by Rawlings at spring training camps. They take an hour each. Players' mitts are also repaired in the facility.

A rotational molding line mounted on a 44-foot trailer turns out one-person kayaks made from plastic. The production line on wheels includes a mold, oven and fans.

A brick-making machine aptly dubbed Brickmaker has been developed in Australia. Designed and built in Sydney, it is said by the inventor to be capable of producing bricks at up to 500 per hour. It was specifically made to use soil or clay. Three versions have been offered: a trailer-mounted, diesel-driven unit; one mounted on a custom-built Daihatsu four-wheel drive Hi-Jet truck with power taken from the 993cc engine; and a free-standing unit.

Two firms, Cherokee Pipe Line Company in Oklahoma and the Pacific Gas and Electric Company in California, have successfully used mobile pipe mills. The 105-ton machines move along the right-of-way with two units: power and steering and rear mill. Electrically driven on Caterpillar tracks, the units are 104 feet long, 16 feet wide and 11½ feet high. The two units are separated for transportation from one jobsite to another and a truck-van accompanies the operation.

Mobile electroplating, 24-karat gold-plating and chrome plating systems enjoy a market which covers bathroom fixtures, automobile emblems and accessories, jewelry, guns and golf clubs.

Some structural fabricating firms can look back to humble origins in trailers before they moved into factories to make trusses, building skeletons for contractors and performing other jobs.

Scrap yards and manufacturing plants with large amounts of scrap metal depend on mobile sheer balers. These are custom-built and self-contained, with their own diesel power and hydraulic crane for feeding scrap into the crusher. They typically are mounted on Overland 38-foot-long step-frame semi-trailers with an enclosed cabin mounted at the rear for the operator.

For dewatering, a trailer-mounted, self-contained filter press of fabricated steel does the job. It produces filter cake on a 48-foot flatbed trailer with swing-open rear doors, walkways, railings and stairs.

To recycle old tires a manufacturing truck picks them up from gas stations, tire dealers and at car shows. They are then transformed into mats, mud flaps, rubber livestock fences, and bed liners for trucks.

When it comes to ready-mixed concrete and asphalt, transit mix trucks are a familiar sight on the streets. These combination material transporters and traveling batch plants can handle fibrous concrete and automatically extrude their product for curbs and gutters. They are mounted on a truck or semi-trailer chassis. Different sizes yield varying numbers of cubic yards.

Agriculture

Farmers depend on mobile units both for crops and livestock. Power take-offs (PTO) require putting a drive belt on a rear wheel and using the vehicle's power to run machines to churn butter, saw logs, pump water, fill a silo or generate electricity.

Mobile zappers discharge high-powered microwaves into the ground with a sled-shaped emitter to challenge weeds and soil pests, all in lieu of pesticides.

In California's four seasons of iceberg lettuce crops in the Salinas and Imperial valleys, custom-equipped, 50-foot stainless steel Great Dane trailers act as mobile processors as they clean, cool, treat, shred and pack the lettuce. They serve harvest areas as self-contained units, only tied to area sewerage, water and power supplies.

Flatbed trailer-mounted portable feed mills and pelletizers roam from farm to farm processing grain, roughage and other additives into livestock feed which is shot into silos for cattle, hogs and poultry. They have either a compact chassis half-cab body or a four-wheel truck drive chassis.

In Utah portable sheep shearing vans are found.

The Concrete-Mobile is a combination materials transporter and complete, mobile concrete materials proportioning, mixing and delivery system that may be mounted on a suitable truck, semi-trailer chassis or other carrier. Water tanks may be front or side-mounted. Four sizes have a carrying capacity to produce four, six, eight or ten cubic yards, with a wide range of extra-cost accessory equipment. *(Courtesy National Concrete Machinery Co. Division, IRL Daffin Assoc., Inc.)*

Fishing

Fishing operations also benefit from mobile processing. Fish caught off the Mexican coast of Baja, California, have a quick-freeze plant structure using seven 40-foot standard diesel Fruehauf trailers mounted with power generating and refrigeration equipment. Storage and ice-making take place on the other units. The plant moves up and down the 800 miles of coastline in line with the offshore fleet. It can be set up in just a few hours.

An automated clamdigger on wheels, a diesel-powered rig, sucks up sand and clams, expelling the sand and harvesting up to two tons of clams daily.

Power

Mobile electric power is a practical reality at sites where electricity is not available, where sufficient quantities are not in place, to meet temporary usage, when power of a different voltage is required, when normal power failure occurs or during rewiring operations.

Mobile units are produced by such makers as United Technologies and Maloney Electric. The former combines a gas turbine and all necessary controls on a truck-mounted power unit which can produce enough electricity for a city of 25,000 people and can be driven almost anywhere. The latter offers a unique custom-designed dual-trailer mobile substation. In England Petbow has introduced sound-proof mobile generating sets mounted on a six-ton truck for temporary power.

In the United States, mobile electric units will be found at such public utilities as Pennsylvania Electric Company of Johnstown; Detroit Edison; Consumers Energy in Jackson, Michigan; and the San Diego Gas and Electric Company. Outside the United States, mobiles are used by the Nova Scotia Light and Power Company and in such countries as the West African Republic of Guinea, where the generating units are housed in walk-in, weather-proof, sound-proof vans. Other mobile power involves compressed air, called upon when compressors break down, for railroad line crews, etc. At some dumps, trailers burn methane from landfills in four engines which turn generators and create electricity sold to public utilities.

Mechanical Testing

Manufacturers, public utilities, other service providers and retailers have long depended upon mobile units for field research to augment fixed-base laboratory operations. These vehicles have been used by individual firms, in cooperative efforts and emanating from a central facility like an educational institution, both here and abroad.

Mechanical testing of products is an ongoing activity which takes place in a variety of mobile settings for transportation equipment, machinery, petroleum industries, rubber and other products.

In the automotive field General Motors has probably had more experience, especially since the 1970s, with mobile units than any other organization because of its many vehicle and related divisions. Typical programs are:

- Electromagnetic Survey Lab Van to locate sources of interference with electronic controls in vehicle engines
- Test vehicles taken to Kapuskasing, Ontario, by Saginaw Steering Gear division to collect data on turbochargers
- Special single-wheel tire noise trailer to study control methods
- Roadside test van to check on overall noise pollution
- Microwave lab van to test the effects of road surface on radar sensors
- Trailer taken to its permanent cold weather test facility by General Motors of Canada
- Mobile pilot truck of Detroit Diesel Allison used to service original equipment manufacturers on installations of engines and automatic transmissions. Tests are made on air, fuel and exhaust systems, cooling systems, unit sound levels and vibrations.
- Mobile radio laboratory of Delco Electronics in a GMC Ventura to monitor station signal strengths in areas where reception is poor in crowded cities like New York. These moving antenna tests were done for the National Quadrophonic Radio Committee of the Electronic Industries Association

For vehicle squeak and rattle prevention Ford recently set up its Transportable Environmental Four Poster (TEFP), a two trailer configuration facility consisting of a utility trailer and a test trailer. The utility trailer supplies the electrical power and climate control along with a hydraulic power supply and an office for on-site engineers. The expandable trailer is transformed into a soundproofed, stainless steel test chamber. A similar system is in place for Ford Motor Company of Europe.

Mitsubishi uses a test van to gauge the effects of altitude and temperature on vehicle performance in such high locations as Denver.

Mercedes-Benz has developed a special brake trailer which simulates mountain driving conditions for testing new systems on level ground.

The Trailmobile division of the Pullman Company has used since 1975 a mobile satellite truck lab to test its trucks for acceleration, force, deflection and pressure on the road, using 36-channel electronic equipment.

Since 1973 Cummins Engine has depended on its Performance Load Trailer to gather data on simulated operating conditions such as long grades and steep hills. The test engineer inside maintains constant communication with the driver through a special headset system.

Bendix-Westinghouse has used a tractor trailer rig in developing its adaptive braking system. Water tanks at either end simulate the weight of a cargo, and electronic test equipment is installed in the center booth.

Grote Manufacturing, maker of automotive accessories, has used Road Lab trailers to test its truck-bus-trailer safety equipment under typical over-the-road conditions since 1972.

In 1964 Lockheed-Georgia began nuclear radiation testing with a space chamber on wheels.

Deere's van full of telemetry gear monitors metal stresses and hydraulics in its vehicles, such as self-leveling hillside combines.

Pettibone since 1978 has used a mobile testing laboratory to check for accurate stress levels and fatigue life of its cranes. The van is equipped with computers which are specially programmed to measure stress data as they are electronically connected to the cranes.

The Blaupunkt Car Radio Division of Robert Bosch has operated since 1978 its Tech Van, a complete shop on wheels in a Dodge Maxivan, to test its radio and competitors' performance nationwide. It is also used on speakers, power amplifiers and CB radios. In major market areas it tests for different signal conditions and strengths, distortion, noise sensitivity and frequency ranges and also tests new concepts in the field, makes car radio installation tests, gathers technical information and is a display unit for promotional events. Engineers from Germany occasionally visit to use the van.

Zenith Radio set up in 1978 a mobile TV field test lab for engineering and development purposes to take televisions and other consumer electronic products into difficult and remote areas to be sure that they get thorough tests throughout the entire country under varying signal conditions. Periscoping antennas 35 feet long are used on the van. Occasionally it is used at stores and in connection with special public events.

Petroleum interests make good use of mobile test vehicles.

The Leak-Lokator division of Sun Oil has had eight Reading Ready-Van traveling mini-labs used for underground leak detection.

Marathon Petroleum's Product Quality Testing Van, a specially-modified

Opposite top: **General Motors used this roadside test van to check on noise pollution. It was developed by Jams A. Hamburg (in van) and Donald R. Whitney. The noise pollution level meter provided direct readings of community sounds caused by jackhammers, airplanes taking off, or accelerating motorcycles, trucks or passenger cars. It was fully automated and could be operated unattended for long periods with a chart or digital recorder.** *Bottom:* **General Motors researchers have developed an unusual single-wheel trailer to study tire noise on the road. It effectively isolates the single test tire from other noise sources and reflecting surfaces. It is located 40 feet behind the rear wheels of the towing vehicle and can be loaded up to 5,000 pounds and rotated at speeds of 70 mph.** *(Both photographs courtesy of General Motors Corp.)*

white 1982 Ford Econoline 350, was used to run tests on samples of different grades of gasoline and diesel fuel at retail outlets and bulk plants. The van's roof line was raised 24 inches to provide adequate head room and custom-made cabinetry was installed.

The Standard Oil Division of American Oil organized a fleet of red, white and blue Amoco Quality Control Patrol Chevy vans in 1972. They are laboratory-equipped to perform on-the-spot quick tests for lead trace contamination of lead-free fuel at service station pumps nationwide. Each van is scheduled to visit unannounced a number of outlets daily. When samples don't meet standards immediate steps are taken to replace the product.

A tandem-axle, 16,000-pound flatbed trailer loaded with computer-like instruments performed on-the-job tests in 1966 on heavy-duty brake linings for P.T. Brake

Lining. The mobile laboratory was designed and specially built by the firm as a self-contained recording center, using permanent record tape for analysis and study. Instruments were mounted console-style in a structure over the rear wheels. It was loaded to the maximum legal limit by three 30,000-pound pyramid-shaped concrete blocks. It appeared at trucking terminals, shopping centers, truck road-e-o's and vocational technical high schools during in-town and cross-country runs. Then in 1969 it initiated a specially instrumented Ford school bus test research laboratory. The monitoring center provided typical data recording of road tests to gauge the efficiency of severe-service brake block applications.

In 1969 research began at the Highway Safety Research Institute at the University of Michigan on the road in a mobile computer lab which tests tires, brakes

This custom built mobile laboratory for testing the efficiency of heavy-duty air brake blocks made an impressive sight on the highway. Developed by the P.T. Brake Lining Company, its findings were shared with state departments of public safety. The driver subjected the load to extreme jolts to lend a realistic reading to the recording instruments. *(Courtesy P.T. Brake Lining Co.)*

and other components on both cars and trucks. The vehicle consists of an instrumented highway tractor and flatbed trailer.

Sometimes it requires the cooperative effort of two or more organizations to get one of these test projects going.

A joint venture of A.B. Chance, producer of maintenance tools, and Pitman Manufacturing, maker of aerial platforms, resulted in a unique research caravan in 1962 to conduct on-the-job studies of utility line maintenance. It consisted of a fully-equipped 50-foot aerial platform with a fiberglass bucket and a trailer of "hot line" tools. Both companies serve the utility industry.

Two British firms have turned to mobile units for product improvement testing.

In England Armstrong Patents, an automotive components manufacturing group, operates an international minicomputer workshop to test shock absorbers in the field at European vehicle manufacturers. The laboratory is housed in a specially converted Mercedes-Benz four-ton van which also contains all necessary equipment for the assembly and testing of shock absorbers on site.

Aveling Barford, a British manufacturer of earthmoving equipment, in 1981 set up its Data Acquisition Vehicle to develop new construction machinery designs and improve existing products. It is a four-wheel drive, cross-country vehicle with a high-rigidity chassis and purpose-built body with all-welded construction. A tubular stone guard, inclined upward from the lower leading edge of the vehicle, provides protection in the roughest terrain. Included are high flotation tires for soft groundwork. Untethered it can be used for "drive-by" noise tests.

Communications organizations and public utilities also find mobile testing units a valuable part of their operations. Since 1971 Toledo Edison has used

for preventive maintenance its Thermovision van for electronic surveillance to check live wires and transformers for potential line failures. The infrared camera-like heat detector on top runs as an operator inside observes a monitor screen that shows temperature differences. Detroit Edison has a roving van to pick up television or radio interference so that engineers can track down power line problems.

Bell Telephone Laboratories uses a Dodge Commercial Traveler motor home equipped as a mobile laboratory with electronic test instruments to conduct field trials on cables before putting new types into service or adding new services to existing cables to be sure performance objectives are met.

Bell South's Mobility Olympic network project was set up in 1996 in preparation for the Olympic Games to test its cellphone capacities using mobile units known as COW (Cells on Wheels). Eighteen sites featured a giant Holstein symbol of the name.

The Teleprompter division of Hughes Aircraft runs a portable sweep spectrum analyzer from inside a van to check signals of cable TV, a program active since 1975.

In retail usage of mobile tests, Chatham Supermarkets in Detroit has used a completely equipped 1975 Dodge quality control laboratory van stocked with special instruments. It has been used to measure sanitation levels and fat content in ground meats, bacteria levels of equipment and to check weight of produce; in all, the van has figured in checking 200 different items. It was also used to deliver refrigerated perishable product samples to the independent USDA certified laboratory. It made nearly 700 visits annually to the 44 chain stores, meat processing plant and warehouses.

In response to accelerated federal and state government activities in air and

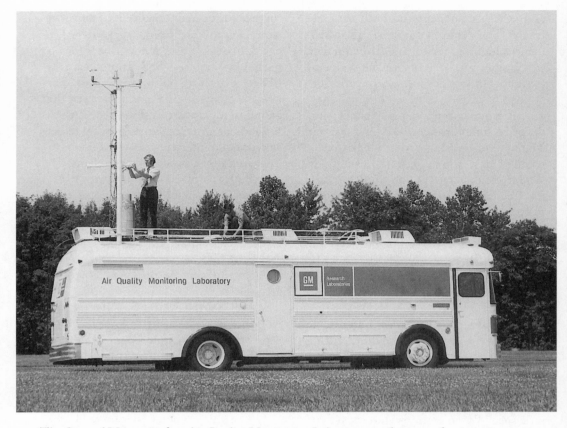

The General Motors 31-foot Air Quality Monitoring Laboratory made a tour of major cities to measure both air pollution and meteorological conditions with a two-man specialist team. The team remained in each area from one to three months with the computerized instrumentation. Results were correlated with measurements obtained by federal, state and municipal agencies. *(Courtesy General Motors Corp.)*

water pollution control legislation, several organizations reacted beginning in the 1970s with mobile test vehicles. These were involved both with individual vehicle exhaust emissions and general air quality around factories.

The companies which set up mobile units to check the air around their properties have included an ITT Rayonier trailer for its Pacific Northwest installations; Gulf water test trailer and air van for its plants and refineries; Exxon's traveling laboratory for power plant testing of boilers and stacks; and Cummins Engine's mobile lab for air tests inside and outside its plants. General Motors and its divi-

sions have employed several mobile air quality monitoring laboratories.

In order to test vehicle emissions General Motors, Ford and Volkswagen have constructed elaborate rolling laboratories.

The General Motors "swing wing" mobile lab has a center section that swings out to provide 11 feet more space for a car inside the 40-foot blue and white van, which is 12½ feet high and eight feet wide when closed for traveling.

Ford's custom-made, self-contained, 29,000-pound test vehicle is expandable also, a 40-foot semi-trailer divided into three sections with test cars driven up a

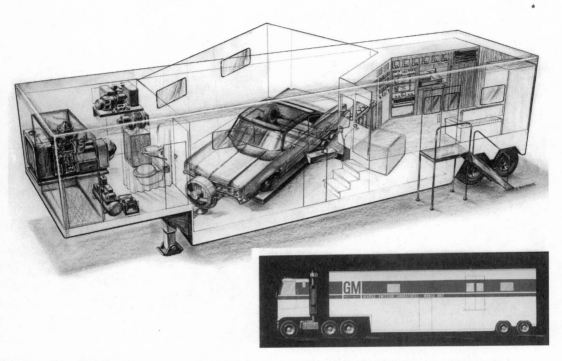

The General Motors mobile vehicle emissions laboratory had a center section which swung out to allow cars and light trucks to be driven into the testing chamber. The three-man crew was from the GM Proving Ground. The vehicle was self-contained with a seven-foot by four-foot control room and two generators. The test arrangements were carried out under controlled temperature conditions. *(Courtesy General Motors Corp.)*

ramp. The 13-foot sections on each side have been replaced by large aluminum doors which drop outward. The expanded floor area section 30 feet across is enclosed by aluminum roof sections and walls carried in the van.

Volkswagen's 44-foot semi-trailer lab is accompanied by a 33-foot Bluebird bus loaded with electronic measuring instruments. Pull-out sides on the trailer allow it to expand to a 16-foot width.

In 1994 Diesel Transit buses in 60 cities such as Cincinnati, Oakland and Baltimore participated in a test in which they burned a blend of diesel fuel and soybean oil to reduce engine emissions. The program was monitored by the National Soy Diesel Development Board and vari-

ous state groups. The research also embraced school buses, military vehicles, marine engines and farm tractors. Vehicles were decorated with pictures of soybeans and signs.

Water testing mobile units have been employed by Union Carbide, Envirotech, Environmental Research Associates and Eastern Kentucky University.

Other functional testing represents an interesting pattern.

Michigan State University helps out farmers with its forage testing van, which operators use to analyze livestock feed with Near Infrared Reflectance Spectroscopy (NIRS).

The Amboseli Elephant Research Project in Africa travels in a special blue-

This Cincinnati, Ohio, bus was part of a three-city, million-mile soybean test of engine emissions. Results of the two-month test in each area were sent to the University of Missouri for evaluation. *(Courtesy of the Ohio Soybean Council)*

green Land Rover through Kenya, funded by the African Wildlife Federation.

The Buffalo Regional Red Cross since 1974 has used a mobile laboratory to make certain blood derivatives at the sites of bloodmobile visits where donations are taken.

The United Auto Workers union monitors members' dental work performed by dental insurance plans to check on discrepancies. Blue Cross–Blue Shield uses motor homes for inspections by a dentist for cost and quality control of the sample reached in the peer-review process.

Marketing Research

Field marketing research studies are conducted in vehicles by manufacturers, consumer magazines and educational institutions.

Beginning in 1955 General Electric used a trailer marketing laboratory to get housewives' reactions to appliance product designs on dishwashers, washing machines, driers and refrigerators. These items were displayed in a model kitchen setting parked in front of houses where women were interviewed initially for background material pertinent to appliance pre-testing.

The Clairol Division of Bristol-Myers sets up research trailers in major shopping centers to interview women shoppers about its hair care products.

Bell-Northern Research in Canada has used since 1982 a high-tech mobile behavioral laboratory for testing prototype office telecommunication products and service concepts with computers. Traveling to key sites in the United States and Canada, the 31-foot, custom-made Airstream trailer is divided into there sections. This industrial research and development organization is jointly owned by Northern Telecom and Bell Canada.

Food and kindred products manufacturers rely heavily on mobile marketing research.

Pioneering in 1948, General Foods even opened a traveling orange juice factory as part of a consumer research taste-test experiment in Florida and California.

Another early user of the method in the 1950s, Standard Brands, has operated a mobile food-testing lab which parks at the curb and attracts consumers from the sidewalk. The interior is a compact kitchen, and coffee and other products have been tested for taste, flavor, strength and aroma.

Philip Morris in 1981 used three white coaches to promote Merit cigarettes and establish brand awareness. The technique was a traveling computerized opinion poll on current issues as a research approach.

Good Housekeeping magazine in 1961 used a mobile office to gather on-the-spot taped information about women's needs and interests at shopping centers as an input to editorial content.

Midas donated a new 28-foot Airstream motor home to Indiana University's Center for Safety and Traffic Education to be used in a field research study of recreational vehicle living. It supported a four-week tour of Southern trailer courts. Funding was by the Indiana Mobile Home Association, the Recreational Vehicle Institute and the Mobile Home Dealers National Association.

Personnel Activities

Mobile personnel employee relations revolve around recruiting, orientation, payroll, health care and communications.

A wide variety of organizations in the United States and Canada has used recruit-mobiles. These include manufacturers, trucking companies, airlines, temporary help firms, banks, publishers, universities, automobile clubs and communication organizations. Employed are vans, minibuses, station wagons, recreational vehicles, tour buses, coaches and semi-trailers. Favorite parking spots are shopping centers, state fairs, truck stops, restaurants, office parks, commuter rail stations and festivals, or even just on busy streets. Some merely are used to take applications while others carry on testing. Many operate during lunch hours and on weekends when more potential applicants are available. Some companies attach recruiting signs on the sides or tops of their regular vehicles.

More and more new cars are becoming "special vehicles" as they are given as perks not only to retain present employees or for bringing in a new hire but as an exciting part of a signing bonus package.

Probably the most ambitious recruiting effort to date is that of the Michigan health Council in Lansing in 1966. Its Health Career Mobile was a 12-ton, 50-foot trailer which was 12 feet tall and 12 feet wide. Its exhibits were aimed primarily at high school and college students, but it also reached parents, teachers and the general public. Foundation grants funded the project.

Greyhound has used a multimedia touring bus to orient employees on a major marketing effort. Operators previewed the company's new television advertising campaign in a 90-minute program for 18,000 employees in 67 cities.

Medical vans have been used to check employee health with tests and physical examinations at small, scattered worksites by Mobil Oil and New York's Consolidated Edison Company. Mobile X-ray units are often connected to the vans.

Mobile communications are used by employers in unique fashions.

The Philadelphia Gas works in 1966 reached employees for the United Fund Torch Drive charity effort with a van for three weeks at street locations where they were working. A slide program was shown to 16 at a time. American Motors at its Kenosha, Wisconsin, plant has used a battery-powered Gab Cab to conduct employee interviews on the shop floor as part of its mass communications radio program. The Buick Motor division of General Motors used an electric go-cart for similar employee interviews.

Transportation

Some transportation applications have involved mobile units: maintenance and service vehicles, workshops, delivery and even as lawn mowers or heliports.

Any organization which has to maintain a fleet of cars or trucks must provide for their upkeep either through internal or outside means. Several different kinds of organizations have chosen to run their own field shops on wheels for on-site work. These range in size from half-ton to over two-ton trucks, and may be either exclusive set-ups or augment service contracts with outside independent shops. "Taking the Mountain to Mohamet" may involve complete workshops or specialty vehicles devoted only to lube, tires, washing or emergency service. Users of these vehicles can be listed as heavy manufacturers, moving and storage companies, contractors, construction companies, mines, leasing organizations, trucking companies and public utilities.

A typical example of these units is that of the McNichols Transportation Co/AIM Leasing in Youngstown, Ohio, which practices mobile maintenance. Its truck was specially designed in-shop and features an 18-foot straight truck van body mounted on a chassis.

The Pacific Telephone Company, part of the Bell System, in 1969 set up a prototype mobile facility as an experimental diagnostic center. It provided both safety inspection and periodic maintenance to its fleet of passenger cars and small trucks. The facility consisted of four basic units: a trailer specially equipped with ramps, an electronic engine analyzer van, a lubrication truck and a parts storage van. Under-vehicle inspections and oil changes were made with the vehicle on top of the trailer which it mounted by a ramp. The vehicle was backed off the trailer at the completion of the inspection. A front end pneumatic lift on the trailer permitted inspection of the front wheel system.

Special job workshops equipped with necessary materials and tools facilitate installation of a variety of products like heating and air conditioning units, doors and windows and screens.

Delivery in a unique vehicle has public relations value. In Japan Domino's pizzas have been delivered on special motor scooters, customized red, white and blue three-wheelers. In 1961 the Bearden Company in Houston, Texas, began gun delivery of circulars to homes from an injection tube. They mounted the tank-and-gun jet cannon in the front seat of the delivery vehicle and shot the missiles up on the front porches of homes in selected neighborhoods.

Prototypes are currently being studied to see if the eight-foot long Daimler-Chrysler Smart Car can be converted to a riding lawn mower equipped with lasers instead of blades. Noise and emissions are problems.

Rounding out the transportation picture in the air, Visco Flying Company in California uses two large Chevrolet trucks adapted as heliports for its crop-dusting

Japanese and Hong Kong pizza lovers order a pizza and the hot meal rolls up to their door in a colorful, trademarked, three-wheeled scooter, much to the delight of the intrigued children in the family. Seldom can functionality and promotional advantage be so cleverly combined in one vehicle. *(Courtesy Domino's Pizza)*

and spraying operations. Their helicopters land on the 12-foot by 12-foot hydraulically operated landing ramp atop the trucks, each of which holds 3,000 gallons of water and is outfitted with a pump and melting equipment to mix chemicals with water.

Communications

Telephones, teletypes, telegraph and Internet operations have all been successfully put on wheels.

In 1977 on the St. Thomas docks, an air conditioned van was set up for phones with eight private booths for direct dialing through an overseas switchboard in the capital city of Charlotte Amalie.

Telephone companies use mobile communications vans in emergencies and disasters, and cellular public payphones in trailers can handle up to six callers at a time. These are self-contained, solar-powered vehicles 12 feet long and six feet, five inches high, weighing 2,420 pounds. Recessed lighting located in the gull-wing doors is automatically activated for nighttime operations. Roof-mounted panels provide for completely independent operation. Callers can line up on both sides.

Temporary homes for teletype departments can be easily set up in trailers while permanent offices are being built or renovated.

In 1952 Western Union had a Traveling Trailer Telegraph Office and by the mid–1970s put its Westar Mobile Earth Station satellite system truck in operation for use by broadcast journalists for such events as political conventions.

In 2001 the Massachusetts Institute of Technology Media Lab and a nonprofit organization in Costa Rica created the LINCOS (Little Intelligence Communities) program for rural dwellers. This mobile digital community telecenter for the Internet and telephone is 20 feet long and made of recycled metal shipping containers.

For the 1984 Los Angeles Olympic Games, Pacific Bell modified and customized 14 trailers fitted with electronics and communications gear which were placed at key sites in the area.

Radio station KRXR in Gooding, Iowa, has a mobile transmitter in a 1970 Buick Electra, the Brave Mobile, equipped with a tail fin and simulated jet engine.

Mobile meter reading saves much time and money. A hand-held device can read water meters from a distance of up to 120 feet. Electric and gas meters are handled by a van equipped with radio transmitting gear which beams microwaves at antennas attached to the meters.

Waste Disposal and Recycling

Ingenious mobile programs have been developed from several sources to address the twin challenges of waste disposal and recycling.

Greer Hydraulics has produced a trash compactor which is truck-mounted on a two-ton pickup or larger vehicle, or it can be trailer-towed. The unit can haul up to 3,000 pounds in a single operation. To dispose of highly radioactive waste, Chem-Nuclear Systems developed a system for pumping radioactive sludge through a mobile unit for preshipment processing. Portable pulverizers with capacities from five to 12 tons per hour have

been built by Heil on Low Boy tandem-axle semi-trailers weighing 53,000 pounds.

When it comes to recycling several well-known firms have participated at a mobile level.

Reynolds Aluminum in the 1970s had a fleet of complete can collection centers on wheels. They purchased directly from the public, as well as soft drink manufacturers, brewers and their distributors. Units were parked in state parks, shopping centers or wherever crowds could see the giant trucks.

In 1977 Pepsi-Cola conducted several mobile reclamation drives for non-returnable bottles. Cola route trucks traveled through neighborhoods picking up bottles and grinding them up ont he spot in high-speed glass crushers. It has also gone on tour with its Mobile Reclamation Center pulverizers with four crushers mounted on a Pepsi route truck adjusted to take the equipment. Canada Dry also has operated a mobile glass reclamation center.

In Tokyo, Japan, since 1977 Chirigami Kogan trucks with public address systems have cruised through neighborhoods picking up old newspapers, magazines, used cardboard and telephone directories, giving in return rolls of high-quality toilet paper.

The nonprofit National Center for Resource Recovery sent out two 40-foot, 19,000-pound Education Vans showing the process of municipal solid waste management and resource recovery systems for trash and garbage. The walk-through exhibits were usually displayed along with a ten-ton per hour, trailer-mounted air classifier which separates shredded garbage and trash.

Emergency Response

Mobile field headquarters are sometimes set up in emergencies when a response is organized by firms in the oil business and other potentially hazardous undertakings.

Standard Oil of Ohio has created a well-equipped fleet of environmental control vehicles to contain and clean up petroleum product spills: four containment trailers and a clean-up truck. Shell manufacturing locations also maintain emergency response programs with mobile field offices.

Offices, Meeting Rooms, Warehouses, Stock Rooms, Retail Areas and Amenities

Instant mobile offices and similar installations are used by a wide variety of or-ganizations: manufacturers, contractors, membership organizations, events sponsors, service stations, resorts, oil-search crews, journalists, truck lines, automobile clubs, public service groups and advertising media.

Mobile amenities cover drop-off centers for children; aircraft boarding stairs; rest rooms; dressing rooms; showers; and hot tubs and spas.

Other Functions

Domiciles and Garages

Mobile dwellers who consider a vehicle a permanent or temporary home include construction crews at remote sites, university students, disaster victims and

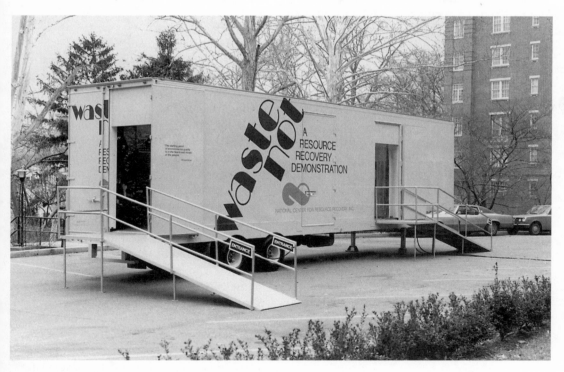

"Waste Not" epitomizes the rationale behind the education vans sent out by the National Center for Resource Recovery, which encourges technology permitting the economical recycling of energy and material resources on a large scale from solid waste. The exhibit featured photographs, models and graphics aimed at both technical audiences as well as the general public. *(Courtesy National Center for Resource Recovery, Inc.)*

homeless individuals and auto tramps and even whole families looking for work and living out of battered cars, as immortalized in the classic Great Depression movie *The Grapes of Wrath*. When the year 2000 approached, the Ark Two Survival Community in Ontario, Canada, set up underground bunkers made of 42 school buses lined up adjacent to each other and connected by doorways.

LIVLAB was introduced in 1981 for truck owner-operators, a big sleeper box mobile home on a truck chassis designed as a whole living arrangement. Attaching to either conventional or cab-over trucks, it provides a 6 × 8 foot bed in the doghouse portion, while the back-of-cab area has a standing-room salon, bath (toilet, shower and sink), clothes closet, refrigerator, stove and microwave, kitchen sink and counter, cabinets, table and built-in television. The all-electric home is airconditioned and has 50-gallon fresh water and 50-gallon sewage tanks. Constructed around an aluminum frame of 1½-inch square tubing, the walls are built of an exterior skin of ⅛-inch fiberglass, ½-inch balsa core, ¾-inch insulation and ¼-inch interior paneling. The 520-cubic-foot home adds about 1,900 pounds to the tractor and requires relocating the exhaust stack and air intake. For engine service it tilts back so that the cab can tilt forward.

Ever hanker for a mobile garage to complement your mobile domicile on wheels? The Wartburg Motor Carriage House was manufactured in Eisenach, Germany, in 1901. It had tiny wheels, a hinged door and could be folded up, weighing about 300 kg., complete with a fire-resistant section for gas and oil.

Food Preparation

The use by caterers of mobile kitchens was described in Chapter I on sales

vehicles. These have evolved from the primitive cook shacks on wheels drawn by mules that once followed the Kansas wheat harvest to Canada in the old days.

The late entertainer Sammy Davis, Jr., boasted a mobile kitchen; cooking was one of his hobbies.

Car engine cuisine, dashboard dining, or, as Chris Maynard and Bill Scheller described it with their book title, *Manifold Destiny* (Villard Books, 1989), is a practical reality. Cooking involves triple aluminum foil wrapping on the mobile stove's intake manifold down by the exhaust manifold, tucking it under the air filter. This is atop the block between two rows of cylinders on a V-8 engine. An oven can be constructed from a five-gallon can with two one-gallon cans fitted inside.

Physical Fitness and Sports

Actor Joe Piscopo is so much into physical fitness that he has a trailer equipped with weights and exercise equipment follow him from one location to another so that he can work out between camera takes.

A love of basketball prompted Jason Parr and Jon Varn Hagen to perfect their patented Pickup Hoops, a portable, collapsible basketball goal that bolts into the bed of any size pickup truck. The aluminum framework of the hoop, which weighs less than 60 pounds, is bolted near the rear and can be set to regulation height of ten feet in less than a minute. After the game is over, the goal can be folded back into the bed for easy storage.

Golfers haven't been overlooked either. The Buick Bengal concept car introduced in 2001 has two standard golf bags in the back seat, inspired by advertising spokesman Tiger Woods. There is also a golf bag door, like those in the classic vehicles of the late 1920s and early 1930s. Engineer Tony Anchors of Oxfordshire,

Jason Parr, right, and his uncle, Jon Varn Hagen, can "play" with their invention, a mobile basketball goal on a pickup truck. The goal requires no tools and one person can set it up or take it down. Seven years are said to have been spent on development. (Detroit Free Press, *photograph by Kirthmon F. Dozier*)

England, has built his own putting green on top of his car, a mini three-holer.

SPECIAL NEEDS

Certain individuals require vehicles with features of a special nature necessitating manufacturing modifications and/or later conversion work.

In 1976 Milton Ruehle's Para-Medic Ambulance Service in Mt. Clemens, Michigan, began to offer a special motor home to transport bed patients several hundred miles for treatment. His redesigned 32-foot Allegro has a five-foot by eight-foot bath in the rear, a private stateroom, large-capacity freezer, oxygen supply and a heart monitoring machine. Wide aisles accommodate a wheelchair and there are separate air conditioning and heating units for the front and rear.

Drivers with disabilities can get cars equipped with joystick drive-by-wire Digidrive II interface controls for gas/brake and steering.

Modified motor homes designed to aid the handicapped are special in every sense of the word. Featured are wheelchair lifts and platforms; four-foot-wide doors and second entry doors; wheelchair lockdown; open floor plan with wide aisles; six-way power seat; hand-controls for acceleration and braking; lounge with roll-under work stations; customized commode; large, roll-in shower and custom bed with electric controls.

Armored cars and trucks are designed for corporate executives, government officials and celebrities for maximum security. The world's largest markets are in Europe, Russia, Brazil and Mexico. The ultimate vehicles are built by hand and feature bulletproof steel armor plating and multiple layers of polycarbonate security glass, 17-inch tires that can run flat up to a speed of 35 miles per hour. Options not usually found include self-sealing fuel tanks, rear power windows; two-way intercom; self-contained oxygen tanks; fire retardation and bomb protection. Sources are vehicle manufacturers and independent security outfitters.

SCULPTURES, MONUMENTS AND CASKETS

Vehicles were never intended to function as sculptures, monuments or caskets, but some have inadvertently ended up as such. In a Western Nebraska wheat field stands Carhenge, set up by Jim Reinders in 1987 with the remains of 31 Plymouths, Fords, Chevrolets, Cadillacs and an old ambulance. It is near Alliance in Box Butte County as a replication of England's Stonehenge monument. Also in a used car dealership near Amarillo, Texas, is Cadillac Ranch, with ten half-buried vehicles. In Berwyn, Illinois, is the Spindle, composed of a 50-foot stainless steel spike on which eight automobiles have been impaled in a shopping center.

Funeral monuments have included granite Mercedes-Benz models; actual cars used to inter include Ferrari, Chevrolet Corvair, Cadillac El Dorado, Corvette, Packard, Dodge and De Lorean. Customized coffins have been ordered in the shapes of sports cars, Cadillacs and the Mercedes-Benz. Grave blankets in the shape of a car have also been reported.

CHAPTER VII

Multimodal Vehicles

Versatile dual capacity hybrid vehicles which can operate successfully both on land and in the air, land and water, air and under the water and on land and tracks are regarded as multimodal. Visionaries have even designed units which can perform in all four dimensions. Such bizarre mobility has always enjoyed a continuing fascination in both peace and war.

Normally to traverse the world you are required to choose one particular segment of the terrain, but multimodality expands these decisions into an exciting range of possibilities.

Skycars

A multimodal skycar for both land and air may be defined as a roadable aircraft with the primary function of a practical airplane and the secondary function of a licensed motor vehicle.

Perhaps the original idea was a gliding carriage built in 1808.

Prophetic vehicle visionaries lead us to such people as Jules Verne, French writer of scientific fantasies, or clairvoyant Andrew Jackson Davis, whose book *The Penetralia* published in 1856 predicted that "aerial cars will move through the sky from country to country."

Around 1900 a French novelty company produced a series of trading cards which predicted life in the year 2000 with people in flying cars.

Developing interest in the 1930s was apparent in the realm of flying cars. Famous designer Norman Bel Geddes predicted a Roadable Flying Sedan featuring retractable wings.

The 1930s films kept pace with the trend. The musical *Just Imagine* saw cars in the sky over New York City by 1980, and the late comedian Jack Oakie, expertly playing the part of tyrant Benito Mussolini in Charlie Chaplin's film *The Great Dictator*, proudly related his plans for a land-sea-air combination vehicle to support his buddy Adolf Hitler.

Both Victor Appleton and Victor Appleton II featured in their Tom Swift series of books for boys, over a period of years, Tom's prolific vehicle inventions and exploits which included fantastic flying cars (*Tom Swift and the Triphibian Atomicar*, New York: Grosset & Dunlap, No. 19).

"Chitty-Chitty Bang-Bang" was a fictional flying car drawn up by Ian Fleming in 1964. It was a five-ton, pre–1914 Mercedes with a six-cylinder Maybach aero engine, capable of over 100 miles per hour. Mud flaps front and rear became dragonlike wings.

Science-fiction literature has perpetuated these fantasies right up to the present day. The *Jetsons* cartoon flying car has been very popular with juvenile viewers.

Provocative names for airborne automobiles have usually focused on the air, the sky or flying ability in their connotations. Unfortunately the media have proved to be notoriously lax in correctly reporting nomenclature, treating individual proper names as confusing generic terms (Skycar, Aircar, etc.).

There have been over 75 different patents submitted to the federal government in Washington. In addition to independent initiatives contests have been the impetus for some entries.

Designers of airborne automobiles usually contend that the vehicles are primarily intended for commuter travel; business trips, particularly by sales representatives and professional people; recreation and sports; crop-dusting; emergency services; military activities; and fire patrol and police work, such as drug enforcement.

So far only a few aircars have been licensed for production, with none successfully made for sales to the public.

Such diverse makes as the Pontiac Firebird, Ford Pinto and Honda CRX have been modified for sky service, and aluminum and fiberglass emerged as favored framing materials.

Several major organizations worldwide have shown an interest in the basic concept, some to the extent of fashioning prototypes. These include British Aerospace, Studebaker, Ford, General Dynamics, Avco, Boeing, Consolidated Vultee, Ling-Temco, and several others. Even a few forward-thinking automobile dealers have given them a close look.

Publicity exposure as a novelty has been extensive but sporadic. These vehicles have been featured in newspapers, magazines, moving pictures, television and cable and by daredevil driving crews as part of their acts. Exhibits have been held at a variety of venues. In 1975 a special flying version of American Motors' Cassini Matador played a spectacular role in the James Bond thriller *The Man with the Golden Gun*, filmed in Thailand.

Even some production automobiles have exhibited unmistakable attributes of aviation styling, like the Lincoln Futura of 1955 or the Tucker, which definitely had the look of a rocket ship.

Several novelty vehicles have been successfully developed as simulated flying cars. David and Irene Major of Benton, Kansas, transformed a small, two-door, 1959 BMW 600 into their unique Rock 'n' Roll Aerocar. It has mounted on the front door a hand-carved, wooden propeller turned by a 12-volt motor, a small tail on the rear roof and two eight-inch wings. The front tires are replaced with Beechcraft 400A nose wheel tires and the rear tires are from the main landing gear of the Beech Starship. Special split-rims from an early Isetta were adapted to fit the airplane tires. The front parking lights and the rear taillights are removed. The custom fiberglass dash holds a working altimeter, air speed indictor and aircraft compass. The front opens to allow the "pilot" to enter. It is shown at many Midwest car shows and parades.

G-Whiz is what graphic expert Bill Carter in Hampshire, England, calls his half-plane, half-car with a top highway

With a vivid imagination you can pretend to fly in David and Irene Major's Rock 'n' Roll Aerocar. The 1959 BMW 600 is ready to take off. *(Courtesy David and Irene Major)*

speed of 150 miles per hour. He combined engine parts from a Hawk Jet and a V-12 Jaguar to power his rocket-shaped, 21-foot vehicle. There is a two-seater cockpit in which the passenger sits behind the driver.

Somewhat of a switch was the Plymocoupe, labeled as a flying automobile because it was an airplane powered by an engine manufactured for use in a 1935 Plymouth.

Before we write off such innovative vehicles with the old riddle "What has wheels and flies?" (Answer: a garbage truck) it is imperative that we recognize that several inherent problems seem to haunt the mating efforts consistently:

- Engine and/or power train design: inadequate power balance, underpowered as airplane, overpowered as car
- Questionable, not streamlined aerodynamics
- Fragility
- Relatively very high development and production costs
- Weight: too heavy for the air, too light for the road
- Difficult to attach wings quickly for safe flight
- Undersized tires
- Hard handling, especially three-wheelers
- Noisy
- Hard starting
- Flight controls of dubious safety
- Difficult climbing
- Unreliable belt drive system
- Strange, dowdy, odd, even ridiculous appearance
- Cluttered, cramped interior
- Undersized passenger compartment
- Small luggage space
- Maintenance and service of unknown availability and excessive anticipated cost

- Anticipated very high sales price and lease rates
- Unproven record, lacking definitive research
- Registrations formidable regarding safety, antipollution, etc. (eight or more licenses required)

The ultimate result of flying automobiles has been mixed for those produced to date: Several have crashed and a few others have ended up as museum exhibits.

Are they really a poor compromise between two distinct forms of transportation? Will innovative technology move the flying car up from its position as an engineering novelty to a practical production vehicle? Time will tell.

A selected list of representative examples of major designs both here and abroad reveals many different approaches.

In a 1911 issue of *The Automobile* magazine, the Metz Air-Car was offered in a modest two-inch illustrated advertisement. The brief copy read: "Bleriot type aeroplanes complete or in the knockdown. Motors 30, 60 and 120 H.P.; propellers and all component parts. Everybody may fly. Manufacturers of Metz Runabouts—lightest and most economical automobile in the world. We want live progressive dealers everywhere. Metz Company, Waltham, Massachusetts."

In 1915 William N. Parrish and his son Russel announced plans for an Aero-Automobile to carry seven passengers with a body resembling that of a touring car. When operated over the road the wings were to be folded into the body.

In 1917 Glenn Hammond Curtiss, an aviation pioneer and aircraft designer, made a prototype Autoplane/Autolandplane. This aluminum-framed touring car with celluloid windows had staggered, removable wings and a boom-mounted tail, and a four-blade pusher propeller at the rear roof which powered the car on the

ground. Up front under the hood was a 100-hp Curtiss OXX engine. It was designed for air speed of 65 mph and road speed of 45 mph. The pilot-chauffeur sat in the front cockpit with two passengers in back in a velvet-curtained, leather-lined compartment with tapestries and brocaded upholstery. It went on display at the Pan-American Aeronautic Exposition in New York City.

In 1925 Virgil B. "Fudge" Moore designed his Autoplane with folding wings in three models: a taxi, truck and salesman's special.

William Bushnell Stout in 1931 designed a series of experimental Sky Cars. Then in 1943 he introduced his Scarab with four wheels and a pusher propeller, designed by George Spratt. It used a removable wing that could pivot and tilt. Speed was announced as 60 mph in the air and 100 on the road.

In the early 1930s six experimental aircraft were ordered by the Bureau of Aeronautics of the Department of Commerce. One of these, the Pitcairn Autogiro, landed in a park near the Washington, D.C., headquarters building in 1935 and drove the short distance on the street for direct delivery. It was called the precursor of the helicopter and had two seats, direct lift, engine in the rear of the cabin with a drive to airscrew through an extension shaft and also to the tail wheel for road traction. The main wheels were steerable and rotor blades folded back to permit passage on the road. Air speed was said to be 90 mph and road speed 20 mph, with 20 mpg fuel economy.

Aviation pioneer Waldo Dean Waterman designed his first Arrowbile in 1937, an outgrowth of his Arrowplane. It had a two-passenger cab mounted on three wheels, a pusher propeller, a single detachable wing and the steering wheel hung from the roof. Air speed was 125 mph and ground speed 55 mph. A later

Top: A pioneer in designing hybrid air cars was William B. Stout. Shown is the Convair Model 103, also known as the Spratt-Stout Model 8 Skycar, on the ground with the wing attached. George Spratt was a Convair engineer. The pilot manually adjusted its wing. *(National Air and Space Museum, Smithsonian Institution [NASM Videodisc No. IA-23170]).* *Bottom:* The roadable Pitcairn XOP-1 direct-lift Autogiiro featured rotating wings and a seven-cylinder radial air-cooled POBJOY engine. The pilot and passenger sat side by side. *(National Air and Space Museum, Smithsonian Institution [SI Neg. No. 88-12578])*

Pilot Jerry Phillips poses with Waldo Dean Waterman's Arrowbile No. 3, "Miss South Bend," after flying cross-country to Floyd Bennett Field, U.S. Coast Guard Air Station, Brooklyn, New York, in 1938. Over 21 years Waterman designed several different versions of roadable aircraft and is often called the father of America's flying automobiles. *(National Air and Space Museum, Smithsonian Institution [SI Neg. No. 78-1875])*

This is J.M. Gwinn's Aircar Model I in flight. It was a two-place, side-by-side cabin biplane built in Buffalo, New York, in the late 1930s and early 1940s. *(National Air and Space Museum, Smithsonian Institution [SI Neg. No. 90-614])*

improved seventh version in 1958 was called the Aerobile, this time with a water-cooled, flat six Franklin engine instead of the original modified Studebaker Commander automobile engine.

In 1938 J.M. Gwinn came out with his Aircar with a tricycle landing gear and no rudder. It featured a simplified instrument panel. The pilot operated the controls with pedals, the accelerator regulating take-off, landing and cruising.

Theodore P. Hall in 1939 built his first roadable airplane which used a three-wheel landing gear, a flathead Mercury V-8, 98 hp engine and a front-mounted propeller. The wings and twin-boom tail could be unbolted and left at the airport. His second version in 1945 had a fiber-glass-bodied small car base and was called the ConvAirCar. The road portion used a Crossley 26.5 hp engine. For flying, a self-contained, rigid aircraft portion attached to the car's roof and had a built-in 190 hp Lycoming engine. This module was supposed to be rented at airports.

The 1940s are recognized as perhaps the heyday of development of hybrids as a sustained resurgence of activity became apparent.

Alex Tremulis in 1944 introduced his teardrop-shaped, aluminum or fiberglass-bodied, four-to-six passenger cars with removable wings. The aircraft engine was four-cylinder, air-cooled and put out 400 hp. Speeds were estimated at 160 mph in the air.

The FA-2 Airphibian roadable monoplane designed by Robert Edison Fulton, Jr. The car and the flight unit have been separated and an unidentified man is shown storing the propeller while the family waits. It was certified by the Civil Aeronautics Administration and was said to take only five minutes to convert from an airplane to a car. *(National Air and Space Museum, Smithsonian Institution [SI Neg. No. 91-13262])*

In 1945 Curtiss-Wright Industries called its craft the Flymobile, a helicopter powered by a four-cylinder, 90 hp Franklin opposed engine. It was of metal construction with wood fairing strips and a fabric covering with a three-wheel landing gear. Top speed was 95 mph.

The Roadplane in 1945 was designed by engineer Norman V. Davidson with detachable wings, tricycle wheels with the front steerable and a 75 hp air-cooled engine.

The H.D. Boggs Airmaster Air Car appeared on the scene in 1945 as a four-place, low-wing monoplane with a pusher engine, twin tail booms, twin rudders and a tricycle landing gear. The nose wheel was fixed, while the main wheels were semi-retractable. Intended was a 145 hp geared-drive air-cooled engine. It seated four with a top speed of 150 mph in the air and 105 on the road and a range of 500 miles. The detachable body containing the power plant was designed to be used on either a plane or car chassis.

In 1946 Robert Edison Fulton, Jr., descendant of the inventor of the steamboat and Thomas Alva Edison, introduced his Airphibian monoplane. This was an aluminum-bodied convertible coupe with a 150 hp, six-cylinder Franklin engine. It had two sections: a wing and tail unit that came off in one piece and stayed at the airport between flights and a narrow, two-seated car with four airplane-sized, semi-enclosed wheels sticking out on struts. For highway driving the three-bladed tractor propeller was unbolted. Air speed was 110 mph and road speed 45 mph. It could fly up to 400 miles on 30 gallons of gas. In all there were six prototypes.

George H. Hervey in 1946 called his design the Travelplane. It had a four-place cabin, pusher propeller, three-wheel landing gear and steerable nose wheel with a 200 hp Ranger engine. Wings and boom-mounted tail section were detachable.

Stanley D. Whitaker and Daniel D.

Zech in 1946 designed a two passenger, three-wheel, high-wing monoplane with a single engine at the rear, the Plane-Mobile. Pivoting wings above the cockpit folded back over the car roof. A wing-carrying frame was in the tail.

The Aerocar was designed by aeronautical engineer Moulton B. Taylor in 1947. He continued experimenting with six more in the series, with two different versions into the 1970s. Outfitted with bucket seats, padded dash and fiberglass bodies over all-aluminum frames, the two-seaters were basically front-wheel drive sports coupes with four-cylinder opposed Lycoming engines. A self-contained trailer towed the 34-foot long aluminum wings, tail and pusher propeller. The Aerocar

Moulton B. Taylor is shown with his Aerocar. It had automobile as well as flight instruments and could accommodate 100 pounds of baggage with a 300-mile range. Conversion took from five to ten minutes with the aid of a single hand crank. The vehicle won federal certification. *(EAA Foundation Library Archives)*

could go 135 mph in the air and 60 mph on the road. In 1961 movie actor Robert Cummings used the Aerocar in his television comedy series *Love That Bob*; the Aerocar also appeared on *I've Got a Secret*, and Portland, Oregon, radio station KISN featured it in its traffic reports.

In 1948 Leland Dewey Bryan's high-wing monoplane Airmobile, or Bry-Car, was introduced. Subsequently improved versions came out in 1958 and 1972. Bryan was a Buick mechanic at the General Motors proving grounds. He ended up with a red and white one-seater using an open skeleton-type frame with a plastic hatch and a hand-cranked engine. He made a yoke to fit over the fuselage and hung Delta wings of a primary glider on the sides. When the wings folded over the cockpit, the plane became an eight-foot wide car. Reversible wing tips protected the pusher propeller. It went 135 mph in the air and 60 mph on the ground.

Industrial designer Henry Keck in 1951 presented a two-place, front-wheel drive car design with twin helicopter blades mounted on the roof which would come apart in sections to be stored in the car.

The Triphibian Aeromarine was designed by J.F. "Skeets" Coleman in 1955. It had a tricycle landing gear, pusher-type propeller, a folding delta-shaped wing, three retractable wheels and a watertight hull for landing on water with a pair of hydro-skis attached to a retractable airbag. Power was a 215 hp Franklin engine with power for the car from a small gasoline engine. Speeds were calculated to be 200 mph in the air and 50 mph on the ground.

In 1960 H.L. Trautman proposed a small, single-passenger, three-wheeler with folding wings and a pusher propeller, the Roadair. Estimated speeds were 90 mph in the air and 70 mph on the ground.

Paul Moller's M 400 Volantor Skycar has some 43 patents making up its construction. As an aeronautical engineer and

For over 40 years Paul Moller has been developing prototype Skycars. The latest is shown, the M 400 Volantor, a designation coming from a Latin root word meaning nimble or agile. Moller claims that it will have a top speed of 390 mph, cruise at 300 mph and have a 900-mile range and get 20 miles per gallon on any fuel. The object of the first liftoff is to hover five feet or more above the ground for one minute or more. A test is planned soon. *(Courtesy Paul Moller)*

college professor since 1965, he has built levitation vehicles. The current three-wheel, fiberglass version is designed to take off and land vertically, has a bullet shape, seats four and is completely computer-controlled by three independent systems. It has been variously described as the iron canary, giant hummingbird, bat-mobile and the flying saucer. It boasts eight, 160 hp rotary engines mounted horizontally, four giant fans and carries two automatic parachutes.

In the 1970s David Heaton developed a 12-foot diameter, disk-shaped, domed flying car which took off and landed vertically. It accommodated two passengers and weighed 1,200 pounds fully loaded. There was one control stick to provide both direction of flight and accelerate the engine to propel the vehicle at speeds of 150 mph.

The Ave Mizar was a 1971 super-customized convertible Ford Pinto integrated with the airframe and pusher-type engine of a twin-boom Cessna Skymaster, conceived by engineers Henry Smolenski and Harold Blake. It had complete aircraft and automobile instrumentation with room for four passengers and normal luggage. The detachable low aspect ratio wings and tail assembly could be connected at an airport. The steering wheel was modified for flight control with retractable rudder pedals mounted under the column. It had a 130 mph cruising speed range of over a thousand miles, and a flight service ceiling of 12,000 feet.

In 1976 former Marine pilot K.P. Rice designed the two-passenger, three-wheel Volante with a fiberglass body, removable canard wings and a pusher propeller. The air-cooled, four-cylinder 75 hp Volkswagen engine was aft of the cabin. Speeds reached 130 mph in the air and 70 mph on the ground. The vehicle was intended to become a home mechanic kit.

In 1992 the Starcar used electric power on the road and a gas-turbine in the air.

Other U.S. roadable aircraft are associated with the names of such men as Reginald Reid and Charles Pritchard.

Outside the United States, there are entries in France, Great Britain, Italy and other countries.

In 1921 in France Rene Tampier designed a roadable biplane with wings that could be folded back against the tail section, with a second pair of wheels dropped. On the ground it was powered by a small, four-cylinder auxiliary engine; in the air by a 300 hp Hispano-Suiza V-12.

In 1932 Caudron-Renault again in France called his vehicle the Aviocar. It was a monoplane with folding wings and a retractable wheel at mid-fuselage. The power to drive on land was furnished by a small auxiliary gas engine mounted on the tail to push the vehicle.

In 1945 in Italy the Erco-Spider was designed by Lt. Col. Ercolano Ercolani. The two-seater, four-wheel-drive car had detachable wings and a tail boom. Intended was an air-cooled, four-cylinder aircraft engine and a two-cylinder engine on the road. Speeds were 110 mph in the air and 40 mph on the ground.

In 1948 Ing Pellarini in Italy made a prototype of a three-place monoplane with a pusher propeller, tail on a boom, twin fins, tricycle landing gear and folding wings.

In 1988 right after British Aerospace had bought England's Rover Group, the new owners conducted secret tests in Norway with a radical Land Rover Whirligig/Personnel Carrier, the Sky Rover. Also in England the Destruction Squad, a daredevil driving troupe, put together a flying car with makeshift wings and tail attached to the top of a small sedan. The propeller was linked to the car's fan belt.

Other Flying Machines

Involvement with flying vehicles has by no means been limited to passenger cars, although most airborne efforts have logically been focused on these vehicles. Also included are trucks, buses, motor homes, tanks, motorcycles, scooters, bicycles, boats and even submarines.

In the 1930s famous designer Norman Bel Geddes combined road and air transport in his Helicopter Community Bus, which would require a floating airport. Again in 1974 the Surtan bus-copter was discussed as a new transportation system connecting the Dallas/Fort Worth Regional Airport with the two cities.

As early as 1932 J. Walter Christie, famous automobile racing driver and inventor in the field of automotive engineering, was trying to develop a workable four-ton flying war tank with a thousand-hp engine for the U.S. Army. It was to have an armored undercarriage, detachable tread and rubber tired wheels. Then in 1935 aviation pioneer Waldo Dean Waterman, who the year previously had designed his Arrowbile flying car (described earlier), turned his attention to tanks with these specifications: all-metal reversible propeller and engine in rear; wing span of 37 feet; steel-armored forward cockpit 14 feet, 4 inches long; bulletproof gas tanks; telescoping gun turret; and a cruising speed of 160 mph and spurt to 180. The single, V-shaped propeller was to be shed in two minutes and the vehicle would go 75 mph on the road, using the pilot's wheel to steer the front wheels. Wings could be stored compactly on an aircraft carrier.

Previous attempts to bolt wings to a motorcycle had proved disastrous when the cycle crashed on takeoff, but Evel Knievel successfully used his thin sky cycle, capable of making 350 mph in eight seconds, to go 1,000 feet up and carry him over the Snake River Canyon in 1973. A so-called hang-bike motorcycle mated with a hang-glider was also created by engineer-designer Douglas Malewicki and associates.

Michael Moshier, an aerospace engineer of Millennium Jet, and NASA are developing a one-person air scooter that can buzz far over the streets. It is expected to go up to 80 mph, climb to 10,000 feet and get approximately 20 miles per gallon with regular gasoline.

Bicycles on the wing have been spurred on since 1935 by a substantial award offered by the Royal Aeronautical Society in London to teams of aeronautical engineers. These contraptions with a propeller are driven by leg power alone. Dozens of efforts have come from Germany, France, Italy, Great Britain, Japan, Australia and the United States.

Norman Bel Geddes and German aeronautical engineer Otto A. Kuhler in the 1930s designed the v-winged ocean liner and airplane, the Transoceanic Airliner. This nine-story high hybrid could have accommodated 600 passengers.

A flying submarine was developed by American engineer and inventor Walter Reid in the 1950s. He claimed that it could submerge or fly wherever the pilot wished. The experimental full-scale prototype torpedo-like craft was 26 feet long and in tests reached an altitude of about 75 feet. It had a 60 hp airplane engine mounted on top of a conning tower, and an electrically-powered boat propeller on the stern. It was designed to submerge and travel at four knots about five feet beneath the surface, and to fly at 65 mph at an altitude of 20 feet.

In the early 1960s the Convair Division of General Dynamics explored the feasibility of a flying submersible, a jet-powered subplane that would be able to dive beneath the waters and cruise. The two-person craft was intended to have an

The very idea of a submarine that can fly may seem just too unrealistic, but not to inventor Walter Reid. Military implications are obviously indicated for such a craft. *(Courtesy Walter Reid)*

aircraft range of 300–500 nautical miles at speeds of 150–225 knots, with an underwater range of 50 nautical miles at five knots and a 75-foot depth. After landing the operators would seal off the jet engines and flood the hollow wings, tail and sides of the hull, causing it to submerge. Underwater propulsion would be provided by battery-run propellers.

Hovercraft

Suspended six to 12 inches between earth and heaven, hovercraft ground-effect machines skim along suspended on a cushion of pressured air, an exciting transportation development in the 1950s. This cross between a boat and an airplane can be operated on any reasonably smooth, unobstructed terrain at speeds of 30 miles an hour over open water, 40 on land and 45

over snow and ice. There are hover cars, trucks, trailers, trains and even lawnmowers. They are said to be the potential motor and marine vehicle, and farm, airport and ranch implement. They are regarded by some as the first new form of transport since the jet plane. As they grow cheaper and more efficient, wheel-less cars may be able to leave roads and take to the countryside or water, provided adequate hover traffic controls are in place. In one sense hydroplanes, the nautical equivalent of the hovercraft, literally are flying when they are above the surface of the water. This vehicle has seen practical uses: The U.S. Coast Guard uses a Husky Nattiqairboat to cross land, ice and water.

In 1959, Curtiss-Wright displayed its Model 2500 Air-Car. The 21-foot-long, eight-foot-wide, five-foot-high hover vehicle had dual headlights and taillights, a hood ornament, chrome trim and a convertible roof. Power came from two 300 hp aircraft engines. Speed was 60 mph in the four-passenger car with a two-passenger Bee also planned. Soon after, Ford was reported to be working on a Levacar. Noise, high fuel consumption, handling and dust apparently doomed commercial possibilities of these types of vehicles.

In Shanghai in 2001 construction began on what is called the world's first commercial railway to make successful use of magnetic levitation, or Maglev. The train is to float a centimeter or two in the air on a cushion of electromagnetic repulsion created between superconducting magnets in the train and coils in the guide track at 20 mph without friction. The only other such service reported as open to the public, a link of less than half a mile between the main railway station and the airport in Birmingham, England, was closed in the mid–1990s after 11 years in operation because of maintenance problems.

Amphibious Vehicles

Aqua-cars are dual vehicles with both land and water capability. They are usually designed for use by public utilities, water search and rescue operations, forestry work, agriculture, boating enthusiasts, fliers, photographers and explorers. They can also function on large estates and for hunting and fishing trips.

Some have developed in connection with contests like the ones sponsored by the Waterbugs of America Racing Association, which has fostered boatmobiles in Portage Lake, Ohio. Garrison Keillor even mentions a fictitious Guy's Boat Mobile on his *Prairie Home Companion* radio show.

A wide variety of automobile and truck makes have been involved, including Mercedes, Studebaker, Morris, Ford, Jeep, Toyota, Land Rover, Chrysler, GMC, Porsche, Packard, Opel and Volkswagen.

By country, the number of different designs produced for amphibious vehicles would probably run, in descending order, from the United States to Germany, France, Great Britain, Italy, Sweden, the Netherlands and Russia.

UNITED STATES

In 1805 Oliver Evans in Philadelphia came out with a 20-ton steam carriage, the Orukter Amphibolos, a flat-bottomed, self-propelled, paddle-wheel dredge or barge equipped with axles and wheels, driving one wheel by belt and pulleys from the flywheel shaft of the machine's twin-cylinder grasshopper beam, five-hp engine.

Many do not realize that the majestic Conestoga wagons used in the French and Indian Wars and later by American pioneers headed west from the Revolutionary War to 1850 were amphibious. These camels of the prairie, drawn by four- or six-horse teams, had boat-bottomed bodies that sloped to the center so that cargoes would not shift, and high raked sides. The wagons were capable of carrying five tons.

In 1883 Terry's amphibious tricycle was designed. When taken apart, reassembled and covered with stretched canvas, it could be converted to a 12-foot boat. In 1894 Beach and Harris produced the Cycle Raft with twin inflatable pontoons. In 1896 Thore J. Olsen's 80-pound tricycle carried rigidly connected twin boats from its axle, and from a yoke on the fore wheel. It could be driven by either engine or treadle power.

Most of the twentieth century amphibious activity in the United States took place before World War II.

The year 1905 saw T. Richmond and his three-wheeler shaped like a canoe, powered by a three-cylinder gas engine. It had a set of hinged paddles attached to the wheels, which automatically opened and closed in the water. As an ice boat it had attached spikes to the drive wheel and a runner put under the forward wheel.

The Hydro-motorcycle was perfected by Eugene Frey. It had an add-on flotation device consisting of three pontoons which could be raised or lowered. Handlebar rudders controlled the steering gear. A sail attachment was provided in case the engine was disabled.

Running backward on the water was George Monnot's Hydro Car in 1914, with special propellers mounted up front under the radiator grille and two steering wheels at opposite ends. It used a Hercules four-cycle engines, and speed was eight mph on the sea and 25 mph on land.

Together William Massel and William F. Purcell called their 16½-foot-long, 3,000-pound invention the Hydromotor or Motor Duck in 1915. Four models were offered: roadster, touring car, delivery truck and limousine with the same chassis used for each type of aluminum body. They were propelled in the water by a 16-inch, three-bladed screw propeller and went ten mph on the water and 60 mph on land.

The 1917 Anheuser-Busch vehicle originally intended as an amphibian for the government ended up as a promotional vehicle, the Bevo Boat Car, discussed fully in Chapter II.

Paul Panketan put all the controls in the front seat of his five-to-seven passenger 1921 Auto-Boat. Shifting levers lifted the four wheels to convert the vehicle to a speedboat propelled by a 90 hp gasoline engine. Speeds were listed as 35 mph in the water and 90 mph on land.

The year 1928 saw George Powels's auto–motor boat with a Ford engine and Ford land running gear at speeds of ten mph in the water and 40 mph on land.

George McLaughlin installed a 70 hp engine in his vehicle in 1931 with an airplane propeller shaft and pontoons under the running boards; it reached estimated speeds of 25 mph on the water and 50 mph on land.

In 1936 Gulf Oil came out with a wader with a Ford V-8 engine, hollow wheels and ten speeds forward and six in reverse.

In 1994 the fiberglass Aquastrada Delta was introduced in California with a 245 hp Ford truck engine and retractable wheels, yielding claimed speeds of 45 mph on water and 100 mph on land.

GERMANY

Amphibious development in Germany has stretched from the 1930s to the 1980s.

Probably the best-known designer, Capt. Hans Trippel, began building in Germany in 1932, producing such vehicles as the Marathon, with the driver in the center in the late 1950s. The most famous of all the civilian amphibians is his Amphicar pleasure boat (originally the Eurocar) available both in a little convertible and sedan models. Between 1960 and 1967 Trippel produced 3,300 for world markets. Regarded as 85 percent car, 15 percent boat, all seams in the body, essentially a steel hull that enclosed the engine but was not built on a chassis, were welded. The undriven front wheels acted as rudders. Axles poked out through holes lined with thick seals, and there were rear deck louvers. Motive power in the water was supplied by the propeller screws in the back beneath the rear bumper tucked up inside the propulsion tunnels, driven through a special gear by the rear-mounted, water-cooled Triumph Herald four-cylinder engine. It contained two transmissions, one for each mode of travel and some 25 different grease fittings. A tall pole with a yellow light on top was intended for night navigation. Speeds were ten mph on the

The Amphicar, which grew out of a World War II military vehicle, was sold worldwide and manufactured in Germany. A typical sports application is depicted in the photograph. The amphibian resembled a tail-finned motorboat when afloat. Its 1.1-liter engine put out 43 horsepower. Amphicars have been used for remote radio broadcasts. An estimated 400 remain. *(The Detroit Public Library, National Automotive History Collection)*

water and 70 mph on the road. The Amphicar proved to be a prime drawing card for advertising, but owners characteristically complained about sluggish performance and lack of local service and parts availability. There is still an active Website of owners supported by lubricant sales.

It features restoration tips and parts sources. President Lyndon Baines Johnson owned an Amphicar and used it on the lake at his Texas ranch. It also starred in several movies.

In 1978 Karl Mayer, who owned a textile machinery company in West Germany, produced his Amphmobil, which could go 75 mph on land. After some market research he decided not to put it into production.

FRANCE

In 1905 Fournier in France combined a boat hull with an automobile chassis, placing the engine in the middle and the propeller on the drive shaft. Passengers faced sideways. Two years later Ravailler's canoe-shaped car, Waterland, was pulled by a 20 hp engine. Driven by a propeller when in the water, it used its solid-tired disc wheels as rudders. The steering wheel was connected both to the front wheels and to a rudder in the stern. Vargoz in 1922 extended a Ford at both ends to hold up two floats. The drive went to all four wheels with discs and paddles.

GREAT BRITAIN

W. Miller Metcalf in England in 1920 had his Amphiglyder with a there-cylinder radial engine driving a tractor airscrew, converted for the water with a twin-float hydroplane. Next year the two-passenger Cyclecar had a two-and-a-half hp, two-cycle engine and paddle blades on the rear wheels to drive it in the water. In 1935 Alfred Burgess's Precursor I was a punt upon which a car was driven and connected to controls for marine use. L.G. Wood in 1956 designed a three-wheeler with paddle blades welded to the rear driving wheels and using a two-cycle Ahzani engine.

ITALY

In August 1988 the late Giorgio Amoretti with his four children took a modified Ford from Italy to New York City on the water. In May 1999 his son Marco and Marcolino De Candia tied together a wrecked Volkswagen Passat and a Ford Taurus filled with buoyant polyurethane to cross from the Canary Islands to Martinique on the Atlantic Ocean in a sea odyssey. In the vehicles the driver and passenger compartments were arranged as a shelter. On top were rubber boats with holes in the middle so that the sailors could climb in and out of the cars, and a tent, sails and solar batteries for the mobile telephone set and the desalinator for making drinking water from sea water. More equipment was on towed boats. The trip took 119 days.

SWEDEN

Swedish contributions to amphibious vehicles include the five-seater, fiberglass, gullwing Allskog Aquacar in 1955.

THE NETHERLANDS

The Dutch DAF had two ends and four-wheel drive. Both driving units could steer.

MILITARY AMPHIBIANS

Some military amphibians were adaptations of civilian designs while others were original vehicles.

Experimental prototype designs for amphibious tanks and other military vehicles were under study in the 1920s and 1930s, but World War II pushed such units into mass production.

The German navy had the four-ton, four-wheel-drive Voran in 1929 with a four-cylinder, 40 hp Opel engine, intended mostly for marsh use, with speeds of seven mph on the water and 15 mph on land. During World War II the Porsche Schwimmwagen, a four-wheel-drive military car which doubled as a boat, saw a production total of 14,265. It featured a hybrid outboard water propeller. Water speed was six mph, with land speed at 50 mph. Hans Trippel built around 1,000 amphibious vehicles for the military.

English military authorities had experimented with several different vehicles (the Mark IV tank came out in 1916 suspended between two steel floats), but it was to the United States that the Allies looked for military amphibians in quantity. Ford built a Seep, based on a Jeep chassis which had a steel hull and a winch to assist in hauling itself up steep banks. Some 18,620 Landing Vehicles Tracked (LVT) were turned out in American plants under the names Water Buffalo and Alligator.

The most famous U.S. vehicles were the DUKWs (popularly labeled Ducks), 2½-ton, 6 × 6, GMC cargo trucks which racked up a total of 21,000 units. They were used to carry troops and equipment between water and land and served a vital role in many battles, most notably in the D-Day invasion, where over 2,000 were employed at Normandy. They also stormed Japanese-held Pacific islands. They enjoyed the unique ability to vary their tire pressure while on the move to suit the terrain.

Subsequently in the 1990s they have been pressed into service as passenger vehicles for tourist sightseeing, billed as "Ride the Ducks." Fully renovated, recon-

Sightseers would probably have a very hard time visualizing their tourist vehicle storming a beach in France, but this surplus amphibious DUCK, seen here in Branson, Missouri, is a renovated DUKW used in World War II. *(Courtesy Branson Ride the Ducks Tours)*

structed and refurbished, they now operate in Branson, Missouri; Seattle; Boston; Chicago; Memphis; Hot Springs, Georgia and the Wisconsin Dells. Functioning as part bus, part boat equipped with watertight hulls, marine propellers, bilge pumps and rudders, they typically support 45-minute narrated land tours and 35-minute trips on nearby waterways.

Light amphibious tanks could swim also by means of flotation screen equipment; when Jeeps were fitted with special canvas sides and snorkels they could cross streams six feet deep.

After World War II Russia produced a modified version of the Duck, the ZIL-485.

AMPHIBIOUS ODYSSEYS

Between 1950 and 1958 Ben and Elinor Carlin circumnavigated the globe in Half-Safe, an Army surplus Jeep. Amphibious and watertight, it was fitted with a keel that could be removed for land operations. The record: 9,500 miles by sea under sail and 40,500 by land. From 1993 to 1998 Karen and Rick Dobbertin logged over 3,000 sea miles and 24,000 land miles in the amphibious surface orbiter *Perseverance*. It was rocket-shaped, built on a 1959 Heil double-walled, stainless-steel milk tanker body. It was 32½ feet long and 7½ feet wide, and weighted 9½ tons. The Dobbertins visited 28 countries, going through the Caribbean and the Panama Canal on this Project Earth-Trek.

RECREATIONAL AMPHIBIANS

Demand in the commercial recreational dual-purpose vehicle-boat market has generated a variety of offerings.

Land 'n' Sea Craft has produced a 28-foot houseboat that becomes the equivalent of a house trailer when fitted to its special undercarriage. Camp-A-Float renders any recreational vehicle up to 31 feet in length and weighing 9,000 pounds a totally amphibious houseboat. In 15 minutes it is driven on board a specially-designed, five-ton cruiser deck and secured in place. The 16-foot Caraboat is towed like a conventional trailer and then launched in the water as a jet-propelled boat carrying as many as five people. It has fitted wheels and a collapsible towbar built into the hull for trailering. The one-piece hull has an open, self-draining forward cockpit. The Otter is a small vacation travel trailer sleeping four that converts into a powered houseboat instantly through a system of roadable wheels coupled with retractable-extendable flotation units. Other entries in this category bear such provocative names as Porta-Bote, Camper Boat, Waterlander, Naut-A-Care, Ship A Shore and Combo Cruiser.

NOVELTY AMPHIBIANS

Several unique vehicles, such as swamp or marsh buggies, qualify as minor prototype entries in the amphibious race.

What is probably the world's first vehicle designed to travel upside-down comes out of Toronto, Canada, intended for exploration of the Polar ice pack. Inventor Doug Elsey, a diver and ocean engineer, has named it Nomad. It is a submersible that will have enough buoyancy to roll around under water, using the bottom of the ice sheets as a roadway. It requires about five feet of ice to hold it down.

At New York City's Guggenheim Museum is on display Claes Oldenburg's sculpture, *Swiss Army Knife*. It doubles as a boat and was successfully floated on a Venice canal.

If you want a real novelty, try the 45-foot floating milk truck made with 6,000 milk cartons by Jack O'Keefe and his family in Seattle, Washington.

Or how about the standard automobile on suspended cables operating as a passenger ferry across the Pudding River near Barlow, Oregon? Two strands support the car, which runs under its own power, while a third, through a pulley cradle, steadies the vehicle at the top. Flat rubber bands for traction replace the tires. The 120-foot crossing only takes a gallon of gas to make 1,760 trips.

A 42-foot, $200,000 British-built luxury super cruiser can reveal a pair of dune buggies coming out of the bow when it is beached. It cruises at 40 mph and burns 45 gallons of gas an hour at that speed.

Pulling a switch on the land to water cycle is Ken London, a Ft. Lauderdale, Florida, realtor. He purchased a Boeing 308 airplane and turned it into a 56-foot luxury yacht, the *Londonaire*. An old boat hull supports the fuselage. The cockpit remains the same as when Howard Hughes owned it. It moves at 40 knots.

Finally sculptor Livio De Marchi in Venice, Italy, in 1999 carved out of pine and walnut a 1,500-pound vessel, a replica of a 1964 convertible Volkswagen Beetle which goes five mph. The Beetle-boat or floating bug is propelled by a ten hp inboard motor housed in the trunk. It is complete with rearview mirrors, roll-down window handles, headlights and taillights. De Marchi has made a similar amphibian to resemble in every detail a Fiat Topolino.

Private amphibians have to be fairly simple in design to enable production and so that retail costs can be kept down. Demand is so relatively limited that this type of vehicle is probably never likely to be much more than an engineering curiosity.

The late comedian Steve Allen attempted frivolously to bring the Wright Brothers at Kitty Hawk, North Carolina, into the amphibious scene:

> Contrary to what you were told in school-books, they did not invent the airplane.

That thing was a propeller-driven boat they were putting together with two outriggers. Haven't you ever wondered why they went to the beach to try it out? They were just trying to push the thing downhill into the water to find out if it would float. So they turned on the propeller and the breeze caught the outriggers and the thing lifted up into the air. They were both terribly embarrassed [*Dumbth*, Prometheus Books, 1989, p. 133].

Land, Water and Air Capability

Some modern Jules Vernes have made mention in their designs on paper of vehicles which have tripartite ability to function on land, sea and air. This is the next exciting dimension to emerge from science fiction to reality.

Two stalwarts have called their inventions Triphibians: Constantios H. Vlachos in the District of Columbia in 1935 and in 1955 J.P. "Skeets" Coleman, who is previously described in detail in this chapter.

Beginning in 1950 Dr. William R. Bertelsen developed eight different amphibious, ark-shaped wing, ground-effect Aeromobiles for land-water-air navigation. His production prototype Gem III was the eighth refined version. It was a four-passenger, 180 hp craft capable of floating 18 inches above the ground at 90 mph maximum forward speed and 70 mph cruise speed. It was made of aircraft alloy tubing, aluminum sheet and fiberglass. The ninth design, Aeromobile 250, was produced for a Universal movie, *Brass Bottle*.

In 1977 the Heli-Home came upon the market, manufactured by Orlando Helicopter Airways and sold by the Itaska Division of Winnebago. The 46-foot, eight-passenger flying camper consisted of a surplus Vietnam War and Coast Guard dual-control Sikorsky helicopter connected to a Winnebago motor home. It boasted an

The Bertelsen Aeromobile 14 hovers over ice in 1969. Lift, propulsion and control are supplied by a single duct-mounted gimbaled 55 hp JLO engine driving a 36-foot, eight-bladed fan. Mechanical linkage to the handlebars allows the operator to tilt the fan duct. *(National Air and Space Museum, Smithsonian Institution [SI Neg. No. 94-13077])*

optional float for amphibious landings, making it a triple-threat vehicle. It could travel on a 350-mile flight at 100 mph. It was intended as a portable cabin chiefly for sportsmen, or as a field office for exploration crews and executives of oil and mineral companies.

Road and Rail

An unusual dual combination is that of highway and railroad or transit tracks for specially-equipped vehicles with two separate sets of wheels, known variously as rail vehicles, rail/highway vehicles, hi-rail vehicles or road 'n' rail vehicles. They range from passenger cars, buses, vans, pickup trucks and station wagons to heavy-duty trucks, truck-mounted cranes and aerial towers. Many were devised in the late 1800s and early 1900s with retractable steel-flanged wheels.

These may be purpose-built or temporarily or permanently converted by independent specialists or railroad maintenance shops, and have been used widely around the world.

Several automobile and truck manufacturers in the United States and Canada have provided versions of these vehicles: Ford (Model T), Jeep, British Leyland (Roadmaster), Toyota, White, etc.

Conversions have involved a fairly wide list of makes and were on the scene principally between 1920 and 1950. The list includes Fords, Pontiacs, Buicks, Jeeps, Lincolns, Packards, Dodges, Willys, Chevrolets, Chryslers, Cadillacs, Checkers, plus White and International trucks.

In the early days numerous attempts to adapt road vehicles to travel on railroad tracks were less than satisfactory because of problems in making the drive system efficient, and with different gage roads. If

This White Motor Company rail bus is one of three put in regular service by the Hawaiian Consolidated Railway, Ltd. They were purchased through the Thompson-Graf Edler Co. branch in San Francisco after a series of trial runs, one with a trailer. All proved to be very successful. Shown is a party of 45 businessmen from Hilo on a trial run to Hakalau. *(American Truck Historical Society)*

friction-drive was used, it also required that the vehicle be driven in reverse to achieve forward motion.

Today makers claim the switch from road vehicle to a fully-operational rail locomotive or vice-versa can be accomplished in only three to five minutes.

Who needs them? Users who may own or lease are railroads, rail contractors, interurban transit lines, industrial plants (chemicals, steel, cement, etc.), ports, airports and the military.

These road-legal hybrids have proved to be a boon to railroad lines, which employ them as an alternate to the traditional switcher/work train for tracks inspection,

maintenance, emergency service, yard shunting and short-haul business trips. Intermodal freight transport also yields welcome flexibility.

Two early examples of their use are interesting. A tramway-boat in 1899 was in service to play across two lakes north of Copenhagen, Denmark. Magrelem, a Swedish engineer, built this 11-ton amphibious steamboat with a 25 hp engine with action transmitted by a triple gear, either to the propeller or to the rimmed wheels. It accommodated 70 passengers.

In 1918 interurban service between El Centro and Holtville, two small cities a few miles apart in the extreme southern part of California, was maintained by a bus built much like a streetcar with wheels designed for both railway and highway. The inner half of each wheel was flanged to follow a steel rail. The outer half was equipped with an ordinary solid rubber tire. It held 17 passengers and driver with a rear luggage rack. Small wedges placed alongside the track permitted it to run on or off roads without difficulty.

Between 1901 and 1908 Charles Glidden of Boston, Massachusetts, took a marathon international tour by car of over 46,000 miles in 39 countries. When his various Napiers ran out of road, he fitted flanged wheels on and bowled over the railroads.

When the first car reported crossing Australia in 1913 it spent much of its time thumping over railroad tracks to avoid being bogged down in sand.

In 1924 the late Austin F. Bement and Edward S. Evans made the first reported automobile trip in Canada from Winnipeg, Manitoba, to Vancouver, British Columbia, fitting their vehicle with flanges to allow them to use the Canadian Pacific Railroad tracks where the roads were too rough for motor travel.

Other vehicles adapted to rails have been motorcycles and bicycles. Colorado inventor William Gillum integrated a bicycle into his railbike. It had a three-wheel outrigger design adjustable to various gages. The wheels were eight inches in diameter with rubber tires with wide grooves cut in so that they would fit on the edges of the rails. Gillum founded the American Railbike Association.

Considering all these exciting developments in multimodal vehicles, when can we realistically anticipate taking our best girl "flyin' and floatin'" in our Merry Oldsmobile? Don't hold your breath!

CHAPTER VIII

Government Vehicles

To provide adequately a multitude of growing services to their constituencies, government agencies at all levels have come to depend in a significant way on special use vehicles of all types. Whether it is a city, county, state or federal government department involved, there is a vast pool of unusual mobile units pressed into service to perform needed functions. The principal uses are in behalf of the armed forces, education, law enforcement, health, social services and transportation.

Local Jurisdictions

FIRE PREVENTION

Most municipal fire departments naturally focus their use of mobile units on fire prevention programs. In 1976 the Lansing, Michigan, Fire Department put into service a custom-designed emergency mobile medical/surgical unit, a GMC Transmode. In 1977 both the township of Cranford, New Jersey, and the Montgomery County, Maryland, Division of Fire Prevention set up fire detection demonstra-

tion vans to educate the public. Audiovisual exhibits were used and smoke alarms shown at shopping centers and other locales.

Mobile fire safety houses came into play in the 1990s. Most of these are 35-foot, two-story, multiroom, four-wheel trailers and can be found in several cities in Washington, Ohio, Pennsylvania and Michigan. To battle chemical spills, quite a few cities now have special hazardous materials command units equipped with computers and communications equipment linked to Chemtrack in Washington, D.C.

SANITATION SERVICES

A boon in the mid–1980s arrived for the sewerage divisions of the departments of public works: a Telespector, which gives a clear, color picture to the viewing stations of underground conditions. The small camera transmits in a special self-contained van which houses all necessary equipment and video facilities in its control room.

In 1989 New York City equipped its

This Skagit County, Washington, mobile children's fire safety smoke house is typical of the units now found in many communities. They are taken to schools and events where children gather and are designed to teach them how to exist safely a home in a fire. Drills in the trailer in simulated blazes offer valuable lifesaving tips on fire and burn prevention. *(Steve Berentson Photography)*

street-sweeping vehicles with public address systems for this message: "This is Ed Koch, your mayor. You know the Sanitation Department cannot sweep this street if you don't move your illegally parked car. Please get it outta here!"

ANIMAL CONTROL

The Ohio County, West Virginia, Animal Control Department has converted a van into an ambulance with emergency equipment. The extensively refitted, customized vehicle is a service both for pets and wild animals, available 24 hours a day at no charge.

ELECTIONS

Mobile voting registration is set up by city clerks in many states in such vehi-

cles as Super Ford Club Wagons. These are parked mostly on weekends at educational institutions and shopping centers. Often they are on loan from local auto dealers. Trailer polling places can also be found in many smaller communities.

COURTS

Improvised, temporary mobile courts are set up for a variety of reasons. For example in 1972 in Los Angeles, California, the chief of police provided a bus at the airport for hijackers who had surrendered in order to expedite immediate legal processing. Subsequently in the 1970s, 1980s and 1990s such courts on trailers or mobile homes were necessitated by wildcat strikes, overcrowding of existing courtrooms and fires. Probation officers also sometimes counsel their clients in vehicles.

PARKS AND RECREATION

The parks and recreation and public works departments in cities in such states as Illinois, New York, Michigan and Ohio have made excellent use of mobile units since the 1950s. Most of these special vehicles reveal their purpose in their names: Skatemobile, Puppet Wagon, Showmobile, Playmobile, Fun Wagon, Fitness Van, Playbus, Movie Mobile, Fashionmobile, Tennis Truck and Zoo Van. In addition to the United States such units can be found in countries like Canada, England and Japan.

The most widely used one is the Swimobile, introduced by Fruehauf in 1969. Especially popular at such civic events as block parties, swimobiles were often funded by local donors such as television stations. They have now found their way to Rochester and Syracuse, New York, and in various cities in Hawaii, Michigan and Illinois. The 30-foot aluminum semitrailer truck chassis is eight feet wide and four feet deep, water-tight with all seams welded, a special surface nonslip floor, a flip-up side platform and a pair of access ladders. They are equipped with a pumper, filter, skimmer and a front-mounted water heating system. They hold about 8,000 gallons of water which is changed twice a day and can be easily filled from fire hydrants in about half an hour. Companion trucks containing portable showers and restroom facilities accompany the mobile pools.

CLERK'S OFFICE

Jennie Nelson was clerk of Seney Township, Michigan, for 64 years before retiring, operating the entire time out of a mobile home since 1921. It is believed that she held office for the longest time of any publicly elected official in the nation's history.

STATE VEHICLES

In 1997 the Michigan secretary of state acquired a mobile branch office. It is a full-service facility, consisting of a van and a 24-foot trailer, handicapped acces-

It may look like only an old gravel hauler, but to an inner-city child in a congested area on a hot day it's a Swimobile! Shown is one of a fleet of four operated by the Detroit Parks and Recreation Department. They can accommodate about 300 to 500 boys and girls a day at neighborhood locations. The crew consists of a driver, two laborers and the lifeguard. *(Courtesy Detroit Department of Parks and Recreation)*

Providing full services in a mobile unit is no mean task, but that is exactly what the Michigan secretary of state does. Schedules are arranged to serve the maximum number of customers. The trailer requires electric and telephone hookups. Staff consists of a manager and clerk. *(Courtesy Michigan Secretary of State)*

sible with a service window at the front. It is taken to both small towns and areas with large customer populations such as auto companies, other manufacturers and businesses and nonprofit agencies, as well as fairs, civic events, senior housing and mall openings. Outside decorations resemble a Michigan license plate, blue and orange with the Mackinac Bridge as a graphic.

Some similar state agencies use a custom-designed mobile automated driver's license testing van. There are two models: a 27-foot fiberglass body and a 34-foot aluminum body.

In the early 1970s several states, including Illinois, Indiana and Ohio, acquired Showmobiles for their lotteries. Drawings are held on portable stages on trailers which unfold; customized vans and motor homes are also used.

National Vehicles

ARMED FORCES

History is replete with accounts of military mobility. According to mythology, the Greeks finally won the ten-year Trojan War by making a huge trick wooden horse on wheels. Julius Caesar's mobile office was a chest carried on a cart. Emperor Napoleon I used a big, green traveling coach or carriage on the road as a command post between campaigns. On January 29, 1776, General George Washington ordered a specially equipped wagon to use as a field headquarters. Famous English nurse and heroine of the Crimean War Florence Nightingale operated in a mobile hospital. In the Civil War there were over 60 mobile military hospitals

The Michigan State Lottery Community Event Team mobile unit tours the state. The 24-foot Chevrolet van body is customized for advertisements, performances and presentations on the ten-foot by 12-foot stage in front. In the rear motion pictures are shown. Favorite sites are county fairs and other community events, shopping centers, games and so on. Nicknames for the unit include Dream Machine and Luck Truck. *(Courtesy Michigan Bureau of State Lottery)*

scattered through the western theater's transient battle lines. The automobile made a dramatic entrance as a weapon of war when General Gallieni's famed Taxicab Army saved Paris in World War I in the course of the first battle of the Marne.

There are at least 75 common, well-recognized mobile units used by the various arms and branches of the service on the home front, in training camps and war theaters. Some units on wheels are common to two or more groups, such as dental, spare parts, repair shops, water purification, recruiting, command posts, etc. Other vehicles are only used for particular functions occasioned by the nature of the objective, such as mobile water pollution laboratories maintained by the Coast Guard; mobile television coaches of the Signal Corps; or alert quarters and flight simulations for the Air Corps.

The Army by far has the most different mobile units, putting wheels on hospitals; gymnasiums; bookmobiles; kitchens; laundries; post exchanges; photography studios; printing plants; radio stations and recording studios; video production; showers; etc. Its new SmarTruck has headlights that detect and disorient the enemy, electrified door handles, smokescreen, pepper spray blasters and bullet-proof glass, with oil slick or tire-puncturing tacks to disable vehicles behind it. All this on a Ford F-350 pickup.

Some unusual military uses of mobile units deserve mention:

- Mobile pigeon lofts for carrier pigeon messages in World War I
- Vans parked on the street in downtown areas like that of Chicago in World War II as a focus to encourage civilians to accept jobs in area defense plants
- *Mobile Army Surgical Hospitals* operating successfully only one-half hour from the front lines, made famous by the film

and 1972–1983 prime time television series *M*A*S*H*
- Wolfmobile, a Persian Gulf War hot dog and fast food stand to supplement nourishing but bland mess hall chow
- Mini jet powered by an electric golf cart motor used in parades and various community events by the Air Force
- Four traveling Air Force theaters, cockpit vans featuring two virtual reality shows simultaneously to educate the public and foster recruiting at schools and public events
- Vegetable garden grown in three trailers by the Navy in space habitat research in Newfoundland, developed by General Electric in 1977
- Mobile labs with air filters for the National Guard anti-terrorism team, for preparedness training to respond to nuclear, chemical or biological attacks
- In 2000 the Air Force launched an interactive display for recruiting in two 53-foot custom trailers with an F-16 fighter jet and six simulators, observation roof deck and searchlights. The display has so far made 66 appearances in 30 cities before 36,000 people
- Traveling exhibit by the Canadian Coast Guard highlighting its varied roles and emphasizing boat safety

It took the Bicentennial in 1976 to bring all the services together in a combined mobile effort. The U.S. Defense Department sponsored the Armed Forces Bicentennial Caravan: four identical traveling exhibits for each major branch of the service (Army, Navy, Marines and Air Force). These became quickly the nucleus of local celebrations and observances. The specially painted 40-foot red, white and blue trucks visited smaller communities in all states. In the exhibits and audiovisual presentations history was emphasized. Expandable sides gave each van over 480 square feet of space. At every site they

The Canadian Coast Guard and Auxiliary use six colorful display trucks to reach the public. They feature boating safety messages in the Central and Arctic Regions, visiting marinas, boat shows, yacht clubs, boating organizations, schools, camps and parks. Viewers are urged to take courses and get wallet cards. The swingout panels provide a wide expanse of exhibit area. Note the bilingual English-French signage. *(Courtesy Mobilexhibit)*

were displayed as a group. Power units were International Harvester II cab-over heavy-duty trucks.

What has been reported thus far on American military vehicles with a few exceptions is representative of the other major powers.

From time to time reports come in accusing various countries of maintaining spy vehicles with listening devices and filming equipment, especially in border areas.

Mobile nuclear missiles can be launched from trucks, railway cars, barges and even dirigibles according to those involved in such operations.

Civil defense and disaster preparedness activities are normally confined to the local community levels and wax and wane depending on the threat of war. When in operation the programs use trailer command posts and communication centers. Disaster programs concentrate on educating the public in such places as California and Japan on how to cope with earthquakes. Vans that realistically tremble and shake get the points across dramatically.

POST OFFICE

To maintain its mobility, the U.S. Postal Service has even had to enlist the aid of animals. Camels were briefly used in 1857 to carry the mail between Army posts and small settlements in the old West. Mules are still used to haul mail along a winding trail into the Grand Canyon to a Native American village. Around the turn of the century rural carriers also delivered groceries and collected and returned laundry. There is also a Great Lakes maritime mail service.

Highway post office buses operated from 1941 to 1974. Today van and house trailer post offices cover special events and operate at peak periods like Christmas and tax deadlines to supplement fixed locations. They often offer special commemorative stamps and cancellations. Mobile repair facilities came in the 1970s, 40-foot redesigned Dorsey trailers whose midsections expanded from eight feet to 16 feet wide.

Overseas postal services report some innovations. France began in 1962 to circulate in Marseilles five days a week on a scheduled route a fully-equipped truck, and in Scotland since 1985 school buses have done double-duty in the postal service. The driver drops off the bus, using its hydraulic lifts and pull-down legs and mates it with a van body as the chassis becomes a mail truck. In certain areas these buses are allowed to carry passengers on their mail routes.

CENSUS

To motivate participation in the national head count was the specific objective of the Census 2000 60-day Road tour of 12 colorful, 28-foot U.S. Department of Commerce Bureau of the Census motor home Censusmobiles. In 400 cities an all-out effort focused on schools, libraries, city halls, community centers, supermarkets, theaters, restaurants, fairs and other places where people gather. On board each vehicle were five kiosk-like portable exhibits in

Under the provocative slogan "This Is Your Future. Don't Leave It Blank," 12 of these U.S. Census Bureau motor homes hit the road to urge full participation in the 2000 census. They carried displays, handouts and prizes in the roadshow production. *(Courtesy U.S. Census Bureau)*

Custom mobile X-ray scans enable the Canadian Customs to detect illegal contraband. The device is a valuable high-tech tool for interdiction and intelligence operations. The machines are built into self-contained Ford vans which can operate at 30 degrees centigrade. They provide maximum security, especially concerning illegal drugs at bridges, tunnels and airports. *(Courtesy Canadian Department of National Revenue: Customs and Excise)*

multiple languages and boxes of handout literature. This effort surpassed the 1990 minivans with loudspeakers.

CUSTOMS

The U.S. Customs Service uses mobile units at border stations at the Canadian border of Washington and British Columbia, Canada, and a trailer at the Mexican border. The Detroit office in 1988 acquired a 53-foot, high-tech firearms training trailer which is used by federal and local law enforcement officers. Video scenes of staged crimes are shown on a screen to get participants to react. The unit travels as far as Minneapolis from its permanent base in Detroit.

Canadian Customs started to use in 1989 Can-X-Scan X-ray vans in all of its ten provinces, available to any law officer from the local police to the Northwest Mounties. Objects to be viewed are placed on a conveyor belt that runs through the vehicle, and the X-ray images show up guns, drugs, knives and other suspicious objects on two monitors inside. They are deployed at commercial warehouses, airports, docks, border crossings, postal stations and virtually any accessible location.

In Belfast, Ireland, the British customs agents use mobile posts. Some have been wrecked by terrorist explosions.

INTERNAL REVENUE

Back in the 1930s the Internal Revenue Alcohol Tax Unit employed "The

Under the catchphrase "Moonshine Kills," Alcohol, Tobacco and Firearms agents of the U.S. Treasury sent this exhibit vehicle on tour to warn against the illicit beverage. Illegal firearms were also covered with exhibits and handouts. *(Courtesy Alcohol, Tobacco and Firearms Division, U.S. Treasury Dept.)*

Dog," a Ford with an air scoop attached to the roof. It was intended to sniff out illegal stills in the woodlands by picking up yeast germs in the air from fermenting mash and relating them to suspected areas.

In 1969 the concept of employing a vehicle to warn the public about the hazards of using moonshine whiskey was originally developed by Alcohol, Tobacco and Firearms agents of the U.S. Treasury Department in Georgia. It was subsequently adopted by South Carolina and Florida and extended then to other states, using trailers and vans. The vehicles have been exhibited at shopping centers, fairs, parades, schools and training seminars. A firearms display trailer has also been sent out for public display.

In the 1970s the agency began to provide Uncle Sam Taxmobiles. These were rented motor homes, vans and trailers used to give free tax assistance in such districts as Philadelphia, Indianapolis, Brooklyn and Chicago. Locations chosen included shopping centers, main streets, high schools, city halls, churches and supermarkets.

FOREST SERVICE

Since 1972 the National Forest Service has operated self-contained crew trailers in the Tonto National Forest in Arizona. These trailers are designed to have separate sleeping areas for four persons, with a rear entrance and inside pocket doors to insure privacy. They are equipped to be hauled over rough terrain.

OTHER AGENCIES

Besides those agencies listed above, the federal government uses various mobile units in operations of the Immigration and Naturalization Service, National Bureau of Standards, Department of the Interior Bureau of Mines, Indian Affairs and Secretary of State.

Examples of foreign government mobile units include mobile immigration registration in Canada and in Saudi Arabia using 40-foot workshop semi-trailers coupled to Mercedes 1926 tractive units with awnings to provide a further 800 square feet of covered working area; a stores recovery unit built on a Mercedes 1926 four-wheel-drive chassis and a small lubrication trailer.

Shared Responsibility

Many agencies with mobile units operate at several local, state or national levels.

ECONOMIC DEVELOPMENT

In 1966 two states sent out promotional vehicles. The Florida Development Commission's Sun Coach Showcase displayed exhibits from various chambers of commerce aimed at vacationers, retirees and investors in property. It traveled to Northern states and set up at travel shows, giving out free orange juice. The Labor and Industry Division of the New Jersey Conservation and Economic Development Department featured omnibus mobile exhibits in a 22-ton van on a trade mission with 105 New Jersey firms involved. It went to Mexico and Central America in cooperation with the U.S. Department of Commerce.

The Ohio Department of Agriculture in 1994 put out an Ohio Proud Van to visit 60 county fairs, festivals and special events to promote the state's number one industry. Some 50 companies that raise, grow or process Ohio products participated.

The Department of Industry and Development of the Alberta Government in British Columbia, Canada, launched a "Buy Alberta" campaign in 1963–64 with a trailer full of samples which visited over 60 fairs and exhibitions under the operation of the Publicity Bureau. This informative undertaking was designed in part to make people of the province aware of the variety of manufacturing; the definitive objective was to encourage new manufacturers. Both sides of the 26-foot-long, nine-foot-high vehicle opened outward, clam-shell style, with one half forming the floor and the other the roof of a porch with steps. The trailer was also used by other government departments.

Again in 1967 Canada's Centennial Commission, to mark the Canadian Confederation (1867–1967), designed eight 23-foot truck trailer exhibits each of 27,000 cubic feet. Canadian Pacific and

This free exhibit was part of a radio-mail-display program urging Canadians in Alberta to purchase goods made in the province. *(Courtesy Alberta Department of Industry and Development Publicity Bureau)*

Canadian National Railway participated. The complete caravan included a train with six cars and three station wagons. At the time special permission to move such large vehicles, said to be the largest on North American roads, had to be obtained.

The Trade Publicity Branch of the Department of Trade and Industry in Australia uses a mobile exhibit, a tandem expandable show van.

In 1970 the Japan Association for the 1970 World Exposition sent out two specially customized exhibit utility vans to the United States and Canada. Fragile displays were transported successfully due to the design of the vehicles.

EDUCATION

Local mobile projects initiated by school districts at the city and county levels began in the 1960s and have maintained a fairly steady momentum ever since, peaking in the 1990s.

Early efforts were largely refurbished school buses and motor homes and similar made-over vehicles. Then new stock models came into play, until today many customized vehicles reflect both expanded budgets and enlightened attitudes. Over half of the states have had mobile educational units with New York, Pennsylvania, California, Tennessee, Virginia and Washington in the forefront of activity.

An older school bus was made into this efficient teaching vehicle for Sylvania, Ohio, public schools. David Stanley, director of computer services for the school district, works at a terminal of the Technology Bus. A custom built unit would run an estimated four times the cost of this refurbishing effort. (Toledo Blade, *photograph by Dave Zapotosky*)

What do schools on wheels teach?

A ranking would probably run computer skills first, followed by remedial reading, science, vocational education and math. Less frequently seen are preschool; speech and hearing; art; special education; safety; music; languages; and adult education.

These mobile schools have been a boon especially to isolated, sparsely populated, remote rural areas, and often are supported by federal money.

Exceptional creativity has gone into some of these vehicles. At Pierce Elementary School in Birmingham, Michigan, a 40-foot, white and black, 1974 Ford Spaceliner school bus has been converted into a mock shuttle craft. The passenger section of the bus was blacked out to simulate the darkness of a shuttle trip and television monitors played a tape of a

launch. The lift-off was simulated by using a fire extinguisher spewing smoke from metal cans attached to the rear of the bus. To complete the metamorphosis the vehicle boasts a nose cone and wings that lower for "landing."

The Sylvania Public Schools near Toledo, Ohio, in 1994 converted a school bus into a technology bus to teach computer keyboard skills at seven elementary schools. To turn the bus into a classroom the windows were replaced with sheet metal, new doors installed, and steps, lights, heating, air conditioning, carpeting and two banks of ten desks and seats were added.

The Phoenix Central School District in Phoenix, New York, also converted a school bus into a maintenance vehicle. The back section was separated with a body-cutting saw and 12 feet removed from the center. The back section was then welded to the front. It is also used for towing and pushing stalled buses.

State departments of education have been active with vehicles since the 1970s, mostly in vocational education and driver training or specialized sight, hearing and speech and addressing the needs of migrants and preschoolers.

During the 1976 Bicentennial Celebration the Ohio Department of Education sent out a Heritage Van as a traveling museum in a converted school bus.

In foreign countries mobile cinema and radio vans were a somewhat primitive but effective means of education going back to the 1930s in Russia, East Africa and Asia. At least 30 different countries were active with these types of fundamental educational presentations, much of it for illiterates. Vehicles used included cars, station wagons, pickup trucks, light delivery trucks and vans. The practice persisted until the 1950s.

Modern government-sponsored training has now emerged in several countries and geographic areas:

- Russia: mobile laboratories available at specified intervals for correspondence students
- Brazil: literacy bus fleets plus trailers and railway cars
- Puerto Rico: narcotics abuse prevention vehicles
- South Pacific Islands: literacy and vocational skills vans
- Australia: teacher training units

Numerous mobile programs of a varied nature are also reported from Japan, the Philippines, Iraq and other nations.

Very extensive use of mobile training has taken place in Great Britain. In 1967, for example, seven 59-foot mobile units were produced for the Ministry of Technology Production Engineering Advisory Service. The trailers were used in a four-year program to show films and for demonstrations and lectures. Engineering works throughout Britain were visited to introduce new techniques in production and engineering. The towing vehicle was a large cab designed as a mobile cinema and lecture room constructed on a Bedford passenger vehicle chassis. On top of the cab was a steel framed Perspex dome to house film projection equipment, fully divided from the main body, which was equipped to seat 28. The bodywork was constructed from patent interlocking extruded aluminum. The towed trailer was designed as a demonstration unit mounted on a four-wheeled chassis with turntable steering and a roof with translucent Perspex panels. When set up for operation the two units were linked with a hinged annex forming an entrance lobby with access from either side.

LIBRARY

Mobile libraries are traced back to Maryland in 1912 with the Washington County Free Library in Hagerstown, whose International Harvester truck replaced the horsedrawn produce wagon which had been visiting farms and villages three times a week. Bookmobiles subsequently have spread across the country and the world using everything from small panel trucks to semi-trailers under city, county and state auspices. There are an estimated 1,200 in the United States alone. Outreach programs bring bookmobiles to shut-ins and migrants and some are used now for computer classes.

Church bookmobiles are covered in the chapter on religious vehicles and public service bookmobiles in the charity vehicle chapter.

LAW ENFORCEMENT

Police and sheriff's departments at the local and state levels and the Federal Bureau of Investigation as well as the U.S. Marshal look to mobile units for many of their special needs. After World War II vehicles began to be acquired and the trend has maintained a fairly steady pace, reflecting some ups and downs due to budget restraints. In many situations all or part of the money required has been donated by local car dealers, fraternal organizations or other sources.

The Chicago Police Department has produced excellent examples of versatile vehicles.

In 1964 its Marksman-mobile Truck was revealed for the first time to the public. It patrols the streets day and night manned by sharpshooter officers from the special operations group. It is stocked with enough heavy weapons and ammunition to handle "any situation that might come up," including hostage-taking. It can be readily converted into a conference room, auditorium, emergency communications station or community service unit, and can be adapted for parades through the use of placards and displays mounted on the roof and sides.

Later in 1973 its Exhibit Cruiser Program for the Bureau of Community Services was a custom-built trailer 40 feet long, ten feet wide, and 11 feet, 6 inches high. The General Body was all-steel construction with sectional Lindsay-type framing, weather-tight seals, shutters and readily demountable exterior fixtures. There were two doors and two rear projection windows. Two sections housed exhibits and audiovisual equipment. The project had three basic objectives: educate the public on the department, enlist support in crime abatement, and promote recruiting applicants.

The most common uses for police units are as field command posts and mini precinct stations, and to conduct drug abuse programs. Whether a van, bus or motor home, it may also serve as a facility for rape counseling, accident investigations or traffic safety. In Los Angeles; Olympia, Washington; and New York City vehicles are actually used to book suspects on site, administer breathalyzer tests for drunks and provide temporary incarceration on the way to the station and jail. Placerville, California, started in 1975 to put on skits for tourists featuring a portable truck "gallows" for members of the Apple Hill Gang of train robbers when they were captured by the sheriff. Some states also use mobile crime labs.

A unique two-wheel portable speed indicator is now used in many cities, operated by battery packs. This SMART trailer (Special Monitoring Awareness Radar Trailer) records and displays speeds of all passing vehicles.

In at least ten states house trailers are used as temporary cells, halfway houses, offices, libraries and for conjugal visits. Prisoners in Michigan trusty farms, camps and outside-the-wall cellblocks are visited by a 22-foot converted house trailer commissary.

The FBI favors undercover surveillance vans and the U.S. Marshal has had a mobile crisis command center trailer custom-built with a meeting room, dual generators, and heating and cooling systems. An eight-foot diameter satellite antenna is stowed into a roof well, and is automatically deployed at set-up.

In 1973 a proposal was made but never implemented suggesting private industry sponsorship of trailer training for prisoners on an on-site, pre-release basis. The hope was to afford them marketable skills as they reentered society.

"When can I call my lawyer?" he seems to be pleading as he is en route to the pokey. Years ago in Los Angeles, California, the police incarcerated miscreants on the spot, as in this case. Other police departments across the nation that have been reported as having similar "sidecar justice" are in Washington state and New York. That padlock looks pretty secure, doesn't it? *(Los Angeles Police Historical Society)*

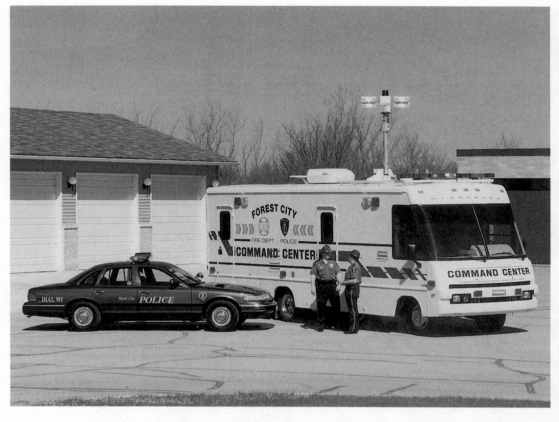

This Forest City, Iowa, combined police and fire Winnebago motorhome command post gives this community a versatile vehicle in every sense of the word. While intended essentially for family recreation, these units have multiple commercial applications. Note the vital communications equipment on the roof. Headquarters facilities can be brought to any emergency situation where mobility is available in a vehicle. *(Courtesy Forest City Police Department)*

HEALTH CARE SERVICES

To take proper care of a variety of health needs, cities, counties, states and the federal government turn to mobility as the logical answer. Units have come on stream regularly since the 1950s. Two of the earliest efforts were those of the American Samoa Public Health Program and the New Mexico Department of Public Health mobile chest X-ray, both in the mid–1950s.

City mobile health care is largely devoted to emergency care, mostly coronary; poison control; speech and hearing difficulties and mental health. Other top-

ics covered are drug addiction, dentistry and X-ray. Counties stress immunization for children, breast cancer detection, dental care and migrant workers' needs. State departments appear to be preoccupied with dentistry, X-ray, speech and hearing, Native American problems and mental health. The national emphases are upon mothers and infants, dental care, food and drug control, research into disease and Native American needs.

A van with a crew of two paramedics and a driver regularly visits remote Papago Native American villages in Arizona. There are 75 villages widely scattered in 4,300 square miles of desert near the Mex-

This is one of a fleet of 12 self-contained mobile laboratories of the U.S. Food and Drug Administration's program of ship-to-shore inspections of imported goods. Each of the specially designed units contains facilities for analysis equipment and instruments for on-the-spot dockside sampling. They are all designed with forward control chassis with insulated aluminum bodies. *(Courtesy U.S. Food and Drug Administration, U.S. Department of Health, Education and Welfare)*

ican border. Health checkups have been provided since 1976. The program known as STARPAHC (Space Technology Applied to Rural Papago Advanced Health Care) contacts through a microwave transmitter doctors at the hospital, who tune in the patient using television monitors, scan X-rays on the screen, or plug into the van microcomputer to consult records.

Outside the United States, Great Britain has probably made the most consistent use of mobile health programs in its health authorities in England and Scotland. Other active countries in this area are Canada, Mexico, Egypt, Russia, Venezuela and many others. Family planning is stressed. India even sends out elephants with birth control devices to remote areas.

SOCIAL SERVICES

The umbrella terms "social services" and "consumer affairs" cover such aids as those rendered to the unemployed, senior citizens and street children. Mobile activity began building in the 1970s and continues.

Locally buses and vans go out to distribute food stamps, hear citizen complaints about products and services, register bicycles, etc. An example is Cleveland's Office of Consumer Affairs, set up in 1973 with a renovated 1955 GMC Transit Systems bus with a staff fluent in 18 different languages. Depending upon the business cycle, mobile help for the unemployed is critical and has taken place since the 1960s, mostly under the state aegis. Applicants are screened, tested and counseled on area openings for which they may qualify in such cities as Norfolk, Virginia; Philadelphia, Pennsylvania; Chicago, Illinois; and Concord, New Hampshire.

Counties typically use their vehicles to hear complaints, distribute food stamps, check health status, counsel on nutrition and the like.

States cater particularly to children, with toy lending libraries on wheels. They also provide clothing and advice on dealing with unscrupulous firms.

TOURISM

To attract visitors to a city or state, promotional buses or trucks are often part of the overall program. They have been employed effectively in such states as Florida and New Jersey and outside the United States in Canada, Wales and Mexico.

In 1999 Louisiana celebrated Franco Fete: the tricentennial, a year-long birthday party honoring 300 years of French influence as a unique cultural experience. It took its show on the road with a gaily-decorated bus full of famous Louisiana chefs, musicians and dancers as a portable party. It was shown in eight different cities and visited over 900 fairs, festivals and special events. To decorate the vehicle a vinyl-type removable wrap was applied with no harm to the existing paint. The project was coordinated by the Department of Culture, Recreation and Tourism with Delta Air Lines, Best Western Motels and Coca Cola as corporate sponsors.

MUSEUMS

Mobile museum projects have involved several counties, states and the federal government in various countries.

In 2000 a mobile sculpture display designed to tell the history of Lenawee County, Michigan, went on the road. It had 280 illustrated panels on seven columns by 100 different artists. Funding was by the Adrian City Commission.

Several states have had so-called Historymobiles, including Wisconsin, North Carolina, New Jersey, Michigan and Illinois. Often commercial sponsors were involved: R.J. Reynolds in North Carolina

This mobile clinic in Cairo, Egypt, offers women contraceptives and family planning advice. Such health and education programs have to overcome cultural barriers and are not always compatible with militant ethnic and religious groups in the country. It is operated by the government's Ministry of Population and Family Welfare *(AP/Wide World Photos)*

The Philadelphia Commission on Human Relations took help for problems directly to the people with this Helpmobile van. Staff members listened to complaints in the neighborhoods about bad housing, racial discrimination, or whatever else was on the citizen's mind. *(Courtesy Philadelphia Commission on Human Relations)*

and Bell Telephone and Ford in New Jersey. In the 1980s the Georgia Council for the Arts had a bus featuring contemporary artists' programs aimed at students, teachers and parents.

In 1987 the Smithsonian Institution in Washington, D.C, featured a Roads to Liberty exhibit cosponsored by the American Express Company. In 1988 a rolling museum in tractor trailers criss-crossed Australia to celebrate its two-hundredth birthday. It reached the most remote Outback communities to bring them the nation's history, culture and accomplishments.

TRANSPORTATION

Special mobile units participate in road, rail and air transportation programs at the local, state and national government levels. These programs cover such topics as safety, road maintenance, traffic congestion and courtesy patrols.

To promote school bus safety, the De Soto County Schools in Hernando, Mississippi, in 1998 developed Sidney's Safety Bus, a fully-equipped vehicle fitted with a television set, videocassette recorder and surround-sound stereo system. It visits area kindergarten and elementary schools and neighboring counties in Mississippi and Tennessee. The Suffolk County, New

York, school districts set up a school bus safety classroom with the help of a federal grant in 1978. Colorado, Missouri and Oklahoma state agencies have all produced mobile exhibits and similar safety efforts.

Nationally the U.S. Transportation Department in 1970 started using a mobile motor vehicle inspection facility, and in 1985 promoted automobile seat belts and child safety restraints with a replica of the Flintmobile from the popular cartoon *The Flintstones*. Traffic safety displays have also been put on wheels by Great Britain and Saudi Arabia.

To implement road maintenance and signage upgrading, local jurisdictions use a special van which photo-logs streets and highways for replacement periodically. In England its PROFLOMETER trailer towed behind a van by the Transport and Road Research Laboratory began in 1983 to aim at preventing crushed pavement by heavy trucks. It measures ruts, cracks and potholes.

To promote carpooling in a most unusual fashion, the California Transportation Department ordered a car made from parts of a Ford LTD, Volkswagen Beetle, Chevrolet Corvair and Chevrolet Vega. The composite vehicle was intended to symbolize four commuters who rode to work in the same car to save gas.

Freeway Courtesy Patrols to aid stranded motorists have been sent out by the State of Colorado, and include the Mexican Green Angel fleet. Since 1968 Dearborn, Michigan, has provided free gasoline to drivers who run out.

Turning to the air, truck-mounted air traffic control towers are used here and abroad on a temporary basis, with other navigational aids, radar units and transmitting stations.

Combined government-industry support backed the planned 1967 Helicopters USA traveling exhibit. This group of eight

educational mobile units was to visit colleges and high school campuses. Sponsored signed were 14 prime industry manufacturers, 24 allied manufacturers and seven government agencies, including the Federal Aviation Agency.

The National Air and Space Administration (NASA) in 1964 displayed its Spacemobile, a traveling space science demonstration unit at universities.

In support of the exotic, one-of-a-kind vehicles actually used in space NASA has used mobile units for testing, staging, radiographic processing, space awareness, final review, quarantine, transfer and tracking.

Conrail took out in 1989 a mobile safety exhibit in a semi-truck which showed up at sites like city parks displaying the slogan "Please don't meet us at the crossing!"

ENVIRONMENT

Ecological concerns have focused since the 1970s mostly on air and water pollution at the local, state and national levels of government in the United States and in countries like Canada, Great Britain and Mexico. Vans, buses and trailers are used to inspect vehicles with exhaust emission tests, and mobile labs are set up at plant sites and other strategic locations to monitor air quality continually. Mobile water testing is also a common activity.

Special units address unique environmental problems. County agricultural extension agents operate mobile labs to determine the amount of nitrogen in farm soil in regard to the need for fertilizer and avoidance of groundwater contamination. The National Severe Storm Laboratory takes weather instruments out in trucks to report on significant meteorological aspects of tornadoes. The Environmental Protection Agency has designed a mobile incinerator that can destroy hazardous

This unique eight-ton, off-the-road NASA vehicle is a mobile geological laboratory that contributed to valuable scientific information for early manned landings on the lunar surface by U.S. astronauts. It was built by General Motors for the U.S. Geological Survey and designed for rugged terrain to test instruments of space ships bound for the moon. *(Courtesy NASA)*

wastes, such as toxic chemicals, on site. It is mounted on three flatbed trailers and stretches for about a block.

ENERGY

Although most mobile energy programs are federally-based, some state departments of commerce since 1985 have developed specially equipped vans to roam through neighborhoods to record heat loss in homes.

Various traveling exhibits from federal agencies have promoted specific types of energy: solar energy by the U.S. Department of Housing and Urban Devel-

opment; nuclear energy by the Tennessee Valley Authority; and atomic energy by the Atomic Energy Commission. These activities began in the 1970s.

AGRICULTURE

Mobile exhibits have been used to promote agriculture.

In 1961 the New Jersey Department of Agriculture used a Farmobile exhibit at county fairs, shopping centers, banks, schools and special events. It was a 20-foot trailer that told the entire story on the outside on three different panels. Hinged sides lifted up to provide cover for audiences. Two rear-screen projectors with mirrors presented a continuous sequence of color slides, and the center area displayed presentations of versatility and quality of 18 different farm products raised in the state. It took 20 minutes to set up. In the 1970s the U.S. Department of Agriculture had a 25-foot traveling exhibit vehicle; England and the Netherlands have also used mobiles for agriculture.

There is at least one other category of "government vehicles," that of heads of state. Americans are familiar with presidential limousines, but few have seen such conveyances in their most extreme forms. When the late President Ferdinand Marcos and his wife Imelda were in power in the Philippines in the 1980s their palace garage boasted 25 different vehicles. A fully-equipped, 40-foot mobile hospital painted in rainbow colors followed the president, who reportedly suffered from a serious kidney disease. His wife traveled in a luxurious bus replete with thick maroon carpeting, cream-colored wallpaper, 14 armchairs facing a bar and television, two beds, a kitchen, bath and the statue of Christ as a boy on the dashboard.

CHAPTER IX

The Future of Special Use Vehicles

Special use vehicles have indeed come of age. It is probably inevitable that the more aggressive organizations would choose literally to chase their audiences out on the road rather than wait for them to come to more traditional fixed-base locations.

Overall there appears to be a reasonably bright future for special use vehicles. Several significant factors presently developing into apparently long-term trends point in a positive direction. They include:

- Improvements in trailer construction as to flexibility and roominess through single and double slide-out expandable units combined with hydraulic operation
- Auxiliary attachments to enhance drawing power, such as giant inflatables and searchlights
- Optional equipment such as complete audio and video capabilities and radio broadcast facilities
- Animated and computer-based interactive displays, 3D effects and simulations
- Dramatic breakthroughs in full-color exterior graphics designed on rivetless sidewalls

With so many technological improvements, it seems likely that businesses will continue to find new uses for specially modified vehicles. Firms presently using the medium may decide to increase their use, and new organizations will probably come into the fold.

Special use vehicles will likely enjoy increasing stature and prestige—and will continue to attract attention while doing business worldwide.

APPENDIX

List of Productmobiles

Novelty advertising vehicles have been built in an astonishing variety of shapes, representing food products, animals, toys, and more. Here is an alphabetical sampling.

Acorn
Airplane
Ale Bottle
Amusement Park Ride
Aspirin
Auto Meter
Banana
Barbershop
Barn
Baseball Cap
Bat
Bathtub
Battery
Bed
Bee
Beer Bottle
Beer Can
Blacksmith Shop
Boat
Boot
Bowling Pin
Bullet
Bungalow

Caboose
Cake
Camera
Candy Kiss
Candy Roll
Canoe
Cash Register
Cathedral
Chicken
Church
Cigar
Cigarette Lighter
Circus
Clock
Coffin
Cola Bottle
Cola Can
Cow
Dog
Drainage Pipe
Drugstore
Egg
Football

Fort
Guitar
Hamburger
Helmet
Horse
House
Ice Cream Bar
Ice Cream Carton
Light Bulb
Loaf of Bread
Lobster
Mailbox
Mattress
Milk Carton
Mouse
Muffler
Mummy
Nose
Oleomargarine Carton
Orange
Orange Juice Can
Ostrich Feather Plume
Peanut
Piano
Pickle

Pinball Machine
Pipe
Pool Table
Popcorn Popper
Refrigerator
Rocket Ship
Roller Skate
Shoe
Skull
Space Shuttle
Spark Plug
Stereo Speaker (Automotive)
Swan
Swimming Pool
Tank
Telephone
Thermos Bottle
Toothpaste Tube
Toy
Train
Vacuum Cleaner
Video Game
Whale
Wireless Set
World Globe

Glossary

Air Car *see* **Sky Car**

Amphibious Able to travel both on land and in the water

Art Car Vehicle decorated with outrageous, whimsical ornamentation to represent the personality of the owner or to constitute a work of art

Articulated Having two or more sections permanently or semipermanently connected by a joint that can pivot for operation as a unit

Beach Wagon *see* **Station Wagon**

Bookmobile Vehicle with shelves of books, tapes, etc., that serves as a traveling library or bookstore

Bus Large motor-driven vehicle designed to carry passengers on a fixed route or under charter

Camper Motor vehicle equipped as a self-contained traveling home, smaller than a motor home; trailer hauled by a car

Camper Trailer *see* **Camper**

Canteen Temporary or mobile restaurant

Caravan Group of vehicles traveling together in a file; covered vehicle; van; motortruck equipped as a traveling living quarters or office, trailer (U.K.)

Cavalcade Procession or sequence of vehicles

Chassis Main frame, wheels and working parts upon which is mounted the body and engine of a vehicle

Cinema Van Vehicle showing moving pictures outdoors

Cinemobile *see* **Cinema Van** (U.K.)

Citizens Band Radio Two-way, unlicensed radio communication device

CB Radio Abbreviation for Citizens Band Radio

Coach Automobile body, especially of a closed model; house trailer; bus designed for long-distance travel or sightseeing

Coffee Wagon Caterer truck

Concept Car One-of-a-kind experimental prototype featuring innovative options, alternative power sources, etc., used at auto shows, parades and the like

225

Conversion Structural changes and modifications in a vehicle to remodel it to go from one use or purpose to another

Convoy Train of vehicles

Custom Design Manufactured according to personal order and individual specifications; *see also* Purpose-Built

Double-Decker One level over another level for additional space in a bus, etc.

Double-Wide Mobile Home Two sections combined horizontally into a single unit while still retaining their individual chassis

Dragster Automobile rebuilt or stripped down for drag racing; *see also* **Hot Rod**

Drop Frame Having most or all of the floor at an unusually low level as the chassis of a truck, van or trailer

Expandable Home Mobile home with one or more room sections that fold, collapse or telescope into the principal unit

Fifth Wheel Trailer Coupling between tractor and trailer of a semi-trailer in the form of two discs rotating on each other for attaching a vehicle body to the front axle so as to support it in turning

Flatbed Motortruck or trailer with a body in the form of a platform or shallow box

Fleet A group of vehicles operated under unified control by an organization

Flying Car *see* **Sky Car**

Full Trailer Weight of trailer carried entirely on its own wheels

Funny Car Specialized dragster that has a one-piece molded body resembling the body of a mass-produced car

Go-Cart Light, open-framed car containing a small engine

Gooseneck Trailer Truck trailer whose forward part is arched like a goose's neck and swiveled to the motor unit

Gull Wing Airplane wing slanting upward from the fuselage for a short distance

and then leveling out

Hand-Made Fabricated manually, as distinguished from a machine or mechanical process

Highway Tractor *see* **Tractor Trailer**

Hot Rod Dragster; automobile rebuilt or modified for high speed and fast acceleration

Hovercraft Vehicle that can travel over both land and water, supported by a cushion of air that it creates by blowing air downward

Intermodal Being or involving transportation by more than one form of carrier during a single trip

Keepsake Vehicle Classic, old, antique, historic

Limited Edition Restricted run, not normal mass-production number

Limousine Automobile having an enclosed compartment seating three or more passengers and originally a driver's seat outside and covered with a roof but later a driver's seat enclosed by a usually movable glass partition; a large, luxurious sedan seating five persons behind the driver

Lorry Motortruck, especially one with low or open sides and sometimes a canvas cover (U.K.)

Lowboy Open flatbed trailer with a deck height very close to the ground

Marque Brand, used especially with sports cars

Micro Vehicle Sub-500-cubic-centimeter engines

Mini Vehicle 500 to 1000 cubic centimeter engines

Mobile Homes Large trailer designed without a permanent foundation and towed on its own chassis with attached frame and wheels

Mobile Library *see* **Bookmobile**

Mobile Media Mobile billboard towed by a car or truck

Mobile Trade Fair Firms ship goods overseas and display them on vehicles in foreign ports and commercial centers, coordinated by the U.S. Department of Commerce

Mobile Unit Vehicle equipped for some special unconventional service

Mock-Up Structural model built accurately to scale for study, testing or display

Modify Alter, make changes in form or structure for a definite purpose in mind

Motor Caravan Self-powered unit converted from standard commercial van, coachbuilt unit, standard chassis cab, car-size van or bus; motor home (U.K.)

Motor Coach Motor bus; automotive omnibus

Motor Home Automotive vehicle built directly on truck or bus chassis and self-contained

Motor Vehicle Automotive vehicle, especially one with rubber tires, for use without rails

Motorcycle Two-wheeled tandem automotive vehicles having one or two riding saddles and sometimes having a third wheel for the support of a sidecar

Motorscooter Low two or three-wheel automotive vehicle having a seat but with smaller wheels and less powerful than a motorcycle

Multimodal Vehicle Capable of operation in two or more environments (land, water and air)

NASCAR National Association for Stock Car Auto Racing, Inc.

Omnibus Public automotive vehicle, four-wheeled and designed to carry a comparatively large number of passengers

Pace Car Car that leads competitors in a car race through a pace leg before the start of the race but does not participate in the race itself

Panel Truck Light motor truck of passenger-car size with a fully enclosed body, used principally for delivery

Pickup Truck Light truck with an open body with low sides and tailboard, usually mounted on a passenger car chassis

Piggyback Transported on another vehicle; reinforced semi-trailer for railroad

Production Model Vehicle mass-produced in a factory

Productmobile Novelty advertising vehicle with the whole body shaped like a huge replica of the product being offered

Prototype First full-scale model of a new type or design of a vehicle

Purpose-Built Designed for a special use, custom, made to order

Recreational Vehicle Motor home, trailer, etc.

Reefer Refrigerated truck

Replica Reproduction or copy of original model

Restoration Bringing a vehicle back to its original condition

Retrofitting Modification, addition of new parts and equipment not available, considered unnecessary or not in place at time of manufacture. May appear in later production models

Rig Trailer truck; tractor trailer

Roadable Capable of being driven like an automobile, usually by power delivered to one or more wheels; airplane capable of being transformed into an automobile by removing or folding wings and tail

Rod *see* **Hot Rod**

RV Abbreviation for recreational vehicle

School Bus Vehicle either publicly or privately owned and operated for compensation, usually conspicuously marked with the words "school bus," and used to transport students to and from school

Self-Contained Vehicle Fully-equipped for extended periods of operation without access to external electricity and plumbing

Self-Propelled Vehicle Powered by its own motor

Semi-trailer A truck trailer supported at the rear by its own wheels and when attached to the tractor is supported at its forward end by the fifth wheel device

Show Car *see* **Concept Car**

Sky Car Roadable aircraft with the primary function of a practical airplane and the secondary function of a licensed motor vehicle

Souped-Up Car Augmented in power or efficiency or made physically more attractive

Special Interest Vehicle *see* **Special Purpose Vehicle**

Special Purpose Vehicle Used for other than transportation involving passengers, goods, raw materials and mail

Special Use Vehicle *see* **Special Purpose Vehicle**

Standard Vehicle *see* **Stock Vehicle**

Station Wagon Automobile that resembles a sedan but has no separate luggage compartment and has a top less rounded in back, a tailgate, and one or more rear seats readily lifted out or folded to facilitate light trucking; beach wagon

Stock Vehicle Regular production model

Tandem Axle Trailer or truck having a close-coupled pair of axles

Tractor-Semi-trailer *see* **Tractor Trailer**

Tractor Trailer Combination of tractor and semi-trailer

Tractor Truck Motive power unit in the form of a truck with short chassis and a cab but no body

Trailer Vehicle usually hauled by some other vehicle

Travel Trailer Vehicular structure mounted on two to four wheels and towed by an automobile or truck

Trolley Street car running from overhead rail or track by means of a trolley pole

Trolleybus *see* **Trolley**

Trolley Car *see* **Trolley**

Truck Vehicle with body mounted on a chassis to carry cargo

Truck Tractor *see* **Tractor Truck**

Truck-Trailer A combination of a truck trailer and its motortruck

Unit Vehicle

Van Motortruck usually enclosed having rear or side doors or sliding side panels

Vehicle Wheeled conveyance used on land on road

Vocational Vehicle Used for a particular line of work or commercial project

Index